THE STORY OF
LONDON'S UNDERGROUND

THE STORY OF LONDON'S UNDERGROUND

John R. Day and John Reed

Historical Consultants: Desmond F. Croome and M.A.C. Horne

Capital Transport

ISBN 978-1-85414-316-7

First published 1963
Tenth edition 2008

Published by
Capital Transport Publishing,
P.O. Box 250, Harrow, Middlesex
www.capitaltransport.com

Printed by CT Printing Ltd

Contents

Picture Credits

Introduction

This is the story of the oldest underground railway system in the world. The first edition appeared in June 1963 as part of the celebrations to mark its centenary. Apart from the wealth of history described within its pages there was also the news that the tube was all set to extend its mileage under London's congested streets for the first time in over fifty years. The previous August, London Transport had received the green light from the government to build the Victoria Line. As the Victoria Line took shape and the Jubilee Line came into the picture, several subsequent editions of the book kept readers up to date on the changing face of London's Underground.

This edition appears just over a year after the maintenance of the extensive infrastructure and train fleet passed to private companies, a switch that has been hotly debated in the press and elsewhere. Benefits have been promised in the longer term and much work was under way as we went to press.

Grateful thanks go to Desmond Croome and Mike Horne for supplying additional material and checking the updated draft; likewise to Brian Hardy for his useful comments and amendments to the text. Staff at Transport for London's archives were very helpful while additional research was being carried out for this new edition. Thanks are also due to the staff of the photographic library of the London Transport Museum and all the people who have supplied photographs for this book.

The Metropolitan Railway

This drawing of 1860 predates the opening of the Metropolitan Railway by three years but gives a good impression of Baker Street station as built. The two small station buildings at the junction of Baker Street and Marylebone Road were replaced just before the First World War. The drawing shows particularly well the proximity of the subsurface lines to street level as compared with the tube lines which came later.

Just as main-line railways first came to full flower in Great Britain, so did underground railways. The world's first public passenger-carrying underground railway, the Metropolitan, opened the gates of its stations to Londoners on 10th January 1863. Its route from Bishop's Road, Paddington, to Farringdon Street at the city boundary was only some 3¾ miles long, but there were queues at Farringdon Street on the first day to see the new marvel. Two months after it opened this small steam-operated line was carrying passengers at the rate of 2¾ million a year for every mile of track; 26,500 passengers a day used it in the first six months.

Even this modest line was the end-product of a long period of planning, counter-planning, struggles, and financial manoeuvres, and the devoted propaganda of one or two men. In the 1830s, a scheme for an underground railway from King's Cross to Snow Hill (near St Bartholomew's Hospital in the City) was put forward. Not a great deal is known about this scheme, or of another tunnel idea of the same period which might have put the London terminus of the London & Birmingham Railway on the banks of the Thames instead of at Euston; but they fired the imagination of Charles Pearson, later to become City Solicitor, and of John Hargrave Stevens, who was to be Architect and Surveyor to the City (Western Division). These two men were to press for an underground railway for London for the next 25 years or so, though Pearson was to die just four months before his vision was realised.

In the mid-1840s there was much talk of railways to reach London, and the Great Northern Railway, an amalgamation of the Direct Northern and the London & York, was authorised by an Act of 1846. These events, together with what would now be called town-planning proposals to improve London in the area between Clerkenwell Green and Holborn Hill, brought a burst of activity from Pearson. He wrote a pamphlet which put forward the idea of a covered way down the Fleet Valley through which trains could be drawn by atmospheric power. This was at the time when experiments with this potentially powerful, clean, and silent form of motive power were being made by the London & Croydon Railway.

Lack of money for the Clerkenwell town-planning scheme brought the City into the picture again in 1851, and its financial help for the scheme gave Pearson, ably assisted by Stevens, another opportunity of putting his case for the railway. Other factors in its favour at that time were that the Great Northern, already at Maiden Lane, was just building its permanent terminus at King's Cross and that the Great Western, far out in the (then) suburbs along the New Road at Paddington, was thought likely to jump at the chance of a close approach to the City.

In 1851 a committee was set up to examine Pearson's 'Railway Terminus and City Improvement Plan'. The plan consisted in essence of a 100-ft wide road to be built from Holborn Hill, which the new Farringdon Street had reached from Fleet Street in 1830, to King's Cross. The road would be supported on the arches of a tunnel which would be wide enough for six standard-gauge and two broad-gauge railway tracks – the latter presumably aimed at enlisting the support of the Great Western, despite the gap between King's Cross and Paddington. A connection with the Great Northern was proposed at a point about a quarter of a mile north of King's Cross and at the other end of the line would be the City Terminus itself. Main-line stations were to be built on both sides of Farringdon Street, a large goods yard was to be provided, and there would be a special station for short-distance travellers. The plan, after able lobbying by Pearson and his friends, was agreed by the committee and put to the Common Council, who also approved. The main-line railways, however, were not interested, and Pearson and his associates of the City Terminus Company were left to keep their plan alive as best they could.

Meanwhile, the remoteness of Paddington had set other, more hardened, minds thinking. The Bayswater, Paddington & Holborn Bridge Railway was promoted to link Paddington with King's Cross and with Pearson's line to Farringdon. Taking advantage of the presence of the wide, reasonably straight New Road route, the cost of this line, despite its greater length, was estimated as less than half that of Pearson's. Furthermore, the traffic potential of the route had been proved by the buses, and the railway could hardly fail to be a success. John Hargrave Stevens became the surveyor of this line, the engineer was John (later Sir John) Fowler and one of the sponsors was William Burchell, a member of the City Terminus Company and a solicitor. The first chairman of the new company, William Malins, always declared that he had first thought of the idea of a railway under the New Road and spent a great deal of money later in trying to prove it and claim compensation from the new railway. These experts went about the job of promoting the line with smooth efficiency. Small concessions were made here and there, and plans were altered a little to meet objections. The advantages of the line were put, salesman fashion, into the ears of local authorities. The Bill went through the committee stage in Parliament in one day in 1853 without a single objection. Its Act secured, and renamed the North Metropolitan, the company began to look round for the £1m capital required.

Meanwhile, Pearson had the mortification of seeing his Bill thrown out without even a Second Reading. This did not suit the North Metropolitan, which wanted the Pearson line as an essential part of its own scheme. The experts went to work, and Pearson's scheme was subjected to corrective surgery, one of the first stages being the amputation of the 20-acre City Terminus itself, the most important part of Pearson's proposals. The route of the line was changed to allow it to serve the General Post Office and thus gain GPO support.

There was opposition in Parliament, but Rowland Hill himself backed the scheme on behalf of the Post Office, and Brunel and Hawkshaw, both famous and respected engineers, supported Fowler. Malins put up a remarkable performance before the Committee, and an Act eventually emerged in 1854 for the 'Metropolitan Railway: Paddington and the Great Western Railway, the General Post Office, the London & North Western Railway, and the Great Northern Railway'. John Fowler was named as engineer and John Hargrave Stevens as architect.

The Metropolitan now had to find the money to build its line, but the Crimean War was in progress and money was short. Eventually, however, Pearson, still eager for even his truncated scheme to be built, advised the company that if it stepped in quickly it might be able to buy, cheaply, land which had been cleared for the Clerkenwell scheme. If the company moved at once, it could get it at a reasonable price before the land was redeveloped. Although it took a threat to wind up the company to do it, and much advocacy by Pearson and others, the City Corporation eventually agreed to subscribe for shares to the value of £200,000. The Metropolitan agreed to cut the cost of the line to £950,000 by not building the section from Cowcross Street to the Post Office.

To have a railway, after the American fashion, passing through a densely-populous district, and crossing on the level our overcrowded streets and thoroughfares, was utterly out of the question; and scarcely less so to carry an unsightly viaduct through the heart of the metropolis. The only alternative was that adopted by the Metropolitan Company – namely, that of an underground communication, by which the most densely-crowded districts could be traversed without the slightest annoyance or obstruction to the existing traffic.

Illustrated London News, 7 April 1860

The works of the great engineering project are now being pushed forward with a considerable degree of vigour by the contractors; Messrs Smith and Knight having undertaken that portion extending from Paddington to Euston-square, and Mr. John Jay that part from Euston-square to the City. The new railway commences from the Great Western line at Paddington and will terminate, according to present arrangements, at Smithfield; and ultimately at Finsbury Circus, embracing a distance of 4½ miles. In briefly giving a preliminary notice we may disabuse the public mind in reference to the correct name of the work, it having been called the 'underground' railway. This, however, is a misnomer, the fact being that the whole of the stations on the line will not only be entirely open to the day but a considerable portion of the line will also be so; for the tunnelled parts will only occur immediately under roadways at present existing, and in all cases where old buildings are to be purchased, open cuttings are to be formed, so that the whole line will thus be well ventilated. Some of the platforms will only be 20 feet below the surface.

Building News, 2 November 1860

A further £100,000 was saved by omitting a spur to Praed Street terminus, so that the new line would terminate at Bishop's Road Station, parallel to the Great Western's Paddington terminus. Another £175,000 was to come from the Great Western Railway in return for connecting the line to the GWR and building it on the broad gauge.

This time there was enough money to make a start, and contractors were appointed. The line east of Euston Square was in the hands of John Jay, who had built the cuttings for the Great Northern Railway's route to Maiden Lane, and the line west of Euston Square was given to Smith & Knight. The Smith & Knight section ran mostly through gravel and was 'cut-and-cover'. It was crossed at Baker Street by a minor river used as a sewer, the Tybourne. Jay's section was in open cutting for a good deal of its length but included the 728yd Clerkenwell tunnel as well as three crossings of the Fleet River, which carried a respectable flow of water.

In 'cut-and-cover' construction, a great trench is cut for the railway and afterwards roofed over, leaving the line in a subway or covered way, the roof of which can form a road or be used for other purposes. If the roof is made strong enough, buildings can span the tracks where required. To save disturbance of property, as much of the Metropolitan Railway's trench as possible was dug along the line of existing streets – Praed Street, Marylebone Road, and Euston Road. This had some disadvantages, because beneath the surface of the roads lay nests of pipes – water, gas, and sewerage in particular as well as, even in those days, the electric telegraph. All these had to be diverted before the trench for the railway could be made.

By March 1860 the contractors were ready to start on the building. In his book of the period 'Our Iron Roads', Frederick S. Williams gave a graphic description of the start of the work:

'A few wooden houses on wheels first made their appearance, and planted themselves by the gutter; then came some wagons loaded with timber and accompanied by sundry gravel-coloured men with picks and shovels. A day or two afterwards a few hundred yards of roadway were enclosed, the ordinary traffic being, of course, driven into the side streets; then followed troops of navvies, horses and engines arrived, who soon disappeared within the enclosure and down the shafts. The exact operations could be but dimly seen or heard from the street by the curious observer who gazed between the tall boards that shut him out; but paterfamilias, from his house hard by, could look down on an infinite chaos of timber, shaft holes, ascending and descending chains and iron buckets which brought rubbish from below to be carted away; or perhaps one morning he found workmen had been kindly shoring up his family abode with huge timbers to make it safer. A wet week comes, and the gravel in his front garden turns to clay; the tradespeople tread it backwards and forwards to and from the street door; he can hardly get out to business or home to supper without slipping and he strongly objects to a temporary way of wet planks, erected for his use and the use of the passers-by, over a yawning cavern underneath the pavement ... but at last, after much labour and many vicissitudes, even the Underground Railway was completed.'

By agreement with the Great Western and Great Northern Railways, whose trains were to have access to the Metropolitan tracks, the railway was laid to the mixed gauge. This means that there were three rails, the outer ones giving the Great Western broad gauge of 7ft 0¼in and the platform-side rail and inside rail giving the standard gauge of 4ft 8½in favoured by the Great Northern (and, indeed, by almost every British railway except the Great Western). The use of the broad gauge meant that the trench, or, in engineering parlance, 'covered way', for the Metropolitan had to be 28ft 6in wide. Later extensions, where only the 4ft 8½in gauge was used, were only 25ft wide. A typical section of the original covered way shows an elliptical brick arch of 28ft 6in span, with the arch springing from side walls resting on 4ft wide footings well below rail level. There was no concrete foundation for the side walls, and there was no invert to the covered way; i.e., if the structure is imagined to represent the sides and top of a box, the box had no bottom. In some later parts of the covered way an invert of brick or concrete was provided, and on other sections they have been added later. Beneath the centre of the covered way, under the space between the tracks (the 'six-foot' way), ran an 18in diameter drain.

In places where there was not enough depth above the railway to build a brick arch, cast-iron girders (sometimes wrought iron) were used to span the tracks. On the original section of the work, the ground was dug out to the full width of 33ft 6in (allowing for the brickwork) and to the full depth, the sides being supported by timber while the brickwork was built. In later sections of London covered way (for

the District Railway) the practice was to dig 6ft wide trenches for the side walls and build these walls up to a height of about 10ft from the bottom of the trench. The excavation was then carried down across the full width of the railway to the top of the new walls and the arch was built from side wall to side wall. The remaining spoil inside the new covered way was not taken out until this had been done, and if necessary, the surface restored. This method caused less disturbance to the soil on each side of the line and this reduced subsidence or cracking in neighbouring buildings, the cost of repairing which could be very high and had to be met by the railway. Sir Edward Watkin, one of the best-known chairmen of the Metropolitan Railway Company, told shareholders that work on the repair of a single London chapel, the fabric of which had been cracked during an extension to the railway, cost £14,500. This was at a time when the construction of the covered way for the railway itself, including brickwork, drains, etc., cost only £40–£50 a yard.

With modern methods and materials substituted for the old, the 'cut-and-cover' method is still the one used for most of the world's underground railways. In most places it costs the least to build, and as the stations are only just below ground level passengers can reach the platform quickly by stairways or inclined ramps. Unless the railway can follow existing streets, however, or be run through an area not yet built up or due for demolition and redevelopment, a great deal of expensive disturbance to property is involved which makes the cost prohibitive.

Pavements each side of the Marylebone Road remain for pedestrians but the whole of the road is dug up to enable the construction of the Metropolitan Railway.

The Clerkenwell tunnel, already mentioned, was built between November 1860 and May 1862. The depth from the surface to rail level varies between 29ft and 59ft. It was near this tunnel that the Fleet River, then carried in a lightly-built brick sewer, 10ft in diameter and resting on rubble in the old river bed, burst through the retaining wall in June 1862, and flooded the workings to a depth of 10ft in some places. This was the only serious accident attending the whole of the original works.

The intention at first was to make the stations completely underground, and Baker Street, Portland Road (renamed Great Portland Street in 1917), and Gower Street (renamed Euston Square in 1909) were so constructed. The platforms at the original stations were about 10ft wide, but the width was increased in later years when the broad gauge tracks were removed.

The Farringdon terminus was built on the site of the City Cattle Market, which had been removed to Islington. The Great Western and Metropolitan between them leased the basement of the new central meat market at Smithfield for use as a goods depot.

A great deal of thought had been given to the way in which the line would be worked. There were doubts about ventilation if steam locomotives were used; some suggested cable traction and others the atmospheric system. Neither of these ideas found favour – which was probably just as well.

In giving evidence before the Parliamentary Committee of 1854, Fowler, who had thought a great deal about propulsion methods, stated that he would use an ordinary locomotive but would dispense with the fire. By using a 'plain cylindrical, egg-ended boiler', which would be charged at each end of the line with water and steam at high pressure, his locomotive would be able to complete a single trip easily. By experiment, he found that even an ordinary locomotive, without modification, would haul a train the length of the line without a fire, provided it had a full head of steam to start with (Sir Daniel Gooch tried the same thing with the same results). I.K. Brunel, of the Great Western Railway, supported Fowler before the committee, but he also said that he did not see why an ordinary locomotive, with a fire in the firebox, could not be used. 'I thought', he said, 'the impression had been exploded long since that railway tunnels required much ventilation'. All the experts agreed at the time that 20-ton trains would be enough to carry the traffic. In fact, 120-ton trains hauled by 45-ton locomotives proved to be needed, so that ventilation had to be improved.

Fowler went ahead with plans for his fireless locomotive, and Robert Stephenson & Co, of Newcastle, were asked, late in 1860, to build a prototype. It had, in fact, a small firebox, but there was a large mass of firebrick in a chamber in the boiler barrel proper. The idea was to run the locomotive in the ordinary way on open sections of line, getting the firebricks really hot, and then damp down the fire in the covered section, the firebricks acting as a heat reservoir. This locomotive was a 2-4-0 tender engine with four 5ft 6in coupled wheels and cylinders of 15in diameter with 24-in stroke. Exhaust steam from the cylinders was not allowed to escape into the tunnels but was turned into an injection condenser fitted with an air pump. The locomotive weighed 32 tons and the tender 14 tons, both in full working order with fuel and water.

In October 1861 the engine was taken out on the Great Western Railway. It ran for 7½ miles as an ordinary locomotive and then was turned to run back. The fire was shut off by dampers and the exhaust steam was turned into the condensing tanks. Unfortunately, in 12 minutes the condensing apparatus was so hot that steam was coming out of the air pump delivery pipe mixed with boiling water. In the same period, the boiler pressure fell from 120lb per sq in to 80lb and the firebricks, which had been at 'a clear white heat', were almost black in appearance. The water from the condenser seems also to have formed the boiler feed, so that the failure of this apparatus meant that the boiler was rapidly running dry. The fire was dropped, but the heat from the firebricks could still have caused a boiler explosion. A further trial – also unsatisfactory – took place in the tunnels between King's Cross and Edgware Road.

Daniel Gooch, locomotive superintendent of the Great Western, was eventually asked to design a locomotive for the Metropolitan. He decided on a 2-4-0 tank design with 6ft coupled wheels and outside cylinders 16in by 24in. The heating surface of the firebox was 125 sq ft and of the tubes 615 sq ft. The grate area was 18.5 sq ft. As well as the normal feed tank holding 375 gallons of water, there was a special condensing tank holding 420 gallons. On trial in October 1862 the engine ran with a 36-ton train from Farringdon Street to Paddington in 20 minutes. The locomotive itself weighed 38 tons.

With 22 of these Great Western locomotives and Great Western eight-wheel carriages of a type known as 'Long Charleys', the service was prepared by Myles (afterwards Sir Myles) Fenton, the Metropolitan's operating superintendent. The long coaches were very comfortable for their day and had a very large capacity. All 45 coaches were fitted with gas lighting.

These coaches were not used by the inspection party of shareholders on 30th August 1862, when they travelled, largely in the contractor's open wagons, to see what their money was producing. On an earlier trip, on 24th May 1862, were Mr and Mrs Gladstone, and a well-known photograph shows them sitting in state in a wagon, attended by Mr Fowler. The same wagon held a large number of other notable personages, as can be seen from the reproduction below. The two wagons seem to have been pushed by the locomotive.

At last the line was ready for inspection, and in December 1862 it passed, except for a few minor points, the scrutiny of the Inspecting Officer of the Board of Trade. The final inspection by Colonel Yolland took place on 3rd January 1863 and rehearsals of the full traffic were carried on from 4th January to 8th January. There had been a delay caused mainly by difficulties with the block signalling apparatus. The disc block instruments used were devised by C.E. Spagnoletti, telegraph superintendent of the Great Western.

Fowler's 'fireless' locomotive at Edgware Road on trial in October 1862. It was unsuccessful and when the line opened it used 2-4-0 tank engines designed by Daniel Gooch. Fowler's locomotive, the workmanship of which was said to be superb, was purchased in 1865 by a Mr Isaac Boulton who intended to convert it to a standard gauge saddle tank. His firm went out of business and the locomotive was subsequently scrapped.

A distinguished party of people being conveyed in open goods wagons to inspect the Metropolitan Railway under construction on 24th May 1862. They include the Prime Minister, William Gladstone, and his wife, far right.

The eastbound platform at Baker Street, 1863, from a contemporary lithograph. Today this is platform 5 and has been restored to an appearance close to original including reproductions of the station lighting. Gas lighting was employed in Victorian times and the ventilation shafts doubled as channels for daylight. These shafts were white-tiled to improve the illumination but have long since been covered and now house large light fittings.

The service started running on Saturday 10th January 1863, with the immediate success already noted; the event had been celebrated the day before with a great banquet for 350 guests and about 250 directors, shareholders and others at Farringdon Street. All the stations were decorated. By the time of its completion, the first stretch of the Metropolitan Railway had cost £1.3m to build, a 30% increase over the estimated cost 10 years earlier. The Met claimed that a railway on viaducts, and intersecting buildings in places, would have cost four times this sum.

It soon became evident that the service provided by the Great Western, whose main interest was in through trains, was not good enough for the amount of short-distance traffic offering. Also, nothing had been done about freight trains, although the connection with the Great Northern was nearly ready to be opened. The Great Western steadily drew away from the Metropolitan, which with equal determination was drawing away from the Great Western. The mutual dislike was intensified by the fact that Charles Saunders, secretary of the Great Western, had brushed hard against John Parson, now the Metropolitan's deputy chairman, over the Oxford, Worcester & Wolverhampton Railway's affairs.

This animosity culminated in a letter from Saunders to the effect that the Great Western would not work the Metropolitan line after 30th September. This failed to produce the expected panic, and a second letter was sent advancing the date to 11th August. To make sure that the Metropolitan was properly brought to heel, the Great Western, knowing that the Metropolitan had neither locomotives nor coaches of its own, made it clear that it would not sell the rolling stock then working the line to the Metropolitan. The answer of the Metropolitan was to hire locomotives and stock from the Great Northern (some rolling stock also from the LNWR) until its own equipment was ready. There were difficulties, of course. The train service had to be reduced, and the Great Northern 0-4-2 and 0-6-0 tender locomotives were not ideal for the work, but the line kept going until at last its own coaches, and its own locomotives, arrived on the scene.

A GWR broad gauge train of the type used by the Metropolitan Railway for the first seven months of existence. Through GWR trains of broad gauge stock continued until 1869, and standard gauge GWR trains until 1939. The right-hand tracks in the picture eventually led to Paddington (Praed Street) station and Gloucester Road (opened 1st October 1868). As this section of the inner circle was not built or equipped to broad gauge standard, the third rails in the picture may have been artist's licence, or a mistake, or a short broad-gauge stub.

The coaches, based on the Great Western model but adapted to the narrower gauge, were said to be a great improvement on anything used on the line before and better than many main-line coaches of the era, and the locomotives, designed by Fowler, were certainly better than the rather strange assortment provided by the Great Northern, though these had saved the day for the Metropolitan.

The new locomotives were 4-4-0 tank engines with outside cylinders. The coupled wheels were 5ft 9in and the leading wheels 3ft in diameter. The tube heating surface was 841 sq ft, that of the fire-box 101.6 sq ft, and the grate 19 sq ft. The boiler pressure was 120lb, but this was raised to 130lb in later locomotives. The cylinders had a diameter of 17¼in and the stroke was 24in. The weight, with 1,170 gallons of water in the tanks, was 45 tons. Tractive effort at 80 per cent boiler pressure was 13,100lb. The Fowler locomotives were so successful that they remained, with a few modifications, the motive power of the tunnel lines until electrification. The first were known as the 'A' type, but the 'B' type were very similar. Between them, they eventually numbered 66. When the District came to need its own motive power, it bought engines of the same type from the same builders and this added another 54 to their numbers. One of the 'A' class (No.23) is now preserved by London's Transport Museum. The fuel at first was coke made from the finest Durham coal, but this was superseded after six years by South Wales semi-anthracite coal.

The Metropolitan's own locomotives began to arrive in 1864. Loco No.18 was one of the first batch and is seen in original condition. It carries the name 'Hercules', later removed.

An engraving of Portland Road station viewed from the south side, giving a reasonably accurate impression of its ornate design, but with a rather out-of-scale bus. The two domes on the north side were demolished in 1869/1870 to improve ventilation.

THE ATMOSPHERE OF THE UNDERGROUND RAILWAY.—Sarah Dobner, aged 56, died at the Bishop's-road Station of the Metropolitan Railway on Tuesday before last. Deceased had complained of a great difficulty of breathing while on the underground, and while waiting for the second train she said she was in great pain. A medical gentleman advised her removal to the hospital, but it was then believed she was dead. Mr Anderson, one of the surgeons at St Mary's Hospital, who made the post-mortem examination, said the deceased was labouring under disease of the bronchial gland, and undoubtedly the suffocating air of the Underground Railway had accelerated death. The coroner, at the inquest, said he had experienced the depressing effects of that railway, and he therefore avoided it as much as possible. The tunnels and stations should be ventilated, but he supposed that would not be done until some shocking loss of life from suffocation had occurred. The jury returned a verdict of 'death by natural causes, accelerated by the suffocating atmosphere of the Underground Railway'.

The Builder, 17th August 1867

When the railway started its public service there were outcries about poor ventilation. A fan had to be provided at what was then Portland Road station and glazing was removed above tracks at Baker Street, Portland Road and Gower Street stations. Later, portions of the covered way were opened up to improve ventilation still further, and in 1871–72 'blow-holes' (an idea of Pearson's originally) were made in the tunnel roof to the road above on the section between Edgware Road and King's Cross. The sudden eruption of air, steam, and smoke from these holes as a train passed below was said to have been very disturbing to horses in the roadway above. The ventilation on the railway appears to have been somewhat less than had been promised before the line was built as the station design had been based on the assumption that the fireless locomotive would work properly.

This experience led to stations on extensions and on the District Railway being built as far as possible in the open. There was also, where possible, an intermediate open section between stations. Some of these remain today.

Meanwhile, Fowler had been busy building another railway, the Hammersmith & City. This was built by a separate company with the backing of the Great Western and the Metropolitan and was conceived as a feeder to the Metropolitan line. The new line ran from the Great Western main line about a mile out of Paddington and formed a quarter of a circle round the suburbs of the day to end pointing almost south at Hammersmith. There were intermediate stations at Notting Hill (now Ladbroke Grove) and at Shepherd's Bush (not the present station). A branch left the main line at Latimer Road (the station of that name did not open until 16th December 1868) and ran to Kensington (Addison Road – now Olympia). The main line opened on 13th June 1864 and the branch on 1st July the same year. The 'branch' was in fact a connecting line with the West London and the West London Extension Railway, which gave a route from Paddington via West Brompton and over the Thames to Battersea and the south, including a connection with Victoria. This later resulted in such curiosities as the London, Brighton & South Coast running trains to Brighton from Paddington and broad-gauge Great Western trains working regularly to Victoria (on the London, Chatham & Dover side). The Hammersmith & City became a joint responsibility of the Great Western and Metropolitan on 1st July 1865. The track was mixed gauge. Because of delays to trains on the section of Great Western main line, two extra tracks were put down for the Hammersmith & City, coming into use on 30th October 1871.

So much for the western side of London. Farther east, the Great Northern had started running through trains to Farringdon Street on 1st October 1863, and on the same day the Great Western started running broad-gauge trains between Farringdon and Windsor. In the next month the Metropolitan let the contract for an eastwards extension to Moorgate Street. Powers for this had been obtained in 1861, and the preliminary matters had been taken care of while the earlier part of the line was still being built. The contractor, John Kelk, started work early the next year, but in the meantime a further decision had been made. To keep the Great Northern trains clear of the Metropolitan's and give them proper access to the goods depot and meat market at Smithfield two extra tracks would be laid on the Moorgate extension, and the existing lines would be quadrupled all the way back to King's Cross. This was an undertaking of some magnitude, because it meant building another double-track tunnel at the side of the long Clerkenwell tunnel. The work was authorised in 1864 and

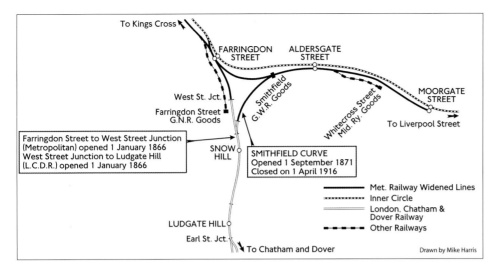

also went to John Kelk. Fowler, of course, was the engineer. The 'Widened Lines', as they have always been called, run north of the Metropolitan tracks from King's Cross to the 'new' Clerkenwell tunnel. Built between November 1865 and May 1867, the tunnel is 733yds in length. At its eastern end the mouth is some 16ft lower than that of the original tunnel, and the Widened Lines dip under the Metropolitan tracks and run from there to Moorgate on the south side of the other lines. The Metropolitan lines were carried across the Widened Lines by an unusual wrought-iron bridge which also acted at a strut between the walls of the deep cutting. The bridge was well known in railway circles as the 'Ray Street Gridiron'. It was replaced by a concrete raft in 1960, but the girders of the original bridge had already been renewed in 1892/3.

A new station was built at Farringdon Street for the extension, and the line was open from that station for passengers to Moorgate on 23rd December 1865. The Widened Lines were opened for passengers from Farringdon to Aldersgate Street on 1st March 1866 and to Moorgate on 1st July of the same year. The new Clerkenwell tunnel held up the Farringdon–King's Cross opening for passenger traffic until 17th February 1868. Meanwhile, the London, Chatham & Dover had been building towards Ludgate Hill and Snow Hill. This line met a short spur from the Metropolitan at West Street Junction, just south of Farringdon, and a new cross-London route (today used by Thameslink trains) was made available on 1st January 1866. Smithfield market, for the traffic of which so much preparation had been made, was officially opened in November 1868, but not served by trains until 3rd May 1869. A connection had also been made between the newly built Midland Railway line to London and the Metropolitan. This was opened on 13th July 1868 and carried local trains from Bedford into Moorgate. As St Pancras was not to be opened for another 2½ months, Moorgate was in fact the Midland's first London terminus.

The Great Western broad-gauge trains had been projected from Farringdon to Aldersgate and then to Moorgate over the new Widened Lines when they were opened – they were mixed-gauge lines. In August 1868, however, it was agreed that the broad-gauge passenger trains should be withdrawn from the Metropolitan, and the last train on the 7ft gauge left Moorgate on 14th March 1869.

Before we leave this area, it is worth noting that in 1871 a connection from Snow Hill to the Widened Lines in the Moorgate direction was opened – the earlier ones faced King's Cross. London, Chatham & Dover trains reached Moorgate by this route from 1st September 1871, and they continued to use the route until 1st April 1916. The tunnel was demolished in the general clearance of the site of the Smithfield Poultry Market, burnt down in January 1958.

Another Metropolitan move towards expansion, small in itself, was to have much significance later on in the railway's history. In 1864, the Metropolitan & St John's Wood Railway was incorporated, with Fowler as engineer. This was to run from Baker Street to meet the Hampstead Junction Railway near the latter's Finchley Road station. In fact, the line got into financial difficulties and finished up – and then only with the help of the Metropolitan – as a single-track line which left the Met by a junction at Baker Street and ended at Swiss Cottage. It was opened on 13th April 1868. When, in the following year, the St John's Wood proposed to increase its through services over the Metropolitan line to six trains an hour instead of three, the Metropolitan declined. Following two small accidents and other difficulties at the Baker Street junction, the Met closed the junction and refused to allow through trains.

The District and the Inner Circle

Above **In this view of the building of Gloucester Road station, the two trenches each side of the path of the railway have been dug, the retaining walls have been built and the roof is being constructed before the central part of the station is excavated. This was the standard method of building the line.**

Facing page **Later stages of construction at Paddington (Praed Street) (upper picture) and Gloucester Road (lower).**

The Metropolitan was not alone in wanting expansion of the London lines. So many promoters came along with schemes that a Select Committee of the House of Lords was set up in 1863, and a joint committee of both Houses in 1864, to sort out the tangled mass of applications before Parliament. The 1863 committee wanted all the main-line termini linked by rail and suggested that the best way would be to extend the Metropolitan at both ends and form an 'inner circuit' by a new line linking the ends of the Metropolitan but running nearer the Thames. For many years there had been agitation for an embankment on the north side of the Thames which could be used as a new through road to reduce the congestion in the traffic-choked Strand. It was also wanted as the route for a new trunk sewer.

Fowler first put forward a line from Farringdon to Blackfriars and then to a Westminster terminus under the new embankment road, powers for which had been granted in 1862. Another new line would run from Paddington to Notting Hill and then, through Kensington Gardens, back to Westminster to meet his other proposed line. Before powers could be sought for this route, the House of Lords had changed its mind and wanted a line to run east from Moorgate to Tower Hill and then to turn to Cannon Street and Blackfriars – a much more expensive route than Fowler's.

The Metropolitan did its best. It applied for powers to build from Moorgate to Trinity Square (Tower Hill) and, separately, from Paddington to Notting Hill Gate, Kensington, and Brompton. These two applications were both granted, the enabling Acts – the Metropolitan Railway (Notting Hill and Brompton Extension) Act and the Metropolitan Railway (Tower Hill Extension) Act – both receiving the Royal Assent on 29th July 1864.

The intermediate section needed to complete the 'inner circuit' – from South Kensington (Brompton) to Tower Hill – was handed to a new company. This was the Metropolitan District Railway Company, also incorporated by an Act of 29th July 1864, making its first appearance on the London scene. Its name came from the title that Fowler had given his inner circuit plans, 'Metropolitan District Railways', and the Metropolitan's chairman, W.A. Wilkinson, and three other Metropolitan directors were on the board. The engineer-in-chief was again Fowler. It was clear that the Metropolitan District, as a company, was a device for splitting the effort of raising capital for the work. It was expected that the two companies would amalgamate as soon as possible, and the terms of amalgamation were actually drawn up for use when required. It did not however work out like that.

As well as the 'Circle Completion' section, the new company had powers to build alongside the Metropolitan from South Kensington to Gloucester Road and continue through Earl's Court to a junction with the West London Extension Railway at West Brompton, and to build a line from Kensington High Street, also through Earl's Court, to join the West London Railway near Addison Road. Work started at Kensington on 29th June 1865 and at several other points simultaneously, and the western section of the Circle was under way.

The Metropolitan, having taken a look at the cost of its City extension, started at the other end on the extension from Paddington. Fowler's original idea had been to build this in easy territory through Kensington Gardens and Hyde Park, but the opposition was too strong and the present route was selected instead. It entailed cuttings 42ft deep and a 421yd tunnel at Campden Hill as well as considerable sums in compensation to property owners. In Leinster Gardens, where the railway runs under the road, the railway had to rebuild the façade of two houses, Nos. 23 and 24, which are just false fronts, to act as screens for the line. They remain to this day and have figured in many stories and, no doubt, in many practical jokes. The line was opened to Gloucester Road on 1st October 1868 and to South Kensington on 24th December of the same year.

A further example of cut-and-cover construction blocking the whole carriageway, this time looking east along Craven Hill towards its junction with Craven Terrace.

These two pictures of the same location show early and advanced stages of work. The retaining walls are of buttress and horizontal arch design for strength and many can still be seen on the Circle Line today. The houses above the tunnel are Nos. 23 and 24 Leinster Gardens, Bayswater, demolished in the second view to be replaced by false fronts to maintain the street's appearance. 23 and 24 Leinster Gardens remain to this day as dummy houses.

This engraving, of High Street Kensington station, made for publication in the *Illustrated London News* of 10th October 1868, looks north and may be taken as more accurate in its depiction of the gothic architecture than its representation of the trains and passengers. The Metropolitan Railway side of the station (at right) was opened on 1st October 1868. There was no regular service over the District Railway terminal tracks (left) until 3rd July 1871, although they were completed in 1869. The station, at first known as 'Kensington' or 'Kensington High St', was renamed 'High Street Kensington' by about 1900.

NSINGTON STATION

METROPOLITAN RAILWAY

TERN EXTENSION: INTERIOR OF THE KENSINGTON STATION.

Building the District Railway in Victoria Street. Each of the iron girders had to withstand a 45-ton load in the centre to be suitable for cut-and-cover. The girders remained in place until the latter part of the 20th Century, when 44–tonne lorries required their replacement by stronger ones.

The District had its difficulties because of the built-up nature of the land through which its covered way was being cut. It also met London's rivers just as the Metropolitan had done to the north. The West Bourne, constricted and fouled and renamed the Ranelagh sewer, had to be carried in a 29yd conduit over the station at Sloane Square. The District found itself mixed up with the widening of Tothill Street and a slum clearance scheme near the present London Transport headquarters; it had to take special precautions for nearly 100 yards as it passed by Westminster Abbey; and at the end there was a frantic rush in which 3,000 men worked day and night to get the line open to Westminster Bridge in time for the Christmas traffic of 1868. They just captured the fringe of this traffic, the line being opened from South Kensington to Westminster Bridge on Christmas Eve.

The trains and motive power were supplied by the Metropolitan, running on from South Kensington. There were three intermediate stations, as there still are – Sloane Square, Victoria, and St James's Park. Westminster station, from 1870, had a subway to the nearby Houses of Parliament. In 1871 Mr Gladstone is reported to have said: 'The convenience of the line had an influence of remarkable efficiency in removing the members of the House of Commons from their seats at a certain hour of the evening'. On his death in 1898 Mr Gladstone's body was carried at midnight through this pedestrian subway for the lying-in-state in Westminster Hall.

On 12th April 1869 the line to West Brompton, where there was a station next to that of the West London Extension Railway, was opened. It was worked by a shuttle service from Gloucester Road. The District tracks between South Kensington and Gloucester Road were ready but not used regularly until the line was also open to Blackfriars and there was a through service from that station to West Brompton.

The line from Kensington High Street to the West London Railway was ready by 7th September 1869 and, after some thought of building its own station, the District made arrangements to use the West London's existing Addison Road station, but regular traffic did not begin until 1st February 1872, and was provided by trains operated by the London & North Western Railway.

The District now ran into money troubles and wanted work on the Embankment, with which its own works were inextricably mixed, to be held up until the South Kensington-Westminster section was bringing in some money. The Metropolitan Board of Works, on the other hand, wanted to get its sewer working and the Embankment completed. The impasse remained until, in 1869, authority was given by Parliament to issue preference stock for the remaining money required. The railway could then proceed, and although it had to be re-excavated from the filling behind the completed embankment wall it was opened to Blackfriars on 30th May 1870, with intermediate stations at Charing Cross and the Temple. As far as possible, stations were in open cuttings with vertical retaining walls. The platforms were 300ft long and the elliptical

Completing the cut-and-cover form of construction over the Metropolitan and District Railways near South Kensington Station; the low building in the left background is Pelham House. When construction here was completed a new road, Harrington Road, was built on top of the railway.

arched iron roofs had a 50ft 6in span. At Temple station a special flat form of roof had to be built because an agreement between the railway and the Duke of Norfolk, whose property the line crossed here, stipulated that this station should not have a raised roof.

The remaining section of the line from Blackfriars to Mansion House was opened formally on 1st July 1871, and to public traffic two days later on Monday 3rd July. On the 10th of the same month the District opened its own station in South Kensington, which it had built, together with a stretch of track, to avoid using the Metropolitan's facilities, and also to cope with expected extra traffic.

The last move arose from an argument between the District and the Metropolitan. The Metropolitan had worked the services for 55 per cent of the gross receipts. Any extra trains had to be paid for out of the District's percentage, and as it always wanted more trains its actual receipts fell to about two-fifths of the total. The District decided that the only thing to do was to run its own trains and gave the necessary notice, due to expire on 1st July 1871, to the Metropolitan.

The District line was originally worked by the Metropolitan with Metropolitan locomotives and coaches, but the District needed its own when it made its bid for independence. It bought four-wheel coach stock measuring 29ft 2in over the buffers. The initial order was for 152 coaches, half of which were third class and the rest first and second class in equal numbers. The first class compartments seated 10, five on each side, and there were four compartments to each vehicle. Second and third class compartments were similar, but narrower, so that five were squeezed into the space occupied by four in the first class. No other type of coach was purchased by the District for steam services, but it bought more of the original type from time to time. At the end of the steam operation it had 215 third class coaches, 92 second, 87 first and one composite coach. According to accounts of the time, the first class was in fact very comfortable, but the second and third probably left much to be desired by modern standards. The coaches were provided with gas lighting, the gas being carried in bags in the roof, replenished as required at Kensington High Street (which was the coaling and watering point for District locomotives) and at Mansion House. Oil gas was substituted in 1878 and was safer, as it was carried compressed in cylinders. Both the Metropolitan and the District were exempted from the requirement of the Regulation of Railways Act of 1869 that a smoking carriage had to be attached to any train with more than one carriage for each class of traveller. The act provided for railways to be excused in special circumstances, and the fact that the District and Metropolitan were underground lines was evidently special circumstance enough. In fact, however, both railways introduced such carriages on 1st September 1874 in deference to popular demand and difficulty in enforcing the ban, which was widely flouted.

The Metropolitan during summer months runs three [workmen's] trains up and down, and in winter two, the latest to the west, and arrives at King's Cross at 5.40. They are so far of some advantage, and I am not going to disparage their value. These trains are always over-crowded, or were when I used to ride. I now prefer walking two miles night and morning rather than run the gauntlet to get a place. Compartments constructed to carry ten persons have often fifteen pushed into them; and, what with tobacco-smoke and other exhalations, the condition of the carriages on a summer's morning is something fearful to contemplate.

The Builder, 7th January 1871

In the meantime, the Metropolitan directors who were also on the board of the District had resigned and a new director had been brought in. He was James Staats Forbes, who had trained under Saunders on the Great Western, been general manager of a railway in the Netherlands, and was now general manager of the London, Chatham & Dover. He became chairman of the District in November 1872.

When Mansion House station opened, the District worked its own lines and also half of the trains from Mansion House to Moorgate. It purchased its own rolling stock and built a depot for it at what is now called Lillie Bridge. The agreement as to which railway should work which trains was concluded only at the last moment, less than a week before the District was due to assume complete independence. To make matters worse, after a very critical report on the Metropolitan's affairs, the Metropolitan shareholders forced the Board on 7th August 1872 to accept Sir Edward Watkin as chairman, and John Parson had to resign from the board to make room for him. Watkin was already chairman of the Manchester, Sheffield & Lincolnshire and of the South Eastern Railway. In his latter capacity he was already at daggers drawn with Forbes, and the situation was not improved when, in 1873, Forbes became chairman as well as general manager of the London, Chatham & Dover.

But we are anticipating. When the District achieved independence it found that this was not an automatic passport to success. Results were disappointing, and the company's stock fell so low that there was talk of amalgamation with the Metropolitan. There was still expansion in the air, for all that. An Act was obtained in 1872 to build a line from Earl's Court to join the London & South Western at Barnes, and in the following year an independent company, known as the Hammersmith Extension Railway Company, was given powers to build a line from Earl's Court to Hammersmith Broadway. The independent company was a creation of the District's, which doubted whether it could raise the money under its own name. The line was built and opened quietly on 9th September 1874. The LSWR agreed to give the District running powers from Hammersmith to Richmond as long as it promised that this should be the only route used to connect its lines with Kew, Richmond, and Barnes. The necessary agreement made, the District was able to scrap its own scheme, which it could ill afford, for an independent line to Barnes. Instead, the District received powers to build the 'Metropolitan District Richmond Extension Railway' (separate capital again) to connect Hammersmith Broadway with the LSWR lines at Studland Road Junction, near what is now Ravenscourt Park station but which before 1888 was Shaftesbury Road. The Midland Railway took a financial interest in this, as it saw the possibilities of the line in carrying its goods trains between Acton and Kensington.

The Hammersmith Junction line was opened on 1st June 1877, and the District's trains began to work through from Mansion House to Richmond. The District made further use of its running powers by obtaining permission in 1877 to build a line from Turnham Green to Ealing Broadway, and this was opened on 1st July 1879. In 1883 it made an agreement with the Great Western whereby a short connecting line was put in between the District and the GWR just east of Ealing Broadway. By this line District trains worked from Mansion House to Windsor for about 2½ years, but the service did not pay.

Another extension, opened on 1st March 1880, was the so-called Fulham extension to Putney Bridge from West Brompton. There was a good deal of muddle over what was to happen farther south. At first there was a scheme which would have taken District trains to Surbiton and LSWR trains to South Kensington, but eventually the LSWR decided on a Putney–Wimbledon line instead. This was to be built by a separate company, but powers were obtained by an Act of 1886 to transfer the powers to the LSWR. In due course, the line was built from Putney Bridge to Wimbledon by the LSWR. It included a trellis girder bridge over the Thames which had a public footbridge on one side of it. The District service began on 3rd June 1889, and the LSWR working from East Putney to Wimbledon started on 1st July. The East Putney–Putney Bridge section, which included the bridge itself, was used only by District trains.

Before we leave the District's 'west country', it is worth noting that for a time it worked, for 50 per cent of receipts, a locally-promoted line from Mill Hill Park (renamed Acton Town on 1st March 1910) to the old Hounslow Town station, on a spur from Osterley. The authorised line should have gone to Hounslow Barracks, but the spur was opened first. Through trains worked from Hounslow Town to Mansion House for a few months after the opening on 1st May 1883, but in December they were cut back to Earl's Court. When Hounslow Barracks station was opened on 21st July 1884 it was served by a shuttle service from Osterley. On 31st March 1886

Except between King's Cross and Edgware Road, open sections were a feature of the whole of the original Circle Line tunnels to provide a necessary escape for smoke and steam. These two drawings, originally published in 1893, show scenes near Paddington and near Sloane Square. Most of these sections have been built over but daylight still punctuates the tunnel darkness at a number of stations and at certain other points including between Bayswater and Notting Hill Gate and between Embankment and Temple.

Aldersgate Street station (today's Barbican) c.1880 with a mix of gas and electric lamps, showing the superior illumination given by electricity. In October 1879, Victoria station on the District Railway had been the first to be lit by electric lighting when a trial using ten lights was mounted for a few days by the Société Générale d'Electricitié of Paris.

Hounslow Town was closed, being 'replaced' the next day by Heston Hounslow on the main line, when a through service started to run between Mill Hill Park and Hounslow Barracks. Hounslow Town station was, however, to come to life again in 1903.

On the east side of London there was no such picture. The shortage of money for the more expensive construction in the City was acute, and neither the Metropolitan nor the District made a move. The Metropolitan had served notices to purchase on the owners of property east of Moorgate in 1865, but nothing was done except that the railway managed, in 1869, to get an extension of time. The powers granted to the District, which had no extension of time, lapsed in 1870. It looked as though the Circle would never be completed.

When the Liverpool Street terminus of the Great Eastern was being built, the Metropolitan managed to extend its lines to join the Great Eastern's. At one time, after the connection had been made in 1875, trains from Hammersmith ran right into the main-line station. The Metropolitan was continued to Aldgate the next year, but this may have been something of a forced move as City interests, tired of waiting for the two railway companies, had formed a Metropolitan Inner Circle completion Railway Company in 1874. This company formed some sort of agreement with the District and it issued a prospectus in late 1877. Sir Edward Watkin used all his influence to prevent the money for the line being raised, and he succeeded, but he must have realised that the writing was on the wall and at last he came to what might be called an armed peace with the District.

The Metropolitan and District (City Lines and Extensions) Act of 1879 authorised the two railways to complete the circle jointly and also to build a line from Aldgate to connect with the East London Railway at Whitechapel. The Act also obliged the two companies to work the Inner Circle when it was completed. Even now Sir Edward Watkin was determined to be awkward. The Metropolitan hastily built its own line under its own powers to Tower Hill and built a station of sorts there at high speed, opening it on 25th September 1882. It was abandoned two years later, but this line caused a lot of trouble when taken over by the joint Metropolitan/District undertaking as compensation had to be discussed. Objections of various sorts were also brought up by the South Eastern, of which, as we know, Watkin was also chairman.

Despite all this, Sir John Hawkshaw and J. Wolfe Barry, the engineers, finished the Circle and it was opened on 6th October 1884. In the meantime, the District had built an independent terminus at Whitechapel which opened on the same day and some of its trains terminated there. The Metropolitan ran from Hammersmith (Hammersmith & City) via the northern half of the Circle and thence over the East London Railway to New Cross (South Eastern). The District through trains ran from Hammersmith also (District station) over the southern side of the Circle and then on to the East London to New Cross (London, Brighton & South Coast). There were both north and south curves at Aldgate; that from the northern side of the Circle was purely Metropolitan property.

Although the lines were now operating, there was constant bickering between the two companies. One frequent source of trouble was the division of receipts on the Circle, each company trying to claim as much traffic for itself as possible. This was aggravated in 1884 by an astute move on the part of the District. The original authorisation for the District did not include a direct connection between Kensington High Street and Gloucester Road. The Metropolitan had such a line and opposed one for the District. In 1870, however, without Parliamentary authority, the District built such a line and the Metropolitan agreed to its use as a relief line. It was little used until 1884, when the District diverted its Circle Line trains over it and claimed it as part of the Circle. By doing this it was able to claim a higher percentage of receipts because it was making, it claimed, more use of its own lines and less of the Metropolitan's. The matter went to the courts and, despite the practice continuing for only five weeks or so, it took until 1903 for the courts to rule that the 'Cromwell Curve', as it was known, was not part of the Inner Circle.

There were also Middle and Outer Circles, though neither was ever a complete ring. The Outer Circle, worked by the London & North Western, was from Broad Street (North London Railway) to Camden Town, Willesden, and the West London Railway, Addison Road, and Mansion House. The Middle Circle was worked by the Great Western, running from Moorgate via the Metropolitan and the Hammersmith & City to Latimer Road and then through Addison Road to the District and Mansion House. These services faded away to nothing in the course of time, with the final blow being dealt by enemy action in autumn 1940.

Like the Metropolitan, the District Railway also utilised Beyer Peacock 4–4–0 locomotives, eventually owning 54; this picture shows one from the 1880–81 batch at Lillie Bridge works together with contemporary carriages. Normally trains were eight carriages long, later increased to nine.

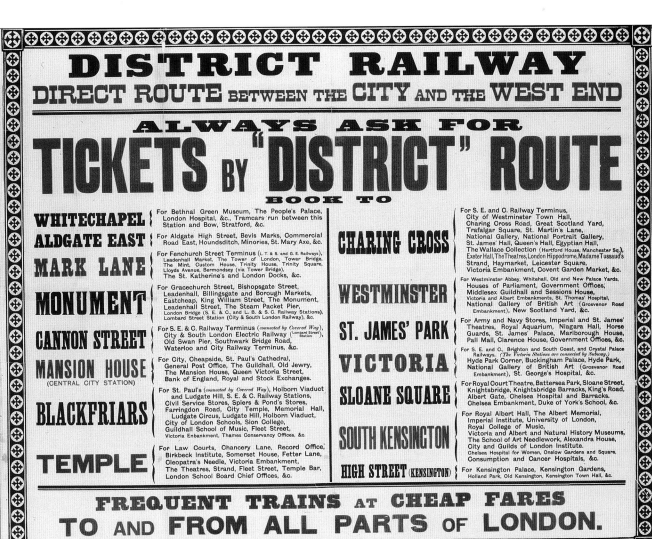

Competition between the District and Metropolitan is well evident in these adverts from the 1880s.

Steaming Ahead

At Aldgate the platforms were very tightly confined within the western side of the triangular junction. This view shows a Hammersmith train (which did not call at Aldgate) emerging from the tunnel from Aldgate East and passing the northern end of the platforms at Aldgate. This loco, a 'B' class built in 1879, is running tender first; locos were not routinely turned at the end of their journeys (though they were turned at intervals to reduce uneven wheel wear occasioned by continuous working around the Inner Circle service).

So far we have seen the Metropolitan under Watkin as a disgruntled parent doing its best to obstruct and control an upstart child, the District, which persisted in kicking over the traces. This is a long way from being the whole picture; probably Watkin considered it not much more than an irritating sideline. He had his mind on bigger things.

It will be recalled that there was a short single-track line, the St John's Wood, running north-west for nearly two miles to Swiss Cottage from a junction with the Metropolitan at Baker Street. This line had double track at the two intermediate stations, St John's Wood and Marlborough Road, and was complete to within a short distance of the North London's Finchley Road station. It had been opened, as already described, on 13th April 1868.

Sir Edward Watkin had appeared on the Metropolitan scene in 1872, and in 1873 the St John's Wood line obtained powers to extend to Kingsbury (the station now known as Neasden). The reason for this, Watkin explained later, was two-fold. The cramped works at Edgware Road were to be moved out into the country and the Metropolitan was to break through 'the iron barrier which the skill and acuteness of the larger railway companies had constructed' around it. They wanted to cross the Midland and the North Western lines so that, if an extension was called for at any time, it would go to the Metropolitan and not to the others.

Watkin was a main-line man, and he looked on the Metropolitan as a potential main-line railway. In 1874 he asked the shareholders to approve a proposal to carry the St John's Wood line on to Harrow, and he tempted them by speaking of 'disjointed pieces of railway which will hereafter help to connect your great terminus with Northampton and Birmingham and many other important towns.' The shareholders must have had their field of vision suddenly enlarged. They had put their money in a small, busy, London railway; here was the chairman talking in familiar terms of the Midlands.

The extension was put in hand. On 30th June 1879, the St John's Wood line was open to West Hampstead; it was doubled from Baker Street to Swiss Cottage on 10th July 1882, the new track running in a separate tunnel alongside the old. On 24th November 1879 it was opened to Willesden Green and on 2nd August 1880 to Harrow-on-the-Hill, powers having been granted for this in an Act of 1874. The Metropolitan, through its St John's Wood company, had now reached out 9½ miles from Baker Street. Among many proposals for building new links and joining existing lines at this period was one, in which Watkin had a hand, for making a new route from the Midlands which would enter London via the Metropolitan. This plan eventually reached Parliament as the Buckinghamshire & Northamptonshire Railways Union Bill, but it was rejected.

Although the Metropolitan was granted powers in 1880 to build on to Rickmansworth and in the following year to Aylesbury, Pinner was not reached until 25th May 1885 and Rickmansworth on 1st September 1887. The Metropolitan, which by now had taken over the St John's Wood line completely, had its railhead 17½ miles from Baker Street. Meanwhile, in 1886, Watkin was accused at a general meeting of concealing the real reason for this advance to the north-west. Watkin dismissed the implication as a 'phantom of the imagination', having conveniently forgotten his promises of 1874 about the future of the Metropolitan's 'great terminus'.

Nevertheless, although the Metropolitan could not at once raise the money to go on to Aylesbury, it did continue to Chesham. The main line from Rickmansworth to Amersham and north-westwards to Aylesbury was authorised by the Aylesbury & Rickmansworth Railway Act of 1881, and the Chesham branch by the Metropolitan Railway Act of 1885, which empowered the Metropolitan to build a branch railway 2½ miles long from the point where it diverges from the main line, some three-quarters of a mile from Chalfont & Latimer station.

Most of the land for the new sections of railway was purchased at the time from the Duke of Bedford and Lord Chesham, but the land for the final half-mile of the Chesham branch was presented to the railway by the inhabitants to ensure that a station could be built in the centre of Chesham instead of on the outskirts, as was originally intended. The Metropolitan subsequently purchased further strips of land extending almost 1½ miles north of the station in the direction of Berkhamsted, land it never used.

In May 1889 the double-track railway from Rickmansworth through Chorleywood to Chalfont Road (as Chalfont & Latimer station was known until November 1915) and the single-track branch to Chesham were almost complete; so, in recognition of their generosity, the people of Chesham were invited to a ceremonial opening on 15th May and were entertained to a banquet. Seven weeks later, on 8th July, the line from Rickmansworth to Chesham was opened to public traffic. The main line

Metropolitan 4–wheeled compartment carriage No. 321, built in 1889 (Jubilee stock) and one of the 27 carriages modernised in 1908–1909 and fitted with electric lighting. There are roof ventilators above the smoking compartments only. Nine-coach trains of this stock were hauled by electric locomotives but withdrawn from Metropolitan service in 1912.

Chesham terminus on the official opening day, 15th May 1889.

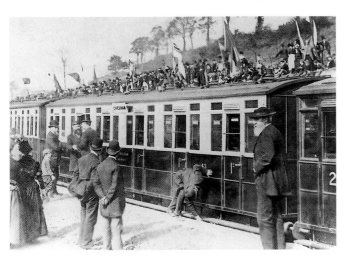

from Chalfont Road to Amersham and on to Aylesbury was not opened until 1st September 1892; for more than three years Chesham was the northern terminus of the Metropolitan. Even before the line was opened to Chesham, the Metropolitan Railway Company catered for travellers from and to Chesham by running special omnibuses between Chesham (Crown Hotel) and the railhead at Rickmansworth.

The opening of the line to Aylesbury had a significance beyond the fact that the Metropolitan now served the town. From Aylesbury there ran onwards, in the same north-westerly direction as the Metropolitan, the Aylesbury & Buckingham Railway. Opened on 23rd September 1868, this ran to Quainton Road and then swung to the north to join the Bletchley–Oxford line of the Buckinghamshire Railway. The junction, which was where the Buckinghamshire Railway's own branch to Buckingham and Banbury left the main line, was called Verney Junction after Sir Harry Verney, chairman of the Buckinghamshire Railway; there was not much else in the locality to provide a name.

From the Aylesbury & Buckingham there turned off at Quainton Road a light railway built by the Duke of Buckingham as a private venture. The Duke was active in railway affairs and controlled or helped to guide many companies. He was a director of the Buckinghamshire Railway, among others. His private estate railway ran at first to Wotton and was formally opened on 1st April 1871. Later that year and in the following year it was extended to the foot of Brill Hill, with a passenger service, but the primary purpose of the line was to carry supplies and produce connected with the duke's own estates. It was long known locally as the Wotton Tramway, whatever its official name at the time. It was 6½ miles long single-track and of standard gauge; it was worked for many years by two tiny Aveling & Porter geared locomotives.

The Aylesbury & Buckingham was a single-track line, and if it was to be of use to the Metropolitan something had to be done about it. The Metropolitan therefore took over working (with hired GWR locos and stock) from 1st July 1891 and started to double it in readiness to connect with the approaching Metropolitan metals. When the link had been achieved, through trains were run to Verney Junction, and the Metropolitan's reach was now just over 50 miles from Baker Street.

In 1883 there was a scheme to build an Oxford, Aylesbury & Metropolitan Junction Railway from Oxford to connect with the Wotton Tramway at Brill, only 10 miles or so away, and continue over the route of the Tramway. The scheme came to nothing, but it was revived as the Oxford & Aylesbury Tramroad in 1888. An Act was duly obtained; but all that happened was that the Wotton Tramway was taken over and worked under the new name in October 1894 – no new lines were built. The Oxford & Aylesbury remained the owners of the line, but the Metropolitan leased and worked it from December 1899. From April 1906 this responsibility was assumed by the Metropolitan & Great Central Joint Committee, but the Metropolitan always operated the trains. The London Passenger Transport Board continued the service from 1st July 1933 until the line closed at the end of November 1935. During the Metropolitan days it was called the Brill branch, and it was normally worked by one of the original 'A' class Fowler locomotives, hauling one passenger carriage and such goods wagons as were necessary. At level crossings the driver or fireman got down and opened the gates; a large key, carried on the footplate, was used to unlock any points that had to be changed.

What connection was there between this rural curiosity and the busy line between Paddington and the City? Sir Edward Watkin told the shareholders in 1889 that 'negotiations have been entered into with the South Eastern Company to the south and with the Manchester, Sheffield & Lincolnshire Company to the north, with a view to the development of traffic by existing and future routes.' The chairman of the South Eastern was, of course, Sir Edward Watkin, and the chairman of the MS&L was also Sir Edward Watkin. In 1890 Watkin showed the Metropolitan's shareholders a great map on which the trunk route over his three lines was displayed. The shareholders were invited to give the Manchester, Sheffield & Lincolnshire running powers over the Metropolitan from Quainton Road to Baker Street on the basis of one-third receipts going to the MS&L and the other two-thirds to the Metropolitan. Manchester to Dover via Watkin lines was the main prize – and it might not have stopped at Dover, for Watkin was also very active in advocating a Channel tunnel and had dreams of connecting his native Manchester with Paris by rail all the way. Dreams were perhaps an appropriate term, for the practical and financial problems of runing main line trains over the cheaply engineered Metropolitan tracks from Quainton Road to London and to a junction with the South Eastern do not appear to have been given much consideration by Watkin or anyone else.

By now, however, Watkin was leaving more and more of the running of the company to John Bell, who became his successor on 5th May 1894 when Watkin retired, through illness, from the boards of the Metropolitan and his other lines. Bell did not get on with William Pollitt, general manager of the MS&L, and relations between the two companies grew steadily worse. After a good deal of argument in which an unfinished tower built at Wembley by Watkin to rival the Eiffel Tower figured prominently, the agreement on running powers was modified, and the MS&L ran over the Metropolitan's tracks from Quainton Road to Canfield Place, near Finchley Road, only. Two extra tracks were built south of Harrow-on-the-Hill specially for MS&L traffic, and that railway built its own London terminus at Marylebone.

With the extension of the Metropolitan Railway into Middlesex, Hertfordshire, and Buckinghamshire during the 1880s and early 1890s, came the need for additional locomotives. Three more small classes, all tank engines, were added to the stud. Four 0-4-4 'C' class locomotives were built by Neilson's in 1891, very much to South Eastern Railway design. These were followed, in 1894/5, by six Sharp, Stewart 2-4-0 tanks, known as the 'D' class, which much resembled Barry Railway designs. Then, in 1896, the Metropolitan put into service the first of the 'E' class 0-4-4s, designed by its own locomotive superintendent, T.F. Clark; the first three were built in the Metropolitan works at Neasden, and one of them was given the number '1', replacing the original 'A' class locomotive of that number which was cut up after an accident. Four more 'E' class tanks were built by Hawthorn, Leslie in 1900-01, and in the latter year the 'F' class also appeared. This consisted of four 0-6-2 tanks built by the Yorkshire Engine Company specifically for freight working. Meanwhile, in 1897 and 1899, two Peckett 0-6-0 saddle tanks were put into service for yard work at Finchley Road and Harrow.

Beyer Peacock class 'A' locomotive heading a down train. The loco has been considerably rebuilt and fitted with a cab (compare with photo on page 15). The train consists mainly of 'rigid-eight' coaches, but the leading first-class coach (white above waist) is half of a so-called 'twin carriage', four-wheeled stock of 1869–70. The spoil heaps on the right of the picture are probably for the Great Central extension to Marylebone whose passenger service started on 15th March 1899.

The Whitechapel & Bow Railway was promoted and incorporated under an Act of 1897 to build a sub-surface connecting line between the District's Whitechapel terminus and the London, Tilbury & Southend Railway's line at Bow. It was opened on 2nd June 1902 and was jointly owned by the District and the LTSR. It was worked by the District, some trains running over it to the LTSR station at East Ham and some right through to Upminster until 1905.

An Act of 1894 gave powers to a separate company, the Ealing & South Harrow Railway Company, to build a line between the District line north of Ealing Common and South Harrow. The company made an agreement with the District and started to build in 1898, finishing the line the next year. The line did not come into use, at this time, however, since the District was in no position to provide a service over it. Another authorised line, the Harrow & Uxbridge Railway (Act of 1897) was intended to make an end-on junction with the Ealing & South Harrow; this also had a working agreement with the District. The work was slow in starting, because of lack of money, and the scheme came under the control of the Metropolitan. A new Act of 1899 added a connecting line from Harrow-on-the-Hill to Rayners Lane and allowed the Metropolitan to build the line from Harrow to Uxbridge, which was publicly opened on 4th July 1904, with steam traction. The connecting line from Rayners Lane to South Harrow was built but not used for regular public traffic because the two companies could not agree about the powers granted in the Act for the District to run over the Uxbridge branch or the costs involved. South Harrow had its first services on 28th June 1903, by District electric trains thanks to its new American owners. The Rayners Lane–South Harrow line was used for District excursions to Ruislip in summer 1909 and regular District electric trains began to run through to Uxbridge on 1st March 1910.

Uncle Lexy met me at Cannon Street Station. There was a big hole in the pavement from which yellow smoke was pouring, but we walked right into it and down some stairs. I choked and, I suspect, was rather frightened till I saw that people were taking the fumes as a matter of course. Below was a cavernous railway station, with soot-filled air dimly lit by a few naked gas jets. A long coal train rumbled by, its engine belching smoke. I noticed the engine had no cab. The footplate men stood in the open, fully exposed behind the funnel's blast. The was the underground railway. It had been going in a cut-and-cover tunnel for many years. The original Inner Circle was intended to link up all the main-line termini. Bits of it were still being used for goods traffic.

Ralph Bagnold, c1903

The East London Railway: the Birth of the Tunnelling Shield

A train leaving the north portal of the Thames Tunnel and entering Wapping station, shortly after this section of the East London Railway opened on 7th December 1869.

The East London Railway owed its existence to what was intended to be a pioneer road tunnel under the Thames. Thames tunnel schemes were put forward in 1798 and 1802 and work started on the second scheme, which was for a tunnel between Rotherhithe and Limehouse. The first shaft struck snags, and Robert Vazie, whose idea the tunnel was, called in Richard Trevithick, the amazing Cornish engineer who left his mark on locomotive development as well as many other things, to help him. The Thames Archway Company, which had been formed to exploit Vazie's plans, soon dismissed Vazie and gave Trevithick full charge. He decided that a team of Cornish miners should first drive a pilot tunnel 5ft high and 3ft wide. Starting from the Rotherhithe bank, he got to low water mark on the Limehouse side, with 84% of tunnels out of 1,220ft built, before, on 26th January 1808, the river broke in and ruined the works. Although Trevithick put forward an idea which has since been used with great success – laying large pipes under the protection of cofferdams to make the tunnel – the company's consultants said the tunnel was impossible to build in this way, and the whole idea was abandoned.

In 1818, however, Marc Brunel patented a shield for tunnelling. One of the Thames Archway promoters heard of it and talked to Brunel, following which a new company, the Thames Tunnel Company, was formed to build the tunnel between Rotherhithe and Wapping, using the shield. An Act received Royal Assent in 1825, but the work was already in hand by then.

Marc Brunel's shield was the world's first, and it was a development of it which made all the London deep tube lines possible, so it is worth describing in some detail. The original idea for this method of constructing tunnels came from a common ship worm (a mollusc) that Brunel had observed while at Chatham Dockyard. The shield was built in Henry Maudslay's works at Lambeth and consisted of 12 massive frames, each 3ft wide and 21ft 4in high, in cast iron. Each frame was divided into three compartments, one above the other, making 36 compartments in all. Massive plates below the frames served to support them, and other plates held up the ground above. Similar plates were provided at the sides of the outer frames. The whole formed a rectangular box with an open front. This opening was closed by stout oak planks across each of the 36 compartments, the planks (or 'poling boards') being pressed against the face of the excavation by adjustable 'poling screws', one end of which fitted in a recess in the plank and the other in a recess in the frame. Each plank had two poling screws to support it, and the screws could be adjusted within a range of 4½in.

One man worked in each compartment, the method being to remove one plank, cut away the ground behind to a depth of 4½in, put the plank back with the poling screws extended, and then repeat the performance until all the ground beyond the compartment had been cut away for 4½in. A staging on wheels behind the shield had a hoist for carrying away the spoil.

Bricklayers building the tunnel lining worked back-to-back with the men at the shield, and, when the earth had been cut away, jacks, using the newly-completed brickwork as an anchorage, thrust the whole shield forward 4½in. As the frames could not be moved with the poling screws in place, arrangements were provided which allowed the poling screws of one frame to be supported on those on each side of it. The frame itself could then be moved forward, the retracted screws put back on their proper frame, and the process repeated for the neighbouring frames until all had been moved forward. The entire cycle then started again. Except for the 4½in ring left when the shield was thrust forward, the tunnel was thus supported at all times by the shield or the brickwork.

The first resident engineer was William Armstrong, but he resigned because of ill-health the following April (1826), and his place was taken by the 20-year-old Isambard Kingdom Brunel, later to become famous for his work on the Great Western Railway. He was the son of Marc (afterwards Sir Marc) Brunel.

The tale of the struggles of the tunnel builders has been told elsewhere. The river broke in, the money ran out, and the incomplete tunnel became a sideshow known derisively as the 'Great Bore'. Eventually work started again, and the break-through was made in 1841, the first person to pass through the narrow hole being the three-

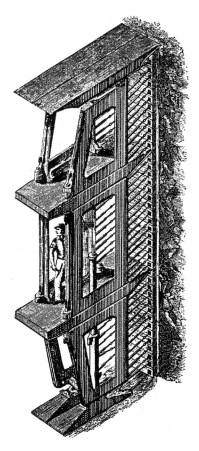

An idealised depiction of construction work in progress in the Thames Tunnel. The two-floor stage in the centre supported two opposing flows of material – excavated spoil from the shield, and bricks, cement and other building materials for the tunnel lining.

EAST LONDON RAILWAY

AND LINES IN CONNECTION THEREWITH.

MIDLAND RAILWAY

GREAT NORTHERN RY.

LONDON RAILWAY

CANONBURY

HIGHBURY

DALSTON JUNCT^N

HACKNEY

HOMERTON

VICTORIA P^K

BARNSBURY

OLD FORD

LONDON & NORTH WESTERN RAILWAY

CAMDEN R^D

KING'S CROSS STAT^N

BOW

ST PANCRAS STAT^N

EUSTON ST^N

METROPOLITAN RAILWAY

SHOREDITCH

BETHNAL GREEN

METROPOLITAN STATION

GREAT

EASTERN

RY.

GREAT EASTERN

NORTH LONDON RAILWAY

WHITECHAPEL

BROAD ST STAT^N

MOORGATE ST STAT^N

GREAT EASTERN & EAST LONDON CITY TERMINUS

COMMERCIAL R^D

LONDON & BLACKWALL RAILWAY

CHEAPSIDE MANSION HOUSE

BANK

HAYDON SQ

STEPNEY

SHADWELL

CANNON STREET

CANNON ST STAT^N

FENCHURCH ST STAT^N

LONDON

WAPPING

POPLAR

BLACKWALL

WEST INDIA DOCK

CHARING CROSS ST^N

CHARING CROSS RY.

RIVER

THAMES

METROPOLITAN DISTRICT RAILWAY

WATERLOO STATION

LONDON BRIDGE STAT^N

BRA ROAD

ROTHERHITHE

SURREY COMMERCIAL DOCKS

DEPTFORD R^D

VICTORIA STATION

WESTERN RAILWAY

BRICKLAYERS ARMS STAT^N

NEW CATTLE MARKET

NINE ELMS STATION

DEPTFORD

GREENWICH

YORK R^D

SOUTH

OLD KENT ROAD

WARDSWORTH R^D

NEW CROSS

NEW CROSS

NORTH

KENT

RY.

CHARLTON

CLAPHAM R^D

SOUTH

QUEENS R^D

BLACKHEATH

BRIXTON

LONDON

RAILWAY

PECKHAM RYE

BROCKLEY

LEWISHAM

DENMARK HILL

HONOR OAK

LADYWELL

LONDON &

CHAMPION HILL

LEE

HERNE HILL

NORTH DULWICH

LORDSHIP LANE

FOREST HILL

ELTHAM

WEST END & CRYSTAL PALACE RAILWAY

TULSE HILL

DULWICH

SYDENHAM HILL

CATFORD BR^E

DARTFORD LOOP LINE

BALHAM

SYDENHAM

SIDCUP

WIMBLEDON

STREATHAM HILL

LOWER NORWOOD

CRYSTAL PALACE

SOUTH

CHISLEHURST

TOOTING

STREATHAM COMMON

SOUTH EASTERN RAILWAY

PENGE

NEW BECKENHAM

EASTERN

LOWER MERTON

THORNTON HEATH

ANERLEY

MORDEN

SELHURST

RAILWAY

MITCHAM

MITCHAM JC^T

NORWOOD JC^T

BEDDINGTON

WEST CROYDON

ADDISCOMBE R^D

HACK BRIDGE

CARSHALTON

WADDON

CROYDON & EPSOM RAILWAY

WALLINGTON

CROYDON

LONDON BRIGHTON & SOUTH

SUTTON

CATERHAM JUNCTION

EPSOM

TO DORKING

REDHILL

TONBRIDGE

EAST LONDON RAILWAY AUTHORISED LINE COLORED RED

SECTIONS ALREADY OPENED

FURTHER SECTIONS TO BE OPENED

RUNNING POWERS

LINES CONNECTING THEREWITH FOR THROUGH TRAFFIC

TO BRIGHTON

TO HASTINGS

year-old son of I.K. Brunel. The boy's grandfather was knighted for that day's work. The opening ceremony was held on 25th March 1843, and an official procession, with band, marched through the western arch of the tunnel, which was divided internally although it had been cut as one tunnel, and back along the eastern arch. The procession had to climb up and down stairways at each end, for the approaches which would take vehicles down to and up from the tunnel had not yet been built. They never were built, for the money was not there, and the Thames tunnel remained for many years a pedestrian subway and something of a white elephant.

In 1865 the tunnel was acquired by the East London Railway (which, in common with many railway companies, never ran a train of its own) and in 1869 the railway through the tunnel was opened from the south to a station at Wapping with a train service of 23 trains a day in each direction, the service being worked by the London, Brighton & South Coast Railway, with which there was a physical connection at New Cross. The East London opened a branch between Surrey Docks and Old Kent Road in 1871, and in 1876 the line was extended from Wapping to Bishopsgate Junction on the Great Eastern Railway, enabling the LB&SC service to be extended to Liverpool Street. The East London was also connected to the South Eastern Railway and the LB&SCR up line in this year. Some trains were projected southwards to Croydon. In 1876 through trains began to run via the East London to Brighton; these continued for eight years, though in the later stages the service was reduced to through coaches only.

In 1880, the South Eastern Railway started running from Addiscombe Road to Liverpool Street via New Cross (SER). The service was later diverted to terminate at St Mary's. Trains to St Mary's ran over the Metropolitan and District joint Whitechapel curve, 485 yards in length, from the East London Railway. This curve was opened on 3rd March 1884, and St Mary's station was opened on the same day. The station was renamed St Mary's (Whitechapel Road) on 26th January 1923, and was abandoned on 30th April 1938. The Whitechapel curve was closed from 3rd December 1906 to 30th March 1913 inclusive and was again closed to public traffic from 6th October 1941.

The Metropolitan and District railways began providing services under a new working agreement on 6th October 1884, and the SER trains were withdrawn. Also represented on the joint committee established were the LB&SCR, the SER, the London, Chatham & Dover Railway, and the Great Eastern, which worked all freight services through the tunnel and, from 1886, the passenger trains which terminated at Liverpool Street.

The District services ceased on 31st July 1905, because of the electrification of the District Railway, but the LB&SCR increased its existing service between Peckham Rye, New Cross, and Shoreditch. For the same reason, the Metropolitan services were replaced in December 1906 by a limited SER service between New Cross and Whitechapel. The Shoreditch–Peckham Rye service was withdrawn in 1911, as were through trains south of New Cross.

In 1913 the East London line was electrified, without interference to traffic, and the passenger service was taken over by the Metropolitan from 31st March. Electric trains passed through the tunnel for the first time, running from New Cross to South Kensington via Baker Street, and also between Shoreditch and the two New Cross Stations. (The LB&SCR station at New Cross was renamed 'New Cross Gate' on 9th July 1923.) The western terminus was changed in February 1914 to Hammersmith (Hammersmith & City). The Metropolitan Railway took over the management of the line from 1st July 1921, and in 1925 the East London was acquired, under the Southern Railway Act, 1925, by the newly-formed Southern Railway, but was leased to the joint committee, then consisting of the SR, LNER, Metropolitan, and District. The London Passenger Transport Board became responsible for passenger service operation in 1933; in 1941 the service to Hammersmith ceased and trains terminated at Whitechapel (Shoreditch in peak hours).

When the railways were nationalised in 1948, the line passed to the London Transport Executive. It is a tribute to the sound design of Marc Brunel and to the good workmanship insisted on by I.K. Brunel that the tunnel has withstood for so long the vibration (entirely unforeseen by the builders) of frequent steam and electric train services. Major work on it did not become essential until 1994.

Access to the platforms at Wapping station is by one of the circular shafts of the original Thames Tunnel and the pillar facing the entrance of the station carries a granite plaque in memory of Sir Marc Brunel. There is also a plaque at Rotherhithe station, placed there by the American Society of Civil Engineers.

Facing page **Prospectus map of the East London Railway and its proposed connections to other railways at north and south ends, some not unlike extensions to the line at the start of the 21st Century. The East London Line closed in December 2007 in preparation for it to become part of a new London Overground network.**

The Tower Subway

Workmen entering the 12–14 seat cable-hauled car of the Tower Subway, each carrying a bag with his tools and (presumably) a packed lunch.

We now come to a different sort of underground railway. Those we have considered so far were all built near the surface. Where they could, they used the cut-and-cover method of construction. Where they had to tunnel they used the traditional railway tunnelling methods – except Sir Marc Brunel with his Thames Tunnel.

When the iron cylinders for the Lambeth suspension bridge were being sunk in 1862, the resident engineer, Peter William Barlow (a former railway engineer) had the idea that similar tubes of iron might be built horizontally to form tunnels. Working on the earlier Brunel shield idea, Barlow devised a new form of circular shield which he patented in 1864. He also thought of a transport system which could use his new tunnels, and in 1867 he published a pamphlet setting out an idea for a network of tunnels in which small cars would run – the tunnels would be only 8ft in diameter – each holding 12 passengers. The cars would be pushed by hand where gravity would not supply the force. He intended to have all the stations at a constant depth below ground and suggested that the tunnels should be built in sections at different levels to make this possible. The cars would be raised or lowered from one level to another by lifts.

This idea was too good to waste, and in 1868 a company, the Tower Subway Company, was formed to build a tube tunnel beneath the Thames. The company started construction early in 1869, and it built, with Barlow's son as engineer and a pupil of his father's, James Henry Greathead, as contractor, a tunnel 1,340ft long which ran from Great Tower Hill to Vine Street, Southwark. The single tunnel was lined with cast-iron segments giving a clear internal diameter of 6ft 7¾in. It was reached at each end by shafts 10ft in diameter and more than 50ft deep. The ironwork

was slightly smaller than the bore made with the shield, and the space between the iron and the earth was filled with liquid cement (blue lias lime) – a principle which has been retained for this type of work ever since. The shield itself was a cylinder which was pushed forward by screw jacks as miners inside it cut the earth away. As the shield moved forward, the segments were erected at once to support the new tunnel, and the shield was pushed forward again, the jacks now pushing against the newly-installed segments. The tunnel sloped downwards to a point under the centre of the river and then rose again as it approached the other bank. At its greatest depth it was 66 feet below high water level.

Once the tunnel had been completed the machinery was installed. The shafts received steam-driven lifts and a 2ft 6in gauge railway track was laid along the tunnel itself. On this track was placed a car 10 feet long with seats for 12 or 14 at a pinch, if accounts of the day are to be believed. Barlow now had the track and car he had envisaged, but he stopped short at using manpower to move the car and installed cable haulage operated by two 4hp steam engines. The formal opening took place on 2nd August 1870, although the line had been working on an experimental basis for some months before that.

The Tower Subway offered two classes of ticket, though not of travel, the more expensive (2d as against 1d) ticket merely giving priority in the lift cages. Unfortunately, the ingenuity of this first tube was greater than its capacity. Not enough people could be carried in the small car to pay for the cost of the equipment and its working. There were also mechanical troubles, and after a few months the cable car ceased to operate. The car was removed, the track lifted, and lifts dismantled. Then a spiral wooden staircase was put in each shaft with a footway along the tunnel, and from 24th December 1870 the first tube railway became a toll subway for pedestrians who paid a halfpenny each to use it. In this guise the tube played a useful part in the lives of Londoners until Tower Bridge opened in 1894 and Londoners could walk over the river instead.

There might have been other such subways, for Barlow had powers to build one between the City and Southwark and later actually began work on one between North and South Woolwich. The financial failure of the Tower Subway, however, caused both these schemes to be abandoned.

An impression of the Tower Subway cable car and its passengers, later in the working day than the previous picture.

The Tower Subway in use as a pedestrian tunnel after the abandonment of cable haulage. The rails for the cable car are still in place.

The First Electric Tube Railway

Barlow had sown the seeds and also had fired the imagination of Greathead, whose name has become attached to the shield which Brunel and then Barlow had laboured to perfect. Greathead was soon to use it to build the first major underground railway in deep tube tunnels.

The first deep-level railway, with electric traction, to be authorised was the Charing Cross & Waterloo Electric Railway, which obtained its Act in 1882. This line was to run from Trafalgar Square to Waterloo station and to have twin tubes under the Thames, though there would have been double-track tunnels clear of the river. The civil engineering work was to be carried out under Henry Law and George Chatterton; the electrical engineer was Dr C.W. Siemens. This was progress, indeed, for it was only in 1879 that Dr Werner von Siemens had demonstrated the first electric railway in the world at a Berlin exhibition.

Another proposal, for a London Central Railway Company line from the northern end of the Charing Cross & Waterloo line to St Martins-le-Grand, via Oxford Street, came before Parliament in 1884 but was turned down on the grounds that Parliament wished first to see whether the earlier part of the line was successful. This setback affected the earlier company, which saw chances of swift expansion to be unlikely, and work on its scheme was abandoned in 1885 after about 60ft of tunnel had been built under Northumberland Avenue and the Embankment.

When Greathead came on the scene in 1884 it was not as an advocate of electric traction. He had been impressed with the cable tramway introduced by Andrew Hallidie in San Francisco, on the Clay Street Hill Railroad, in 1873, and with other lines built afterwards on the same system, including the Highgate Hill tramway in London in this same year of 1884. He now joined in applying for an Act to build a twin-tunnel tube railway from near the northern end of London Bridge to the Elephant & Castle. It was largely Greathead's performance when giving evidence in committee which made sure the Act was passed, despite great opposition.

The City of London & Southwark Subway Company, as the promoters of the new scheme became, was incorporated on 28th July 1884. Greathead was the engineer with Sir Benjamin Baker and Sir John Fowler as consultants. The prospectus of the company promised 12 per cent dividends.

The terminus at the City end was at the junction of King William Street and Arthur Street (now Monument Street); the station building itself was No.46 King William Street. In those days the tubes, like the sub-surface lines, found it expedient to avoid legal arguments and compensation by following the line of the streets above. This meant that the City terminus had to be built to run roughly east and west and that the line had to curve round just after leaving the station to pass under the river (see map). It ran under Arthur Street, which was so narrow that the two tunnels had to run one above the other to keep beneath the street itself, and then under Swan Lane, at the end of which stood Old Swan Pier. South of the river, the line was to pass under Borough High Street and Newington Causeway to the Elephant, a total distance of 1½ miles. Intermediate stations were to be built at Denman Street (London Bridge) and Great Dover Street (Borough).

In February 1886 the main contract for the tunnels and stations was placed with Edmund Gabbutt, a Liverpool contractor. Preparations began in May, and work started in October from a shaft sunk from a temporary staging behind the Old Swan Pier. From this shaft the driving of the upper (up line) tunnel southwards began the same month. The lower (down) tunnel was not started until the following March, and then it was driven so that it rose to the same level as the up tunnel, and to the west of it, on the south side of the river. These tunnels were 10ft 2in in diameter and accommodated a standard-gauge railway track.

In 1887 powers were obtained to continue the line southwards to Stockwell, making the line just over three miles in length. It was decided that the tunnels on this section should be 10ft 6in in diameter because the gradients were easier and the trains could be run at a higher speed. The engine house to be built at the Elephant would drive one cable for the City section at 10mph and another for the Stockwell section at 12mph. The contract for the new section of the line was let to Walter Scott & Company, of Newcastle, the same firm also completing the City section when ill-health caused Edmund Gabbutt to withdraw.

Contracts for the lifts had been placed, and so had those for the cable apparatus, but doubts began to be expressed about the wisdom of cable working. Electric traction had already been mooted for other lines, as we have seen, and what really seems to have turned the scales was the success of the electrically-operated Bessbook & Newry Railway in Ireland, opened in 1885. That electric traction was practicable had already been shown in Great Britain, for Magnus Volk had opened his electric railway at Brighton in 1883.

The technical press was already drawing the attention of the chairman of the City of London & Southwark, Charles Grey Mott, to the advantages of electric traction, and he sought professional advice. In its report for the half-year in August 1888, the board told the shareholders that experiments were to be made with electric traction pending a decision on its use. One of the most famous signal engineers of the day, C.E. Spagnoletti, who has already been mentioned in connection with the signalling of the Metropolitan Railway, was called in as consultant on electric traction. This caused some comment at the time, as he had had no experience in this field, but there is no reason to doubt that his advice was sound.

In January 1889 a contract was placed with Mather & Platt Ltd, who undertook to supply the power necessary to run a three-minute service from each station and to run the trains at a higher average speed than those of the Inner Circle. They also gave a guaranteed cost per train-mile for a period of two years – lower than the cost of steam working if steam working had been allowed. An experimental train was to be provided by the contractors.

Meanwhile, work proceeded on the stations and tunnels. The King William Street terminus site was reached by a shaft from above, but eventually most of the debris from the station works and the City end of the tunnels went out by the shaft in the river at Old Swan Pier. When the work was completed, this shaft was sealed and made watertight over the tunnels and the staging was removed. At platform

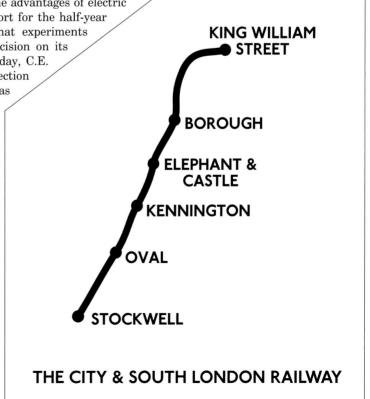

KING WILLIAM STREET

BOROUGH

ELEPHANT & CASTLE

KENNINGTON

OVAL

STOCKWELL

THE CITY & SOUTH LONDON RAILWAY

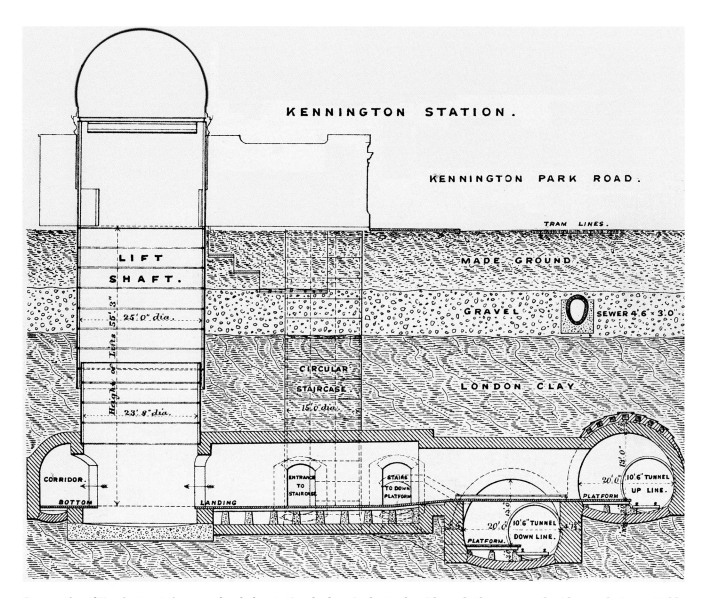

KENNINGTON STATION.

KENNINGTON PARK ROAD.

TRAM LINES.

MADE GROUND

GRAVEL

SEWER 4'.6" × 3'.0"

LIFT SHAFT.

25'.0" dia.

Height of Lifts 55'.3"

CIRCULAR STAIRCASE.

15'.0" dia.

LONDON CLAY

23'.8" dia.

13'.0"

CORRIDOR.

BOTTOM

LANDING

ENTRANCE TO STAIRCASE.

STAIRS TO DOWN PLATFORM.

20'.0"

10'.6" TUNNEL UP LINE.

PLATFORM

20'.0"

10'.6" TUNNEL DOWN LINE.

PLATFORM.

Cross section of Kennington station as originally built. The station tunnels had a 3ft deep brick lining, and the terminal stations had tunnels 26ft wide and 20ft high. At intermediate stations there were tunnels for each line, each tunnel being 20ft wide, 16ft high (13ft from platform level), and 200ft long. Stockwell terminus differed from the layout shown and had an island platform with a track on each side. The reason for the different heights of platforms at intermediate stations was to reduce the number of steps between platform and lift landing. This was achieved completely at Oval, with low-level inclines to both platforms.

level the station had a single track with a platform on each side – a design suitable for cable operation but not electric. The street was reached by two hydraulic lifts running in a single 25ft diameter shaft. The gas-lit station was modified in 1895 (while still operational!) and became a two-track layout with an island platform between the two tracks. At the Stockwell end a 1-in-3½ incline led from the station to the rolling stock depot at the side of Spurgeon's Orphanage in the Clapham Road. Cable haulage was needed to take stock up this incline. The intermediate stations were Borough, Elephant & Castle, Kennington, and Oval.

Experimental running began in September 1889 with one locomotive and two coaches. The track was not yet complete, nor was the generating station at Stockwell, so current was taken, on the three-rail system, from a temporary generating station at the Borough, from which point the rails to the City were complete. The first tunnel went through to Stockwell in January 1890, and a second, geared, locomotive arrived for trials in February. On 7th March the company felt sufficiently confident of progress to take the Lord Mayor and other guests from the City to the Elephant. They also proposed to take them back again to a special luncheon, but the water company, having found some defect, turned off the supply of water to the temporary generating plant, which had to be hastily shut down. The party did get back by rail, an hour late, but the effect on the food – and tempers – is not known. Everyone had recovered enough to take Metropolitan Railway directors on a similar trip the following week.

The formal opening was on 4th November 1890; it was performed by the Prince of Wales (later King Edward VII). In the meantime, the company's name had been changed to the City & South London Railway to match its enlarged status – still further enlarged by the granting of Parliamentary authority to continue the line to Clapham – and it was under this name that the line was opened. The party travelled

The City & South London construction site at Stockwell where, as at many other locations, property had to be demolished to make space for work and for the later erection of a surface station.

from King William Street to Oval to look at the works and equipment, and then on to Stockwell for lunch in a marquee in the rolling-stock depot. The general manager had been appointed – T.C. Jenkin, a former London, Tilbury & Southend Railway accountant – and so had the resident engineer, who was Basil (later Sir Basil) Mott. Pleased as they no doubt were with the ceremony and the electric locomotive specially painted for the occasion in cream and grey and named Princess of Wales, they were

The Prince of Wales arriving at Stockwell station after formally opening the railway – 4th November 1890. The party was walking towards the lifts.

probably even more pleased to receive on the same day permission from the Board of Trade to open the line for public traffic. The first electric tube railway was in business at last. Even now, however, there was a delay while the staff familiarised themselves, but public service started eventually on Thursday 18th December 1890.

The line started working with 14 locomotives built by Mather & Platt at their Salford Iron Works to the design of Dr Edward Hopkinson. They had doors at the ends, measured 14 feet over the centre buffers, weighed 10.35 tons, and were carried on four 27in wheels. Each of the axles was driven by a 50-hp motor with its armature built directly on the axles, the first time this arrangement, obviating gearing, had been used. The second trial locomotive, which was geared, was so noisy that it was tucked away and used only in emergency. It was said to be audible at one station when starting from the next down the line. The two motors were connected permanently in series and took power at 500V d.c. through cast-iron flat collector shoes from the third rail. This was a channel-section steel rail carried on glass insulators and mounted between the rails about a foot from the eastern rail.

The locomotives had air brakes but no air pumps, relying on large reservoirs which were recharged at Stockwell on each trip. There was no 'dead man's handle' in those days to ensure that power was cut off and that brakes were applied if anything happened to the driver, so an assistant had to be carried on the locomotive. Originally these locomotives were in the works livery of dark red, or red-brown, but they soon blossomed forth in orange chrome in three panels on each side, with black and yellow borders to the panels.

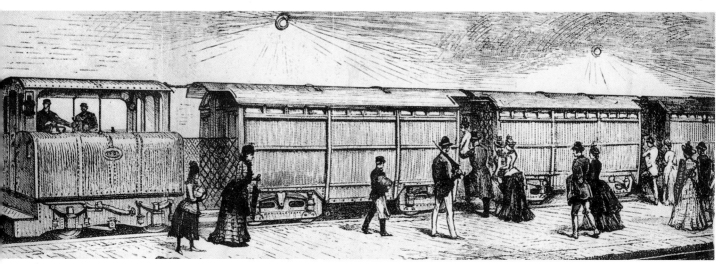

These little locomotives, one of which survives, pulled three-car trains. The cars – 30 of them – were built by the Ashbury Railway Carriage & Iron Co. Each car had seats for 32, arranged in two long seats facing each other across the car, and the bogie frames were extended beyond the wooden body to provide platforms for the guards or attendants, and incidentally to give a semi-circular end to the frame in lieu of headstocks. As there were no buffers on the cars, this arrangement also served as a bumper if required. The attendants rode between the ends of the cars on their platforms and opened and closed lattice gates, letting people into or out of the cars through doors in the ends of the wooden bodies via the platforms and the lattice gates. The attendants also told passengers where they were, for the upholstery was carried up nearly to the roof, leaving only slit windows for ventilation. This was done, apparently, on the assumption that there was no need for windows because there was nothing to see. These cars quickly earned the name of 'padded cells' – perhaps the company thought passengers needed them, because it also felt it necessary to forbid passengers to ride on the roof of the train, although this appears to have been a standard railway regulation applied rather thoughtlessly to the CSLR. One car of each train was set aside for smokers, and it is said that ladies were forbidden to enter it. Each car had four electric lamps, but they were only of 16 candlepower each and not very efficient. They were always short of current, a situation which also made it necessary for the stations to be provided with gas instead of electric lamps.

At first there was a train every five minutes and the average speed was about 11½mph including stops. The hydraulic lifts at the stations, power for which was produced at Stockwell and carried along the tunnels in a main at 1,240lb per sq in,

Turnstiles in a station ticket office, to allow the original system of ticketless flat fare travel, but return tickets were issued from spring 1892.

Right The interior of a 'padded cell' car, with the attendant on the end platform, keeping an eye on the passengers and preparing to announce the name of the next station.

Facing page centre **Car No. 30, rebuilt into 'padded cell' configuration for the Darlington railway centenary celebrations of 1925.**

Facing page bottom **A Bristol Carriage & Wagon car of 1901. Successive batches of carriages built after 1890 had increasingly larger windows.**

took away the disadvantages of a deep line, and the railway prospered. Its two-penny fare seems to have been well calculated, and in its first two weeks it carried 165,000 passengers. It was safe, using a version of Spagnoletti's lock-and-block signalling apparatus with mechanically-operated signals, and, of course, it was clean and quick. It did not run on Sundays until 5th April 1891, and not on Sunday mornings until 1st August 1909.

The first extension to the railway after the opening date was to Moorgate, forming part of an extension to the Angel which had been authorised in 1893. The Act concerned also gave powers to replace King William Street, which was so awkwardly placed that the down line had to negotiate a 1 in 14 gradient on leaving it, by a station at the Bank. It also provided for a station near the south side of London Bridge. The avoiding line needed to connect these two stations left the original line north of Borough station and passed under the Thames east of London Bridge, leaving the original tunnels under the river and the original terminus deserted. The line to Moorgate was opened on 25th February 1900. The deserted tunnels were blocked off from the rest of the line during the Second World War to avoid any risk of flooding, and parts of the tunnels were used as air raid shelters.

The extension used an improved signalling system which had also been applied to the 'main line'. Electric lamps had replaced oil and gas in the signals, and the original long block sections, which extended from the starting signal at one station to the starting signal at the next (or the buffer stops at the termini), were shortened by adding an outer home signal to the home signal which protected a train at a platform – really only an emergency signal. To make sure that a section was clear, an ingenious form of 'last axle' indicator was used. This consisted of an insulated plate mounted on each side of the tunnel and a special brush on the last car of each train. When the brush touched the plate it completed a block release circuit through the rails. This was the first apparatus of this type on an underground railway. The effect was that as soon as a train was known to have come within the protection of the outer home signal, that signal could be put at danger and the starting signal at the station in rear could be lowered to allow another train to follow. There were no distant signals on the line. Repeaters were provided for the signals where necessary, and there were some minor changes, but broadly this form of signalling lasted until replaced after the 1914–18 war by automatic signalling.

The extension tunnels were 11ft 6in in diameter, this size being adopted in an effort to improve ventilation, but it seems not to have had the desired effect, as it was only carried out to Moorgate. London Bridge and Bank stations were built with two platforms on the same level and connecting passages, now a common plan. These three stations had electric lifts from opening, following a successful conversion to electric operation at Kennington in 1897. The intermediate stations on the original line had platforms at different levels, staggered so that one overlapped the other by many yards. Where site conditions allowed, the different platform levels allowed slopes to be substituted for steps between the lower lift landings and each platform.

The extension was opened to the Angel on 17th November 1901. Meanwhile, the southern extension to Clapham Common, authorised in the 1890 Act, was opened on 3rd June 1900. Powers to extend from the Angel to Euston were obtained in 1903 and the line was opened officially to this station on 11th May 1907, public traffic beginning the next day. The Angel extension had two intermediate stations, Old Street and City Road (the latter closed in 1922); there was one station, King's Cross, between the Angel and Euston.

The new stations had electric lifts. At Euston, Angel, Clapham Road (now Clapham North) and Clapham Common there was a single island platform in a 30ft diameter tube. Electric lights were placed all along the tunnels at about this time so that a signalman could turn them on if a train was an unusually long time in any section and might be in trouble. At about the same time, two bare wires were affixed to the tunnel walls so that a train driver could lean out of his stopped train and fix a telephone handset to the wires anywhere in the tunnel. He could then speak to the signalman ahead and tell him what was wrong.

More locomotives and rolling stock were needed for all these extensions, and by 1907 there were 52 locomotives and 165 cars by various builders. The locomotives retained much the same appearance as the original 14 but were smoother in outline. They also had better control arrangements, air pumps for the air brake system, and electric headlamps. In an attempt to work four-car trains into King William Street, a four-car motor coach train, with the motors incorporated in the cars instead of in a separate locomotive, was tried in 1894. Not much is known about this train, which seems to have been a 'do-it-yourself' effort at Stockwell depot. The main reason for failure seems not to have been mechanical or electrical, but the time taken by the driver and his assistant to change ends at the terminus. By the time they had pushed their way through the crowds the train was already late in leaving.

The coaching stock seems to have improved slowly, the main step forward coming with the building and delivery by the Brush Company in 1906–1908 of 25 all-steel cars of a greatly improved type.

Other improvements were a hydraulic car lift to obviate the use of the cable slope at Stockwell and the introduction of four-car trains in 1900 and five-car in 1907. In 1913, the C&SLR became part of the Underground Group, and a new chapter opened in its eventful life. Before we look at that, however, we must go back and see what other tubes were being built.

A Crompton 1901 locomotive, probably No. 36, which was repainted for the Darlington Railway Centenary Celebrations of 1925, and was subsequently displayed at Moorgate station until damaged in a Second World War air raid and later scrapped.

City & South London car interior. A design from the intermediate period, with larger windows than the original stock, but with some way to go to the rectangular windows and full height draught screen glazing of the Brush cars of 1906/1907. The mirrors on the end bulkheads and the deeply upholstered seats give almost a touch of luxury.

The Waterloo & City

A train of the original 1898 stock of the Waterloo & City. Trains were normally of four-car length, and were not increased to five cars until enough extra trailer cars had been delivered in 1922. To the rear of the cab and equipment compartment is a hand operated sliding door for passenger use. This would have sped boarding and alighting each end of this short railway and represents the first use of sliding doors on a tube train. It was this door which required the floor height to be excessively low to give headroom (and probably why it wasn't pursued on other early tube stock).

The next tube railway to appear on the scene was one which remained independent of London Transport until 1994. It was built as an extension to the London & South Western Railway, which had always wanted to push into the City but had somehow missed its chance. It considered a full-scale deep-level line to take its trains into the City and also an elevated line, but both these solutions were turned down as immensely costly, and a deep-level electrically-operated tube railway seemed the only practicable answer if LSWR patrons were to be taken where most of them wanted to go – the City. An Act for a deep line, with twin tunnels, starting under Waterloo station and ending at a point near Mansion House was obtained in July 1893. The Act was obtained by the Waterloo & City Railway Company, but this was a matter of name only, the LSWR being the force behind it. Greathead was the engineer in partnership with the LSWR consulting engineer, W.R. Galbraith. The resident engineer was H.H. Dalrymple Hay.

Work on the line began in mid-1894. It ran under Stamford Street and then diagonally under the Thames to the north bank, reached near Blackfriars Bridge. From there it was a straight run up Queen Victoria Street to the Mansion House terminus (which was called City when the line was opened and renamed 'Bank' on 28th October 1940). The under-river section was excavated from shafts sunk right through the river bed down to working level. Spoil was loaded direct into river barges from the top of the shafts.

The Act allowed either electric or cable working, but the success of the City & South London ensured that electric working was adopted. The tunnels were much larger than those of the CSLR, being a minimum of 12ft 1½in in diameter and allowing larger stock. The gauge was the standard 4ft 8½in.

The Waterloo and City decided from the first not to use locomotives; four-car trains made up of motor cars and trailers were decided on. The cars were built in America, assembled at the LSWR Eastleigh Works, and brought up to Waterloo by steam power. Trains drew power from a third (centre) rail, current being supplied from a

Interior of one of the 1898 motor cars with a raised section at the far end to clear the motor bogie.

small power station next to the line's low-level workshops at Waterloo. One unusual feature (which was soon considered too dangerous to be allowed on new tube lines) was that power cables ran through the cars. (The modern multiple-unit principle is that low-voltage control lines only are carried through a train.)

The work was completed in 1897, and on 11th July 1898, the 1½-mile line was opened by the Duke of Cambridge. It opened for public traffic on 8th August.

There are no intermediate stations on the line, and it has no running connection with any other underground line. When stock needed overhaul, it was raised by the hoist at Waterloo to the main lines. The railway was taken over by the London & South Western Railway in 1907 and came down into the hands of the Southern Region of British Railways. The original stock survived until 1940, when it was completely replaced by modern cars with power-operated doors, and standard Southern Railway current collection.

This photograph of a female gateman on the Waterloo & City Railway in April 1917 provides a good view of the sliding doors at the end of each carriage. The post holding the open gate can be seen to the right of her. Manning the trains had always been a male-only preserve and this was the rule on the Underground until the 1970s. This exception to the rule, made also by the Underground Group lines, was because of a shortage of men during the First World War.

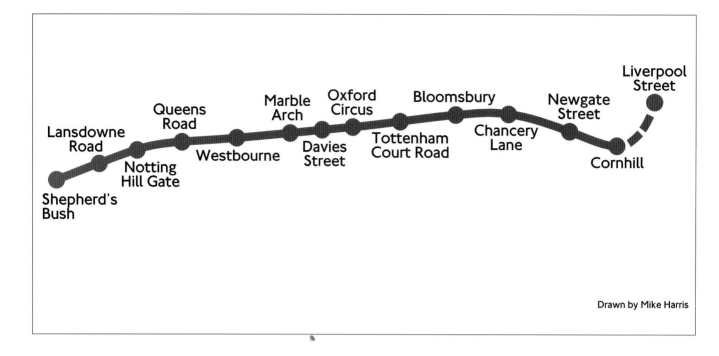

Drawn by Mike Harris

The Central London Railway

The third tube line was destined to make a much greater mark than either of the earlier ones. The Central London Railway thrust itself impudently right across London to reach the City from the west, and Londoners took it to their hearts at once. Like the other lines, however, it was a long time being born.

The original Central London Railway Bill was drawn up to include three railways, the first from a point in the Bayswater Road to a point in Oxford Street just west of the junction of Old Quebec Street; the second from the end of railway No.1 to a point in King William Street and the third from the end of No.2 to junctions with the City of London & Southwark Subway at Arthur Street West. The scheme for this last junction was later abandoned. The Bill passed through the Commons in April–May 1890 but was rejected in July by the Lords.

Among the objectors was the Metropolitan Railway, which claimed that the proposed line was badly engineered and that the electric motive power would have to be replaced eventually by steam ('the only efficient form of railway motive power'). The District also objected, for the new line gave a short cut across the Inner Circle. Other objectors included the City Corporation, the Dean and Chapter of St Paul's, and landowners and frontagers along the route.

Undismayed, the promoters made some concessions to the objectors and returned to Parliament in the next session with a new Bill which combined their original scheme and one originated by the London Central Subway, giving a railway running from Shepherd's Bush to Cornhill. The Bill passed through all its stages and received the Royal Assent on 5th August 1891. In 1892 a scheme for extending the line from the Bank to Liverpool Street, with a station at the Royal Exchange instead of that originally proposed to be in Cornhill, was approved by Parliament.

As soon as the 1891 Act was passed, the Central London Railway Company was able to prepare for the start of work. Greathead was an obvious choice as one of the engineers; so were Sir John Fowler and Sir Benjamin Baker as the others. The original chairman was Henry Tennant, formerly general manager of the North Eastern Railway, but in 1898 he retired from the chairmanship – he was by now an old man – in favour of Sir Henry Oakley, former general manager of the Great Northern Railway. J.H. Greathead died soon after work started, and his place was taken by Basil Mott, whom we first met in connection with the CSLR.

After some delay, contracts for the tunnelling and structural work were let in the spring of 1896. There were three contractors: J. Price (Shepherd's Bush–Marble Arch), Walter Scott & Company (Marble Arch–Post Office), and G. Talbot (Post Office–Bank). Most of the tunnel was built through London clay, but hard rock, sand, and hard clay were encountered in one area.

'I am one of the five directors who have undertaken to carry out a work of colossal consequence for London, and which, depending upon an endless number of problems which must be solved, is extremely interesting. This is to build the Central London Railway. It will go through the heart of London almost in a straight line in two tunnels ... Whether it will bring in anything for me is questionable, but I have a very large interest in it.'

Frederic E. Warburg, a Swedish-born businessman in a letter of 17th December 1895.

Construction of a Central London Railway platform tunnel, March 1898. The heavy concrete wall would support one edge of the future timber floor, to be replaced by stone slabs soon after opening, after worries about fires on underground lines.

A view six months later at the same site. Progress has been made in installing glazed white tiles on the walls, ceiling and headwall.

Like most of London's original tube railways, the Central London followed the line of roads above, with the result that where the roads were narrow the general scheme of platforms between the tracks at a common level had to be modified. Thus at Notting Hill Gate and Post Office the westbound track and platform were above the eastbound; the reverse arrangement applied at Chancery Lane.

The running tunnels were 11ft 8¼ inches in diameter, with enlargments as required on curves and at stations. They lay between 60 and 110 feet below the surface, the greatest depth being in the middle of the line between Notting Hill Gate and Holland Park. The original intention was to have 11ft 6in diameter tunnels; this measurement allowed for the lining of the iron rings with brick and/or concrete. This lining work was not carried out, except for a few yards at the ends of station platforms. Although the minimum diameter was 11ft 6in in these short lined sections, the minimum diameter of the rest of the line, measured to the iron work, was 11ft 8¼in, the diameter adopted later for the other London tube railways.

With the use of the Greathead shield, assisted by the Thomson mechanical excavator, no special difficulties were met. One of the hardest tasks was the building of the Bank station, where a mass of pipes had to be diverted. All the pipes were arranged in a special tunnel of their own immediately beneath the public subways, which the Central London had agreed to build and hand over to the City Corporation in return for being allowed to build under the open area at Bank free of charge.

The steelwork for the booking hall at Bank was temporarily assembled in a field and was then transferred, section by section, to its site at Bank. This station is built over the dried-up course of the once-navigable Walbrook.

In 1896 negotiations with the Great Eastern and North London railways over the station at Liverpool Street failed, and it was decided to make the Bank station the terminus, although the tunnels were carried some distance beyond for use as reversing sidings.

The line was originally to be worked by trains with electric locomotives at both head and tail – a forerunner of the multiple-unit principle – but the Board of Trade refused to allow the power lines to be carried through the train (even though this had been allowed for the Waterloo & City). Greathead therefore decided on single heavier locomotives capable of hauling seven cars. They were designed (somewhat after an American pattern, built for the Baltimore & Ohio) by the company's electrical engineer, Horace Parshall. The 28 locomotives were built in America by the General Electric Company. The cars, much more massive affairs than those of the City & South London, were built by the Ashbury and Brush companies. There were 168 of these cars, each with longitudinal and cross seats for 48 passengers. They were 45ft 6in long and had straps for standing passengers to hold in common with the two earlier London tube lines. They had gates on end platforms, worked by train attendants or conductors as on the C&SLR.

A Central London Railway train at Shepherd's Bush station, headed by one of the 44–ton locomotives which soon had to be withdrawn because they caused too much vibration at surface level. Originally, the platforms on the Central London Railway were made of wooden planks. From 1909, these began to be replaced by concrete as a fire safety measure.

Bank station in about 1903. The track
formation may be noted, with positive
centre conductor rail, and running rails
comprising bridge rail and longitudinal
sleepers with cross-timbers. The
posters employ a wide range of sizes
(at least six varieties); the days of
standard poster dimensions were still
far ahead.

The station building at the Shepherd's
Bush terminus, where passengers
could interchange to tram services
towards Acton or Kew. The 2d flat fare
is boldly advertised.

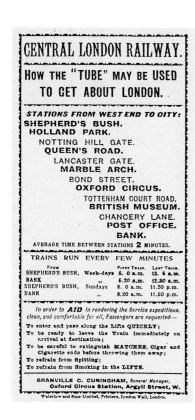
The power station and train depot occupied a large site on the east side of Wood Lane, part of which had previously been occupied by a fine house and garden known as 'Wood House'. The Wood Lane power station generated electricity at 5,000V; it was one of the earliest stations to generate electricity at such a high voltage and to produce alternating current instead of direct.

Three of the original substations – Notting Hill Gate, Marble Arch, and Post Office – were located at the bottom of the station lift shafts. This proved a disadvantage so long as rotary converters were in use and these low-level substations were eventually abandoned. It is now feasible, with modern rectifier equipment, to locate substations in lift shafts again, and it could well be said that in their choice of site the designers of the Central London Railway were well ahead of their time.

The substations fed current to the track at 550V dc. The track itself had three rails, the running rails being 100lb per yd bridge-type rails on oak longitudinal timbers. Cross timbers carried the 85lb per yd positive conductor rail, which was mounted on porcelain insulators between the running rails.

On 27th June 1900, the formal opening ceremony took place. Among the distinguished company was again the Prince of Wales (within a year to become King Edward VII) who took a great interest in the new 5¾-mile tube line between Shepherd's Bush and the Bank. The company travelled westwards from the Bank, and to quote a contemporary account: 'The electric train, with its seven carriages, glided with an ease that was almost magical out of the brilliantly-lit Bank station into the great tube that has been cut into the London clay...slipped through brightly-lighted white-tiled stations one after the other, until, twenty minutes after it had started, it climbed smoothly up into sunlight at Shepherd's Bush.'

At the depot the Prince of Wales made the only speech of the day. He said, 'I have great pleasure in declaring the Central London Railway open. I am sure it will prove a great boon to our great City; and I think Sir Benjamin Baker, its engineer, is to be congratulated on the success with which he has carried out the undertaking. I ask you to drink with me: success to the Central London Railway.' Possibly the shortest opening speech on record!

As the *Daily News* said a month later: 'When a place is royally opened it is not always really opened'; and it was not until Monday 30th July 1900 that the new stations opened their doors to the public. On that day 84,500 passengers thronged the trains and stations, and thousands more looked on. On Saturday 4th August 1900, the *Daily Mail* recorded: 'Meantime London, all agape, crowds to the Twopenny Tube. Thursday's traffic returns completely eclipse the previous day's, as the following list shows; Tuesday – 91,600 passengers; Wednesday – 86,000 passengers; Thursday – 93,000 passengers. Yesterday the crowds swayed and surged to get on to the trains. It was a cosmopolitan throng. Nearly every civilised nation under the sun was represented among the humanity that was struggling to experience London's latest sensation.'

The surface station building at Holland Park. This has been restored in recent years and is the most unspoilt of the surviving original stations.

TAKING THE TICKET AT BANK STATION.

No worry about price 2ᵈ any distance

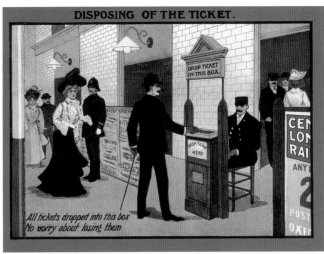

DISPOSING OF THE TICKET.

All tickets dropped into this box No worry about losing them

ENTERING THE TRAIN.

Trains every few minutes. No worry about catching them.

LEAVING THE STATION AT SHEPHERDS BUSH.

The whole distance covered so quickly that there's nothing to worry about.

With its flat fare of 2d and its careful siting to tap a main traffic stream, the Central London proved the potential of tube railway travel. It was the first really modern tube. Its smart trains, hauled by their electric locomotives in crimson lake with gold lining and polished brass-work, opened the eyes of London to the possibilities of underground travel far more than the CSLR or the Waterloo & City had done. In the five remaining months of 1900 it carried nearly 15 million passengers, running from 5am to midnight on weekdays, with a reduced service on Sundays. The route, connecting the residential areas of west London with the City and running the length of Oxford Street to serve the shopping and theatre areas, could scarcely have been better chosen to attract passengers at all times of the day and evening.

It was not long, however, before the Central London ran into trouble. The attractive American-built double-bogie locomotives, with their central cabs, had their armatures built directly on to the axles, obviating gears and making them very silent. Their four motors gave them 800hp (one-hour rating) and a tractive effort at starting of 14,100lb. Efficient as the system of mounting the motors was, it meant that of the locomotive weight of 44 tons only a quarter was spring-borne, and they set up a vibration which disturbed property owners along the line so much that a Board of Trade committee was set up to investigate.

The Central London Railway co-operated whole-heartedly in the enquiry, which confirmed that there was serious vibration, and three of its locomotives were converted to operate with 150hp geared motors. This reduced the weight to 31 tons, of which 21 tons were spring-borne. The railway also made up two six-car trains with two cars in each train converted to motor cars by fitting them with two 100hp geared motors each, giving 400hp per train. Tests with the geared locomotives showed that the vibration was greatly reduced, but no vibration was noticed at any point on the surface when the multiple-unit trains ran below. As a result of these trials the railway decided to replace the locomotives by 64 motor cars and to make the multiple-unit trains up to seven cars although six-car trains soon became the norm. A new motor

These four pictures have been extracted from a larger poster, and show how easy it is to buy a ticket, surrender it on entry, board a train and leave the destination station. The words at the foot of each picture are all on the theme of 'no worry', respectively about price, losing your ticket, catching your train (because the service is so frequent) and taking a long time for your journey.

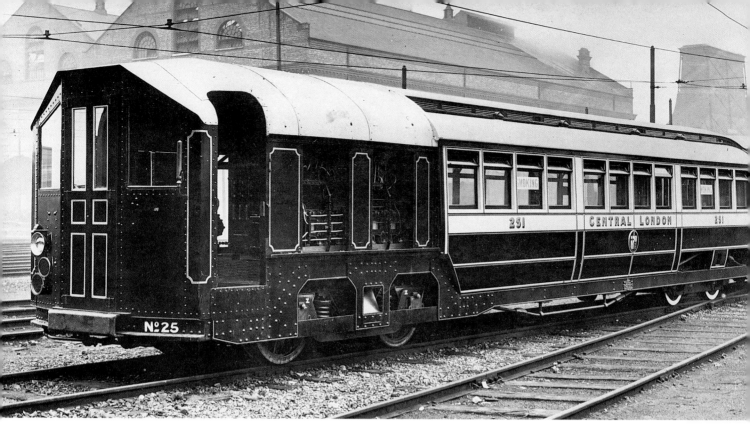

Driving motor car 251 of multiple unit train No. 25 of 1903 is seen at Wood Lane depot when new, one of a fleet of 64 new vehicles that replaced the original electric locomotives after only three years of use. Overhead wiring was installed at the depot so that the remaining locos could haul the stock around the unelectrified track.

At first the CLR trains were very labour-intensive, and eight men were carried on a seven-car train: the driver and his assistant, a front and rear guard, and four gatemen. Starting the train was a complicated ritual, with each gateman facing the front of the train and holding up his hand when the gates were shut. When the front guard saw the correct number of hands he showed a green light to the rear, to which the rear guard responded by showing a green light forward and blowing a whistle. On receiving these signals the front guard showed a green light forward to the driver or his assistant, and the train could start.
J. Graeme Bruce

giving 125hp was designed for the stock, giving 500hp per train. The service was being fully worked with the new trains by June 1903. The easier turn-round made a two-minute service possible against the 2½ minute service which was the best that could be provided with the locomotives. At first, the motor cars had to be manned by a crew of two, but later, after the adoption of the 'dead man's handle', only a driver was required.

An interesting feature of the locomotives was that they had a series-parallel controller of the drum type made up of a wooden cylinder with the copper segments attached. This drum was of no less than 18in diameter and required some physical effort to move it. To assist him with a certain amount of leverage, the driver was provided with a control handle 21 inches in length! After replacement by multiple-unit trains, all but two of the locomotives were scrapped. For a time another two locomotives were used by J.S. Raworth, after adaptation, to demonstrate his regenerative braking system on the Metropolitan, but were soon scrapped.

Just before the First World War, the passenger fleet comprised 64 motor cars, 133 trailers and 38 control trailers. Two 0-6-0 steam locomotives were mainly used to shunt trailer cars in the depot yard but also when power was off in the tunnels. Built to tube loading gauge by the Hunslet Engine Co. Ltd in 1899, these were side-tank locomotives fitted with condensing apparatus. They were oil-fired in the tunnels but coal could be burnt in the open, and a small coal bunker was provided for the purpose. They were sold in 1920 and 1921. The last of the two retained electric locomotives was in service for shunting purposes until 1942.

In 1902 a Bill was submitted to Parliament for powers to extend the line from Shepherd's Bush to Hammersmith, Piccadilly, Strand, and the City to form a 'Central London Circle', on which it was proposed to operate a service similar to that provided by the Circle line. The Bill was rejected, and although revived in 1903 and 1905, was eventually abandoned; the opening in 1906 of the Great Northern, Piccadilly & Brompton Railway from Hammersmith to Finsbury Park (now part of the Piccadilly Line) had removed many of the original attractions of the scheme.

The Central London was now in a settled form, but from 1905 there was a steady drop in passengers, no doubt largely due to the counter-attractions of the Metropolitan and District railways, which had recently been electrified, and also of the motor bus. In 1907, therefore, it was decided that the twopenny flat fare should not apply to passengers travelling more than seven or eight stations and in July of that year a 3d fare came into force. The 'Twopenny Tube' was a twopenny tube no longer, though the name lingered.

The first extension to the railway came in 1908 when on 14th May, the opening day of the Franco-British Exhibition at the White City, the railway opened a loop

line from Shepherd's Bush to Wood Lane. This sharply-curved half-mile line was designed to improve terminal working by eliminating use of the cross-over at the western end of the line, and a station was built on it on Wood Lane to serve the exhibition. The exhibition brought a rise in traffic, but its closing was marked by another decline. Possibly to compete with the motor buses, the Central London introduced a penny fare, for three stations, in 1909.

In 1911 the company started to carry parcels and mails, for which special compartments were provided on four cars. In the compartments rode a parcels porter who sorted the traffic during the journey. A number of tricycle-mounted messenger boys collected the parcels and delivered them; special wicker hampers were used between surface and platform levels. The service lasted until 1917, when the war had reduced the staff to the point where it could no longer be carried on. It was never resumed. The City & South London had a parcels service from 1891 to 1918, and the Metropolitan from 1889 to 1934.

The year 1911 also saw the introduction of season tickets on the line at the same time as they were reintroduced on the Bakerloo, Hampstead and Piccadilly tubes. A short extension at the eastern end of the Central London from the Bank to Liverpool Street opened the following year. Parliamentary powers had been obtained for this extension in 1892, but the scheme had been postponed. Four escalators were installed at the new station, two connecting with the Great Eastern station and two with Broad Street (North London Railway). They were of the early 'side-stepping' variety as were all London Underground escalators until the experimental 'comb' type at Clapham Common in 1924.

The Central London's signalling was mechanical and very much like that on the City & South London, using Spagnoletti's lock-and-block system. There were semaphore starting signals at the platforms, but in the tunnels, where there was less room, the inner and outer home signals were sliding coloured spectacles. Between the Bank and Shepherd's Bush there were 14 signalboxes. These included separate boxes for each direction at the three two-level stations – Post Office, Chancery Lane, and Notting Hill Gate. As on the CSLR, the block section extended from the starting signal at one station to the outer home of the next, the line between the outer home and the starting signal at that station forming a separate section controlled by the signalman at the station concerned. The brush-on-last-bogie system was employed to check that a train had actually passed inside the outer home. There were signalboxes at each terminal station in addition to the 14 mentioned. Track circuits and automatic signals were installed eventually, the work beginning in 1912.

On 1st January 1913, the Central London Railway became a member of the Underground Group.

The *Tramway and Railway World* of 6th August 1908 compares the Central London Railway and C&SLR. The CLR 'spends more on the passengers'. The streets above the CLR are 'perambulated for pleasure by a leisured, well-dressed class of people who have to be attracted to the tube, or they will not ride at all'. The C&SLR is 'mostly patronised by workmen'.

GT NORTHERN & CITY (ELECTRIC) RAILWAY. Finsbury Park Station.

A Bigger Tube –
The Great Northern & City Railway

A wooden-bodied train of Great Northern & City stock as used on the line from opening in 1904 until 1939. In 1906, eighteen metal-bodied cars joined the fleet, making 76 cars in all. This platform at Finsbury Park is now used by southbound Victoria Line trains. The one-time GN&C line was taken over by BR in 1975 on the Drayton Park – Moorgate section.

The next tube railway to be opened after the Central London was, and for many years remained, a curious anomaly. It was the Great Northern & City Railway, built in 16ft diameter tunnels to take main-line stock and carry Great Northern suburban trains into the City at Moorgate from a connection near Finsbury Park. The southern end of this 3½-mile line – the only main-line size tube in London – was deep below the surface at Moorgate. It ran northwards via Old Street (built as a joint station with the City & South London), Essex Road, Highbury & Islington, and Drayton Park to Finsbury Park, where its station was alongside that used by the Piccadilly Line under the Great Northern main-line station.

The aim of running through trains from the Great Northern to Moorgate was thwarted by that company going cold on the idea and refusing to reach an agreement with the GN&C. The plans had envisaged the use of locomotives with axle-hung motors, and the track was laid with both positive and negative rails outside the running rails to allow this. In the late 1930s work was begun on an extension of the line to Highgate and Alexandra Palace, but war interrupted this work and it was never resumed.

The large cars were intended to form seven-car trains when the line was opened on 14th February 1904, using three motor cars and four trailers but the Board of Trade would not allow middle motor cars on tube trains, so the train lengths had to be reduced, until four-car trains were the normal standard. This was true multiple-unit stock, built by the Brush Electrical Engineering Company, and by the Electric Railway and Tramway Carriage Works Ltd, but it was not the first in London, as is sometimes claimed. There were true multiple-unit trains on the Central London by then.

The Great Northern & City was the first tube railway to have automatic signalling throughout using light signals without moving parts. (There were a few electrically-worked semaphore signals where the line came into the open at Drayton Park.) It was also the first tube railway to have an insulated traction current return.

No extensions to this line were ever made, though it had powers to continue at the southern end to Lothbury and may have hoped to turn itself into a main-line link between north and south London by burrowing under the river. The workshops and car-sheds were built at the side of the station at Drayton Park, where the line came to the surface. There were electric or hydraulic lifts at the various underground stations. Escalators replaced lifts at Old Street in 1925 and from 1936 there was an escalator connection with the other underground lines at Moorgate. The line was busy, but it seemed to be stagnating after a while – useful link as it was and still is – and its short independent life ended when it was taken over by the Metropolitan Railway on 1st September 1913. The original rolling stock lived out its full life, but the power station (at Poole Street) was closed down in October 1914, the Metropolitan supplying the current from its own at Neasden through a substation.

Below **Side view of a wooden-bodied car with some of the underfloor equipment, and the permanent bogies, still to be fitted.**

Bottom **A steel-bodied trailer car of 1906, built by the Brush Electrical Engineering Company of Loughborough. The use of steel for the bodies of train carriages was new, having been pioneered in Britain by the Central London Railway in 1903.**

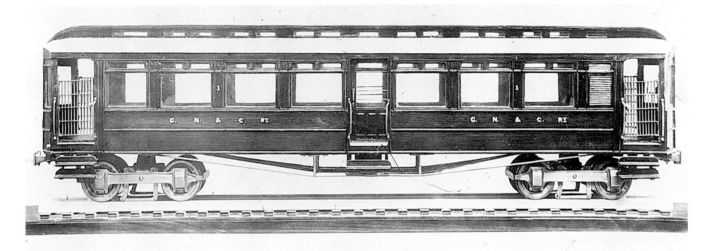

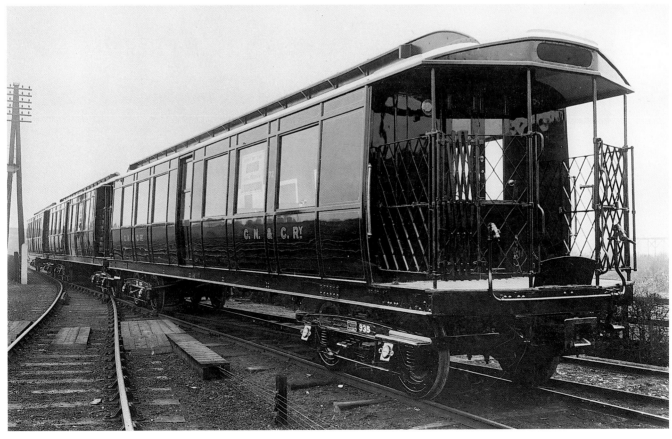

Metropolitan and District Electrification

One thing that the Met had in common with the Underground Group was its purchase of American-style rolling stock for its inner London electric services. They were of composite steel and timber construction and were 52ft 6in long over the centrally-placed buffers and automatic couplers. Built by the Metropolitan Amalgamated Railway Carriage & Wagon Company, originally they had open end platforms and gates, but these were soon enclosed. The motor cars had all four axles driven, each by its own 150hp motor. Trains of this stock were usually made up of two three-car sets, each consisting of a motor car, trailer, and driving trailer. As well as these saloon sets, the Metropolitan had some bogie compartment stock converted for electric working.

On the two original sub-surface railways, all the activity with electrified tube lines was having its effect. To add to the troubles of the Metropolitan and the Metropolitan District, electric trams were spreading and so were mechanically-driven buses. The Central London's short-cut across the Circle Line was also a worry to both companies. The Metropolitan had obtained Parliamentary powers to electrify the whole of its lines in August 1898 and arranged a small-scale demonstration of electric traction at Wembley Park. The District had given some consideration to battery locomotives in 1888 but decided against them. Now great strides had been made in the technique of electric traction and both companies got together, as they were both concerned with working the Circle Line, and spent £20,000 on a full-scale experiment. They electrified the line from Earl's Court to Kensington High Street on the four-rail system and supplied direct current from a temporary power station at Earl's Court. Each company paid for three coaches of a six-car experimental train fitted with Siemens motors.

The experiment went well when it started in February 1900, and passengers were carried on the experimental train from 21st May to 6th November, at first paying one shilling each for the privilege. Subsequently the Metropolitan and the District set up a joint committee which recommended that electrification should proceed, using the three-phase 3,000V ac system developed by the firm of Ganz in Hungary. This used an overhead conductor two-wire system, and the arguments in its favour were much the same as those for ac electrification today – only unmanned substations would be needed and the overhead wires would be much cheaper than conductor rails. The Metropolitan accepted the findings but the District did not. By then it was under a powerful outside influence – Charles Tyson Yerkes.

The name of Yerkes crops up in many places when London's transport is discussed. He was born in the USA in 1837 and became a financier and stockbroker at an early age – for he was only in the middle thirties when he was ruined in the financial panic after the Chicago fire of 1871. He then turned to transport and particularly to tramways, and between 1881 and 1899 he managed to secure controlling interests in and unify the tramways of Chicago. At this time Americans were eager to invest in overseas enterprises, and Yerkes, in partnership with others, bought up in 1900 for £100,000 the powers obtained by the Charing Cross, Euston & Hampstead Railway in its Act of 1893. These powers had remained unused because the railway had never been able to raise enough money to put them into effect. The solicitor who dealt

The experimental electric train of which three cars were owned by the District and three by the Metropolitan. The train consisted of a motor car at each end and four trailer cars between. Both current rails were outside the running rails. It ran between High Street Kensington and Earl's Court from December 1899 to November 1900. Only the motor car *below* at the head of the train was powered (in each direction), the rear car *left* being hauled 'dead'.

with this transaction, R.W. (afterwards Sir Robert) Perks, seems also to have interested Yerkes in the District Railway. Yerkes was also in the market for the control of the Baker Street & Waterloo, which was temporarily in abeyance. Yerkes, aided by Perks, secured control of the District Railway in March 1901 and announced that the line would be electrified and modernised. He also got rid, not too gently, of Forbes, who was still the chairman at that time. Forbes was succeeded for a short while by a stockbroker who had helped in the negotiations – Murray Griffith – but in September 1901 Perks became chairman.

The Yerkes group formed the Metropolitan District Electric Traction Co Ltd to electrify the District and build a power station. It was incorporated in July 1901, for Yerkes had wasted no time, and arranged to build the power station to supply not only the District but also the Brompton & Piccadilly Circus tube railway – another proposed line picked up in passing, as it were, by Yerkes. There was so much activity in this direction that on 9th April 1902 the Yerkes group formed the Underground Electric Railways Company of London Ltd, which took over the Metropolitan District Electric Traction Co Ltd and arranged to take in hand the building and equipment of the Brompton & Piccadilly Circus, the Charing Cross, Euston & Hampstead and the Baker Street & Waterloo underground lines already mentioned, and also the Great Northern & Strand. Yerkes became the chairman and remained so until his death in 1905.

The Ganz system of overhead electrification, which had been tried on only one European line, did not suit Yerkes at all. He was familiar with low-voltage dc electrification in the USA and could see it at work in the newly-opened Central London tube which much disturbed the poverty-stricken District. He decided on low-voltage electrification using conductor rails for his tubes and for the District. This decision brought him against the Metropolitan, a powerful opponent, and the question which system should be used went to arbitration. The verdict went to Yerkes, who offered to take over the Metropolitan on lease and was refused. The Metropolitan had no choice but to fall in with the new system.

The electrification was carried out on the District by the American engineer-in-chief and general manager of the Underground Company, James Russell Chapman. As we have already recorded, South Harrow had its first train services on 28th June 1903; these were by District electric trains. This was because the Ealing & South Harrow was equipped early for electric traction and supplied from a temporary generating station at Alperton. A section of the line was opened in connection with one of the Royal Agricultural Society's shows, at Park Royal, on 23rd June 1903. This section ran from Mill Hill Park (renamed Acton Town in 1910) to Park Royal, and the service was extended to South Harrow five days later. The whole of the District Railway was converted before the end of 1905. The system adopted used third and fourth rails with the positive rail outside the running rails and the negative in the centre. Current was supplied at 600V dc. On the Wimbledon line south of Putney Bridge, which belonged to the London & South Western, the running rails were later bonded to the negative rail so that that railway's trains, working on the three-rail system, could use the same tracks.

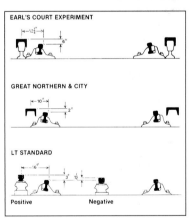

EARL'S COURT EXPERIMENT

GREAT NORTHERN & CITY

LT STANDARD

Positive   Negative

A fairly accurate representation of District Railway B-stock taken from a contemporary poster. The Metropolitan and District had specified varnish for their teak coaches used on steam services. Varnishing was cheaper, but the main reason for avoiding paint was that with so much tunnel working it would be more affected than varnish by the sulphur from the locomotive emissions. With electrification came the use of painted coaches, some of which were steel-bodied. The deep shade of red known as Midland Lake was favoured initially for the doors in contrast to the scarlet bodywork.

Power came from a huge power station at Lots Road, Chelsea, to which coal could be brought by barge to be unloaded at its water frontages on the Thames and Chelsea Creek. Work had been started on the power station in March 1902, even though more than a year and a half was to pass before the whole site was secured. It went into service on 1st February 1905. Its four great chimneys aroused much controversy at the time, and Whistler, the artist, was one of those most against it. A suggestion from Punch that the chimneys should support a large equestrian statue to Thomas Carlyle was perhaps not taken seriously but shows that the dispute was not merely a local one. It was not long, however, before the power station was part of the familiar London scene and artists were painting its reflection in the Thames.

It was built originally to supply the District and, later, the three Underground Group tube lines, but in the end it was supplying the City & South London, Central London, the East London, parts of the Southern and London, Midland & Scottish Railways, the London United Tramways network, and many other installations such as Acton overhaul works and the London General Omnibus Company's Chiswick Works.

Lots Road was improved and increased in capacity from time to time but at first it had eight steam turbines each producing about 7,500hp at 1,000rpm. These were each coupled to generators producing three-phase current at 11,000V, $33\frac{1}{3}$ cycles.

Electric lighting was progressively introduced, both on the trains and at stations. The earliest use of electric lighting on the Underground had been a short trial instituted at the District's Victoria station by the Société Génerale d'Electicité of Paris for a few days in December 1879. Ten lamps were powered by a generator that was being used to light the Victoria Embankment and Waterloo Bridge.

Allied to the District electrification was the installation of automatic and semi-automatic signalling, controlled by the trains themselves through track circuits, and the introduction of pneumatically-operated points. The whole of the District Railway running track was track-circuited, and most of the sidings and yards. Advantage was taken of this to install illuminated track diagrams, controlled by the track circuits, in signal boxes. These showed the position of every train in the area controlled by the signalbox concerned. This is thought to be one of the earliest large-scale uses of such diagrams.

Every stop signal had an associated 'train-stop', which applied the brakes of any train which ran past a signal at danger, a system later used throughout the Underground. Another feature introduced at this time and thought to have been first used on the District Railway was the train describer apparatus which enabled a signalman to pass the description of a train to the next box and so on all down the line. The describer apparatus was capable of receiving and storing train descriptions and presenting them in the proper sequence to the signalman at the receiving point. The description was cancelled by the train itself, through the track circuits, as it left the platform, allowing the next description to appear on the signalman's panel. Normally, the describer showed the next three trains. The apparatus was also used to work illuminated platform signs showing passengers the destinations of trains.

A Metropolitan centre-cab or 'camel-back' locomotive hauling a train of bogie stock (Ashbury stock) carriages.

The electrification of the Metropolitan Railway, with its 'main-line' characteristics, was in some ways more difficult. A power station was built at Neasden on the east bank of the River Brent. It was never as large as the District's power station, which was designed from early days to serve the tube lines as well, and originally had four 1,000rpm turbines coupled to generators producing three-phase alternating current at 11,000V, 33⅓ cycles. The current was fed by high-voltage lines to substations at Baker Street, Neasden, Harrow-on-the-Hill, Ruislip, Bouverie Street, Moorgate, Chalton Street and Gloucester Road, and these first eight were followed by others. All had rotary converters to bring the supply down to 600V dc to feed to the rails. The first line to be electrified was that from Baker Street to Uxbridge, on which electric trains ran from 1st January 1905. In July that year the District electrified from Ealing Broadway to Whitechapel, which included the southern half of the Circle. The Metropolitan had electrified its half of the Circle in readiness for through electric running on 1st July 1905, but had adopted a different position for mounting the collector shoes from the District. When the service began, it was found that the Metropolitan shoe mounted on the end of the bogie would not run properly on the less accurately laid District track and Metropolitan trains had to be confined to the South Kensington to Aldgate section until repositioned shoes could be fitted. A full service of electric trains round the Circle began on 24th September 1905. Electrification reduced the running time of the Circle trains from 70 to 50 minutes for the round trip.

The electric services on the Metropolitan began with multiple-unit trains, but as the volume of traffic on the then rural sections of the line north of Harrow did not justify electrification – the service at the turn of the century was approximately hourly to Rickmansworth and two-hourly beyond – steam-hauled trains continued. To make the best use of the electrified sections of the line, particularly those in tunnel south of Finchley Road, the Metropolitan decided to introduce electric locomotives to work trains on the in-town section, handing over to steam locomotives at convenient points in the suburbs.

Two batches of ten electric locomotives were built by the Metropolitan Amalgamated Railway Carriage & Wagon Co. who acted as subcontractors for the bodywork and framing to the main contractors, British Westinghouse. The first ten were delivered in 1905-06 and the second batch during 1907-08. These were supplied and equipped by the British Thomson-Houston Company, with the same mechanical sub-contractor as for Nos 1–10. The two types differed radically in appearance. Nos 1–10 were of 'camel back' or 'steeple cab' design, having a central driving position flanked by a lower equipment compartment at each end. Locomotives Nos 11–20 were box-like in appearance, with a flat-fronted driving cab at each end and the equipment mounted in the central section on both sides of a central gangway.

When these locomotives were first put to work on Aylesbury line trains, most locomotive changes were at Wembley Park, although electric trains could run to Harrow-on-the-Hill (and Uxbridge). However, from 1st November 1906, all changes were made at Wembley Park and then at Harrow from 19th July 1908.

The District also acquired some electric locomotives, mainly to haul London & North Western Outer Circle trains between Earl's Court and Mansion House. There were 10 of these units, built by the Metropolitan Amalgamated Railway Carriage & Wagon Co. and fitted with four 200hp motors each. The electrical equipment was made in the USA. In appearance these 28-ton machines, which normally worked in pairs with coupled controls so that they could be driven by a single driver (multiple-unit operation), were disappointing, looking like bogie vans with clerestory roofs, but they seem to have been quite efficient. When the Outer Circle service was cut back to Earl's Court (1st January 1909) the locomotives were used on the Circle Line with one at the back and one at the front of a train of trailer cars – much as Greathead had wanted to do on the Central London. When through trains began to run from Ealing to Southend on 1st June 1910, and Shoeburyness from 1911, they were hauled between Ealing and Barking by the electric locomotives.

The District's new multiple-unit electric stock included gate-ended cars used on the South Harrow line in 1903 and also on the Hounslow branch. The Hounslow line was purchased by the District on 1st July 1903 and became the first District line to be converted for electric running (the South Harrow line had no train service before electrification). Electric services from South Acton to Hounslow Barracks began on 13th June 1905. This was the first time that the South Acton branch had been open to public traffic, though the line had been completed in February 1899 and had been authorised 21 years before that to provide a link with the North & South

Below A four-car set of one of the two seven-car trains of the District's first multiple unit electric stock, consisting of motor-trailer-trailer-motor. These cars closely resembled those being built for the Interborough Rapid Transit Company of New York. They entered service on the South Harrow line in 1903.

Bottom End view of the same stock, flanked by a District 4–4–0 tank locomotive of 1871. The location is probably North Ealing, according to evidence of background detail.

Western Junction Railway. The trains ran to Hounslow Town station and there reversed to continue over a newly-laid curve to Hounslow Barracks. Hounslow Town was replaced in May 1909 by a new station on the main line, so that trains no longer had to reverse. (Northfields station had opened as Northfield Halt the year before.) The line from Hounslow Town (renamed Hounslow East in 1925) to Hounslow Barracks (renamed Hounslow West) was single-track for some time with one intermediate station called Heston Hounslow (which became Hounslow Central). The single-track was doubled on 1st November 1912 to Heston Hounslow and to Hounslow West on 27th November 1926.

The greater part of the District's new stock, however, was of American design and made up 60 seven-car trains of three motor cars and four trailers each. All cars were 49ft 6½in over body ends, 8ft 10½in wide and 12ft 3¼in high from rail level. It was open saloon stock, the two end motor cars and the intermediate motor car seating 48, trailer cars 52 and end motor cars with a luggage compartment 40. The general plan was the same as that used for the cars of the Brooklyn Elevated. All the main electrical equipment was British but the cars were built partly by British builders and partly on the Continent. This was the Class 'B' stock, the earlier South Harrow stock having been Class 'A'. Classes 'C', 'D' and 'E' were similar and were obtained in 1911, 1912 and 1913 respectively. All these cars except the E stock had clerestory roofs. The E type had an elliptical roof with 'torpedo' ventilators: the ventilators were draughty and were soon removed.

A four-car train of B-stock in Ealing Broadway station in 1908. The Non Stop disc on the front would have alerted passengers to check which stations the trip would be passing. There was a confusing range of combinations and the number of stations 'Non Stopped' varied between one and seven.

Two of the ten District electric locomotives which entered service in 1905 to haul London & North Western trains between Earl's Court and Mansion House, and were later used to haul Southend-on-Sea trains between Ealing and Barking.

The Yerkes Tubes

We left the Yerkes forces about to build the Brompton & Piccadilly Circus, the Charing Cross, Euston & Hampstead, the Baker Street & Waterloo, and the Great Northern & Strand. Of these, the Baker Street & Waterloo was the first to be started and the first to be opened. It owed its inception, it is said, to a semi-humorous suggestion by some Westminster businessmen that they should have such a line to take them to Lord's as quickly as possible. Examined in a more serious mood, the scheme proved to have merits.

A Bill was promoted in 1891 and came before a Joint Committee of both Houses in 1892. It became an Act in 1893, and work started in 1898. In 1899 the company promoted a Bill for two extensions – to Paddington, and to Euston as well as a deviation in Lambeth. The two northern extensions in this Bill failed, but another was introduced in 1900 and secured authorisation for the extensions to the Elephant & Castle and to Paddington.

Work started in June 1898 with the erection of a staging in the Thames close to Hungerford Bridge. On this was built a small village of workshops and offices, as well as a power station to give power and light for construction work. From this staging two vertical shafts were sunk into the bed of the river so that excavated material could be taken away by barge. It was also intended to take working material in by the same route. The northbound tunnel was started from this point in February 1899, and the shield began to eat its way slowly – 8 feet per day – towards Trafalgar Square, reaching the station site there in November. By then the southbound tunnel had been started and some of the station work had been put in hand, including Piccadilly Circus and Baker Street. The stations were to be, from the south (including some later authorisations), Elephant & Castle, Kennington Road, Waterloo, Thames Embankment, Trafalgar Square, Piccadilly Circus, Oxford Circus, Regent's Park, Baker Street, Lisson Grove, Edgware Road, and Paddington.

As the railway itself put it in the brochure issued to celebrate its opening, 'the advantages which this line will afford for getting quickly and cheaply from one point of London to another are without parallel. It will link up many of the most important Railway termini, give a connection with twelve other Railway systems, and connect with the vast tramway system of the south of London, thus bringing the theatres and other places of amusement, as well as the chief shopping centre, within easy reach of outer London and the suburbs'. But this was in the future, and misfortune was to befall the line before that. In 1900 came the Whitaker Wright financial failure, and with it the collapse of the Baker Street & Waterloo's backers, the London & Globe Finance Corporation. Work on the line slowly came to a stop and the sites remained derelict for some months until Yerkes came along and bought up the remains.

With Yerkes behind it, work started again in 1902 and tunnelling reached a speed of up to 73 feet a week. The same year the Brompton & Piccadilly Circus and the Great Northern & Strand companies were merged as the Great Northern, Piccadilly & Brompton Railway. Similar merging of the Bakerloo and Hampstead railways was proposed in 1903 but these were not merged in the Great Northern, Piccadilly & Brompton until 1910, and the composite company thus formed was named the London Electric Railway. By such means the tube companies were able to further their integration to mutual benefit.

Meanwhile work on the Baker Street & Waterloo continued. One new practice adopted was to fill the lower part of the tubes with concrete on which the sleepers could rest, the ends of the sleepers being embedded in crushed granite. This helped to reduce vibration, but was adversely criticised in the technical press and was not perpetuated. Because the rails had to go down the shafts driven into the river bed they had to be kept short, and no rail on the original line was longer than 36ft 5in. A four-rail system was used, but it was discovered that there was a leakage to earth from the outside positive rail, which was near the cast-iron tunnel lining. This caused difficulties at the large Charing Cross substation, which fed the District tracks as well as those of the Bakerloo, and the solution adopted was to change the polarity of the rails so that the centre rail became positive instead of negative. This change remained until 1917, when the Bakerloo went out to Watford and it was desirable to standardise the current supply. By this time advances in technique had made it possible to overcome the original difficulties.

Automatic signalling with train stops was provided from the start, and there were bare telephone wires along the tunnels. The risk of fire, said the company, was practically non-existent. "The Station Platforms are constructed of concrete and iron, and the Permanent way sleepers of Jarrah, an Australian wood which is non-combustible. The Rolling Stock is built almost entirely of steel, the small quantity

The 'straphanger' as seen in this 1912 poster is a term of American origin and is known as early as 1893. It relates to those members of the travelling public who, unable to obtain a seat, hold onto the flexible straps or hangers, and who sway gently to and fro according to the movement of the vehicle. Straps were common in railway and tramway vehicles of open plan design and allowed a significant extra load to be carried; sometimes the extra load got out hand but it was the great Yerkes who swept objection about his overcrowded Chicago trams aside with the retort that 'it is the straphanger who pays the dividend'. Leather straps were provided on all of London Underground's saloon stock from the early days of electrification. These gave way in the mid 1930s to a ball-shaped device on a flexible rubber stalk. These were found to be too easy to detach, making a handy cosh. An improved design emerged in 1943 with a reinforcing chain and external protective spring, and this design was used on all subsequent Underground stock until 1983. On later stock, and on refurbished stock, the hand grips were replaced by simple grab rails. People do of course still stand, rigidly clutching one of the rails provided, but it is now an artless activity and gone is the gentle formation swaying that characterised a true straphanger.

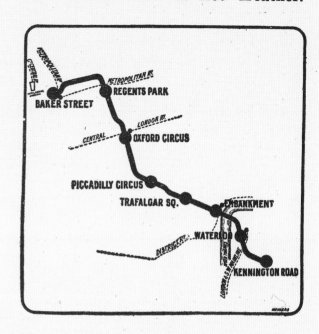
This double sided leaflet was issued shortly after the opening of the Baker Street & Waterloo Railway in March 1906 and shows that the Bakerloo nickname, given to it by the Evening News, was officially adopted very quickly. Kennington Road station was renamed Lambeth North within a few months of opening and Elephant & Castle was opened in August. Passenger numbers would have been somewhat lower than today, which – coupled with draughty trains – probably explains the claim made for a maximum temperature of 60 degrees. Like all the tube railways that preceded it, the Bakerloo began life with a flat fare of 2d, though this did not last long. The City & South London Railway had abandoned its 2d flat fare when the Moorgate extension opened in February 1900. The Bakerloo moved from a flat fare on 22nd July 1906 and the Central London Railway began charging 3d for longer journeys from the end of June 1907.

of wood used being rendered nonflammable. 'There is a lighted footway from end to end of the line. Special Electric Lamps are placed in the tunnels at intervals of 40 feet. The wires for lighting these lamps are entirely independent of the power cables. The space between the rails has been filled in with cement and granite chippings. Should a train come to a standstill and be unable to proceed, the power current would be at once cut off, and passengers would only have to walk a few hundred yards along an easy and well-lighted footpath to the nearest station.'

The lifts had exit gates opened and shut by compressed air, and passengers entered them at one side and left them at the other. The entrance gates were hand-worked. The stations were decorated in different colour schemes at platform level, the idea being that a passenger could recognise his own station by the colour scheme peculiar to it. Externally, the stations were all similar in pattern. They were designed by Leslie W. Green in the form of a plinth, the idea being that offices, etc, could be added above this base later on. They were given strength by a steel frame and were faced with glazed blocks in a ruby-red shade. There were no surface buildings on the Bakerloo at Regent's Park, Trafalgar Square, Embankment or Waterloo.

The multiple-unit rolling stock was, as already mentioned, nearly all-steel in its construction. It was built in the USA by the American Car & Foundry Company and sent over in sections for erection in Britain. There were 36 motor-cars and 72 trailers formed into three-car sets which could run in six-car trains in peak hours and as three-car trains at others. The cars had end platforms with gates and carried attendants, who were responsible for working the gates at the ends of adjacent cars and calling out the station names. A guard (or conductor) travelled in the first car. He was also trained as a driver (motorman) and was expected to take over if the regular driver became incapacitated for any reason. The conductor had to join the attendants in calling out the station names. The rolling stock depot and repair shops were in an open three-acre site at St George's Circus, Lambeth, near the southern end of the line. This became known as London Road Depot.

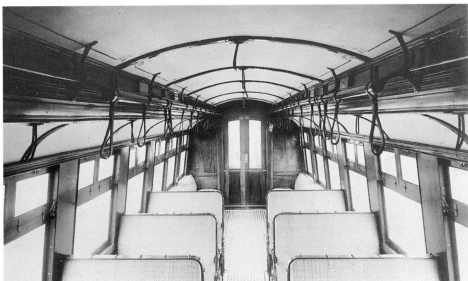

Baker Street and Waterloo ('Bakerloo') driving motor car of 1906 at Trafford Park, where the car was assembled after arriving from the U.S.A. The shoegear and other electrical equipment have yet to be fitted.

The interior of a similar car, awaiting light fittings, route diagrams and advertisements.

The engineers for the line were Sir Benjamin Baker, Messrs Galbraith & Church, and H.H. Dalrymple Hay. The last-named was supervising engineer for the Underground group and the others the consulting engineers. James R. Chapman was responsible for the equipment and was resident engineer. There was also a resident track engineer, W.E. Hanson. The contractors for the main part of the line were Perry & Company.

On 10th March 1906, Sir Edwin Cornwall, MP, chairman of the London County Council, opened the main part of the line from Kennington Road to Baker Street, and the stations were opened for public traffic the same day.

The Kennington Road station was almost at once renamed Westminster Bridge Road (it stood at the junction of the two roads), but it was changed again in 1917 to Lambeth North, originally with brackets round the 'North'. The short southern extension of the 3½-mile line, to Elephant & Castle, was opened on 5th August 1906 (concurrently with the renaming of Kennington Road). At the other end of the line the railway reached Lisson Grove (named Great Central, apparently at the insistence of Sam – afterwards Sir Sam – Fay of the Great Central Railway on whose land the station stood) on 27th March 1907 and Edgware Road on 15th June of the same year. At first there was a 2d flat fare, but traffic fell short of expectations and differential fares were introduced. Whether as a result of this, or not, traffic then steadily increased. The useful portmanteau name of 'Bakerloo' is believed to have originated with 'Quex' of the Evening News and was used officially from July 1906.

C.T. Yerkes did not live to see the first of his tubes opened, for he died in New York on 29th December 1905, at the age of 68. His place as chairman of the Underground Electric group was taken by Edgar Speyer of Speyer Brothers, associates of Yerkes. Speyer Brothers had managed to secure control of London United Tramways in September 1902, when they were a thorn in the side of the District and were even contemplating a tube line of their own, to be fed by LUT trams, from Hammersmith into central London. They had thus turned the powerful LUT into useful allies instead of rivals. It is because Yerkes became the dominant figure in the early development of London's tube railways that American terminology lasts to this day in motorman (driver) and car (carriage).

Perhaps the most astonishing thing to happen as a result of the death of Yerkes was that Sir George Gibb, general manager of the prosperous North Eastern Railway since 1891, gave up that position to become chairman and managing director of the District, and deputy chairman and managing director of the Underground group. It was Gibb who steered the Yerkes tubes into being.

The next of these tubes to open was the Great Northern, Piccadilly & Brompton Railway, which has come into the story several times already. It was opened by David Lloyd George, who at that time was President of the Board of Trade, on 15th December 1906. It was then nine miles in length, the longest and in some ways the most important of the tube railways yet to be opened. At the time of opening it had an authorised capital of £7,206,000 and it brought the length of Underground group lines in operation to about 22 miles.

The Great Northern, Piccadilly & Brompton Railway was an amalgamation of the Brompton & Piccadilly Circus Railway, authorised in 1897, and the Great Northern & Strand Railway, authorised in 1899. Powers to combine the schemes were obtained in 1902, including the building of a connecting line from Piccadilly Circus to a junction with the Great Northern & Strand at Holborn to give a through route between the two railways. This left part of the Great Northern & Strand between Holborn and Strand (Aldwych) as a double-track branch line, opened on 30th November 1907.

There were 22 stations (though not all were ready for traffic) when the line was opened: Finsbury Park, Gillespie Road (renamed Arsenal in 1932), Holloway Road, Caledonian Road, York Road (closed in 1932), King's Cross, Russell Square, Holborn, Covent Garden, Leicester Square, Piccadilly Circus, Dover Street (renamed Green Park in 1933), Down Street (closed in 1932), Hyde Park Corner, Knightsbridge, Brompton Road (closed in 1934), South Kensington, Gloucester Road, Earl's Court, Barons Court, and Hammersmith. There was also Strand station (later Aldwych) on a short branch from Holborn (now closed). The stations from South Kensington to Hammersmith adjoined those of the District. Between South Kensington and West Kensington the new tube ran under the District Railway and in fact formed part of the District's deep-level tube route, authorised in 1897 but never built apart from this smaller-scale version and a short length of tunnel at South Kensington.

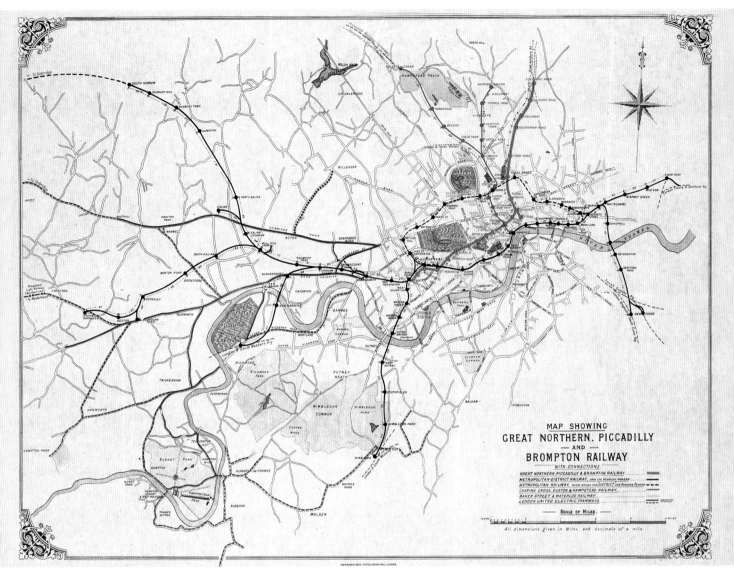

MAP SHOWING
GREAT NORTHERN, PICCADILLY
AND
BROMPTON RAILWAY
WITH CONNECTIONS

The engineers for the line were Sir J. Wolfe Barry, C. A. Brereton, Sir James W. Szlumper, W. W. Szlumper, and Alexander Ross. The engineer-in-chief of the Underground Electric Railways Company, James R. Chapman, was responsible for everything to do with the equipment. The engineer concerned with the tunnelling was H. H. Dalrymple Hay. Work started in April 1902 on the Holborn–South Kensington section, and three months later the South Kensington–Earl's Court section was in hand. The Finsbury Park–Holborn section was started in September of the same year, but the line west of Earl's Court was not begun until February 1904.

The station tunnels were of 21ft 2½in diameter; at a few stations they had to be built above one another to keep within the width of the road above. At South Kensington there is an 18ft difference in level because of the original plan for a flying junction there with the District Deep Level Railway. Generally, however, the tunnels were built side by side, with the stairways, lift shafts, etc, between them. Above ground, the stations followed the general style of those built for the Bakerloo, with flat roofs for later vertical extension. Finsbury Park station was built by the Great Northern Railway and leased to the two tube lines.

The depth of the tubes below ground level varied from 20 feet at Finsbury Park to 123 feet at Covent Garden. Electric lifts were used at most stations to carry passengers to and from the street; in all, 60 lifts were installed in 18 stations. Gillespie Road station, where the railway was close to the surface, had no lifts, and at Finsbury Park, four hydraulic lifts were provided for the use of passengers interchanging with the Great Northern Railway, which, being on a viaduct at this point, was a considerable distance above the tube railway. There were four similar lifts for interchange between the GN & City and the GNR but no mechanical assistance for those passing between tube platforms and street level, and no surface buildings for the underground lines.

Although entitled 'Map showing the Great Northern, Piccadilly and Brompton Railway', the western limit of that line is shown as Earl's Court on this prospectus map for potential shareholders. The western terminus was Hammersmith when the line opened. All other Yerkes Group tubes, as well as the District Railway and the London United tramways, are also shown.

There was an interesting experiment at Holloway Road station in 1906 in the form of a double (up and down) stair belt moving at 100ft per minute. This was installed in one of the lift shafts and was apparently in good working order a week before the official opening of the railway; but for reasons now uncertain it never went into public service. It was five years before the first passenger escalator was opened, also on the Piccadilly Line, at Earl's Court in 1911. Most of the Holloway Road installation was scrapped in 1911 but parts survive and are preserved by London's Transport Museum.

Construction work made such good progress during the second half of 1906 that the company decided, possibly to secure traffic from Christmas shoppers, to open the railway before the stations at Covent Garden, Down Street and South Kensington, and the Strand branch, were finished. Arrangements were made with the contractors for the line to be opened for public traffic before being officially handed over to the railway as completed.

The opening ceremony, as already stated, was duly performed on 15th December 1906, and the service started with 26 three-car trains giving a 3-minute headway in peak

The first method of connecting street level with platform level other than by lifts or fixed stairs took the form of two moving belts installed as an experiment in one of the lift shafts at Holloway Road station, before opening, but not brought into service.

The Great Northern, Piccadilly & Brompton Railway station at South Kensington, photographed when newly completed in 1907. Alongside is the station of the District Railway another member of the Yerkes Group.

periods. Fares ranged in ½d stages from 1d to 3d, with a 4d fare for the whole of the nine-mile journey, which took 38 minutes. As new cars were delivered by the makers, trains were increased in length to six cars. On the Aldwych branch, opened on 30th November 1907, the standard train was one of two cars.

Rolling stock was supplied by two continental companies, one French – Les Ateliers de Construction du Nord de la France (Blanc Misseron) – and the other Hungarian – The Hungarian Railway Carriage & Machinery Works (Raab), Hungary; each built 36 motor-cars, each seating 42 passengers, and 72 trailers, seating 52. There were also two British cars, supplied by the Brush Electric & Manufacturing Company Ltd and the Metropolitan Amalgamated Railway Carriage & Wagon Co. Ltd. The entire fleet of 218 cars was made up of all-steel gate-ended stock, similar to that used on the Baker Street & Waterloo Railway. Two of the French-built cars lasted until July 1956, their half-century of life being due largely to the fact that for many years they provided the Aldwych shuttle service.

South Kensington Station

A depot and car sheds were provided at Lillie Bridge on a site formerly occupied by the sheds, repair shops, and yards of the District Railway before that company opened its depot at Mill Hill Park (now known as Ealing Common depot). The only access the Great Northern, Piccadilly & Brompton Railway had to its own depot was via District Railway tracks. The signalling arrangements, track, safety devices, lifts, etc, followed the same lines as on the Baker Street & Waterloo, except that the current-rail polarity was not reversed.

One of the original Piccadilly gate-ended trailers. The livery carried was reddish brown. Access to the saloon from the station platform was via gates, here shown open, and twin sliding doors, operated by a gateman.

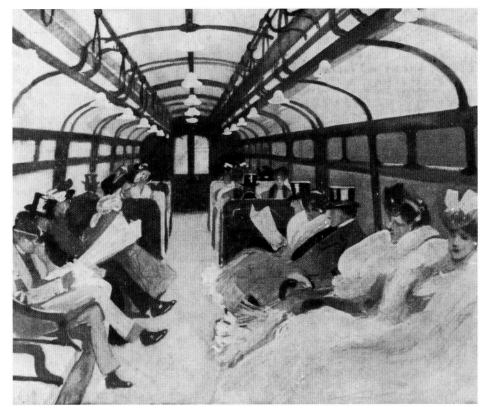

Because initial demand was disappointing, half length trains were operated for a time. In one direction the motorman (or driver) drove from the control trailer seen in this view.

Interior of a Piccadilly car after demand had picked up, from a painting produced for a publicity postcard.

The last of the tube lines to be opened was the Charing Cross, Euston & Hampstead Railway, incorporated in 1893. The Act of 24th August 1893 empowered the company to build a tube railway from Charing Cross (at the corner of Southampton Street and the Strand) to Heath Street, Hampstead. A branch from this line to Euston would end at Chalton Street, St Pancras. The company secured additional powers to buy land by an Act of 1894, gained an extension of time by an Act of 1897, and by another Act of 1898 gained permission to divert the Charing Cross end of the line to a terminus in Craven Street instead of Southampton Street. The next year another Act authorised a one-mile branch from Camden Town to Kentish Town station on the Midland Railway and a deviation to bring Euston on to the main line. A further extension of time was secured by an Act of 1900. All this procedure in Parliament had a slightly academic flavour, for the company was quite unable to raise the money to do any building, even though the 1897 Act gave power to pay interest out of capital during the time the line was being built.

All this was changed when on 1st October 1900 Charles Tyson Yerkes bought up the powers for the Hampstead tube.

There is a story that a Yerkes agent (Lauderbeck) and H. H. Dalrymple Hay, the engineer (afterwards Sir Harley Hugh Dalrymple Hay), drove in the Yerkes private hansom cab along the route of the tube which Yerkes had acquired. Starting from Charing Cross they went all the way out to Hampstead Heath, and then the agent decided to drive on. They went through the fields to Golders Green cross-roads, open and empty, and Lauderbeck declared that there was where the line would end. Powers for the main line extension to Golders Green and for the branch extension from Kentish Town to Highgate (Archway Tavern) were secured under an Act of 1902. This was not, however, the whole story. On that same day another Act received the Royal Assent. This was for the Edgware & Hampstead Railway, originally controlled by a separate company but brought into the Underground Group fold. The directors were replaced by Yerkes nominees in January 1903. This Act was for a railway 4½ miles long from Golders Green to Hendon and Edgware. In the following year another Act incorporated the Watford & Edgware Railway Company, to build another six miles of railway and complete the link with Watford. Although the Underground got to Watford, it was in a different way, as we shall see in due course.

Work on the original part of the line started in July 1902. There were to be stations at Charing Cross (Strand), Leicester Square, Oxford Street (now Tottenham Court Road), Tottenham Court Road (now Goodge Street), Euston Road (now Warren Street), Euston, Mornington Crescent, Camden Town, and then – the line having divided – Chalk Farm, Belsize Park, Hampstead, and Golders Green on the main line and South Kentish Town (now closed), Kentish Town, Tufnell Park, and Highgate (now Archway) on the branch. Its publicity referred to it openly as 'The Last Link' in the London tube network.

Golders Green crossroads in 1904. The opening of the Hampstead Line in 1907 brought about the almost immediate transformation of the area into a modern London suburb. The 'Underground' sign on the right gives a hint of the changes to come. The station and depot were to be behind the single tree in the right foreground.

The line was the work of Sir Douglas Fox & Partners and W.R. Galbraith as consulting engineers, and the tunnel work was carried out under their direction with A. W. Donaldson as resident engineer. The engineer who had ridden with Lauderbeck to Golders Green, H.H. Dalrymple Hay, supervised the work for the Underground Group and also acted as engineer for the construction of Charing Cross station (of which more later). He had J.C. Martin with him as resident engineer. The architect for station buildings was Leslie W. Green. James R. Chapman, the Underground Group's chief engineer, was responsible for the whole of the permanent way and equipment, the surface portion of the railway at Golders Green, and the erection and equipment of the car sheds and repair shops at Golders Green. W. E. Hanson was resident engineer for the permanent way work, and Gilbert Rosenbusch superintended the installation of the lifts.

All the equipment was very similar to that used on the Bakerloo and Piccadilly lines, and there was no special novelty in the construction of the tunnels and permanent way. The only tunnelling difficulties met with were at Euston, where water-bearing sand was struck and work had to be done under compressed air. The quicksand was not a very bad one, however, and a comparatively low pressure proved enough to keep it out of the workings. The contractors were Price & Reeves.

Where the line did differ from the others was in its depth below ground in places because of the rising country through which it ran. There is a 272ft rise between Charing Cross and the tunnel mouth south of Golders Green station. The deepest point below the surface is about 635 yards north of Hampstead station, where the rails are 221 feet below the crest of Hampstead Heath. Hampstead station itself, where there are now high-speed lifts, is 192 feet below ground. The shallowest station on the line, Chalk Farm, less than 1½ miles away, is 42 feet down. Another unusual feature was the station at North End, Hampstead, better known as 'Bull and Bush'. This does not appear in the list of stations already given because, although the station tunnels and part of the station below ground were duly built, no street level building was started. The rail-level facilities were sometimes used for storage.

The stations were again designed as plinths for taller structures, each consisting of a ground and mezzanine floor and framed in steel. The most difficult station was Charing Cross (later Strand, to distinguish it from the District, Circle, Northern, and Bakerloo station on the Embankment). This station was at one time to have been on the northern side of the Strand, but the South Eastern Railway eventually agreed to its being built under the forecourt of the mainline station, where interchange would be easier. The South Eastern stipulated, however, that the surface of the forecourt must not be broken, so that the cab services which brought their passengers to the trains would not be interrupted. This made things difficult, but the Hampstead engineers prepared to dig upwards from the running tunnels until

The Charing Cross, Euston and Hampstead Railway was opened on Saturday last. It has been extensively advertised as 'the last link' of the tube system. That is good enough to catch the public eye, but as a matter of fact the line does not link anything in particular, and it is really the 'last branch' of the system. It goes from Charing Cross to Golder's Green, which is the other side of the Hampstead heights. There is a branch from Camden Town to Highgate, whence passengers can go on northwards by the Metropolitan Electric Tramways, but Golder's Green, the other terminus, is at present situated in a green desert of meadows. The houses and their inhabitants are to come afterwards, as no doubt they speedily will, to the disgust of Hampstead and the other suburbs which at this moment happen to lie between them and built-over London.

Electrical Times, 27th June 1907

Golders Green station and forecourt soon after opening in 1907. On the Yerkes lines the word 'Tube' was eliminated from official notices from the beginning of 1908.

Belsize Park station, Charing Cross, Euston and Hampstead Railway, photographed a few years after it opened in 1907. The semi-circular windows are typical of Yerkes group design, and give daylight to the first-floor rooms, including those accommodating the lift machinery. The left-most arch provides vehicle access to the substation at the rear with the arch next to it the entrance and the right-most arch the exit, maintaining the station's one-way flow system. Roof space allows for future development over. This may be the only station of this period to have a street level garden.

they reached the booking-hall floor level and build the sub-surface facilities in this way. As it happened, however, this topsy-turvy procedure was not required. On 5th December 1905 part of the roof of the South Eastern station collapsed, killing six people and destroying the theatre next door. This tragedy caused the main-line station to be closed for 3½ months and the cab traffic, of course, also stopped. In the circumstances the South Eastern agreed to the Hampstead's having permission, for six weeks, to dig in the forecourt. Work started in January 1906, and before the six weeks were up one shaft was fully excavated and the walls of the booking hall were 12 feet down from the surface. At this stage the steel beams for the roof, supporting the station forecourt, were put in place and the surface was restored. The rest of the work was done under cover, the spoil being dropped down the shaft and carried away by rail.

The station platforms were built, like those of the Piccadilly railway, 350 feet long. (The Bakerloo, having started earlier, had only 291ft platforms.) These platforms were served by five-car trains made up of two motor cars and three trailers. The total fleet, at the start, consisted of 60 motor cars, 50 control trailers, and 40 trailers. They were built by the American Car & Foundry Company and assembled at Trafford Park, Manchester. During peak hours they ran a two-minute service between Charing Cross and Camden Town, with a four-minute service to Hampstead and Highgate, and a 12-minute service to Golders Green. The fare for the whole distance was 3d, with 2d, 1½d, and 1d fares for shorter distances. The power supply came, as with all the Yerkes lines, from Lots Road.

The line was opened on 22nd June 1907, by David Lloyd George. It was a Saturday, and the line was thrown open for the rest of the day for free travel by Londoners: about 150,000 of them took the opportunity. The Yerkes pattern was now complete, and the Underground network in central London was very much as it was to remain for the next 60 years. All the lines had extensive interchange facilities, and London had the finest underground railway service that could then be imagined. It was generally assumed that no more needed to be done.

In June 1907 the London Passenger Traffic Conference was established with Gibb, Yerkes' successor, as its chairman and, indeed, as its originator. The Underground railways were not doing well financially and the objects of the conference were the co-ordination of fares across the central area (reducing competition between them and allowing necessary increases) and an increase in through booking facilities whether the lines were in the Underground Group or not. The Great Northern & City Railway and the City & South London Railway were not represented at this first meeting but did take part in a further meeting the following month.

In February 1908 another meeting agreed on the use of a distinctive name and symbol at all stations. The word 'Tube' was displayed on many station frontages at this time and this was one of the names considered for wider use. The Metropolitan and District Railways would undoubtedly have objected to this. Despite the modern, and probably irreversible, habit of referring to the whole Underground system as the 'Tube', they are not, after all, tube lines. In the earliest days of the Met, the railway was often referred to as the 'underground' (without a capital U) and this word, though ignoring those parts of the integrated system that were on the surface, was nevertheless more accurate than 'tube'. Underground thus became the official title and a logotype was soon designed with large initial and last letters. The equally well-known bullseye or roundel sign owes its origin to a device adopted by the London General Omnibus Company in 1905, which incorporated a wheel across which was a bar bearing the word GENERAL. Its first appearance for railway use was in 1909 as a solid red disc behind station names, and in 1913 with the word UNDERGROUND, with large first and last letters, across the middle. The bullseye evolved down the years to become the 'roundel', still the symbol of London's public transport today.

Also in 1907, just before the conference was formed, a new personality arrived on the London scene. Albert Henry Stanley had been born, as Albert Knattries, in Derby in 1874, but his family went to the United States when he was still very young and his father changed their surname to Stanley. He started his transport career very humbly with the Detroit Street Railway Company but rose rapidly to become assistant general manager, Street Railway Department, Public Service Corporation of New Jersey, in the autumn of 1903. In February 1904 he became manager, and less than three years later he was general manager of the Corporation. Soon after this he was invited to become general manager of the Underground Group and he took over in the spring of 1907. Sir George Gibb evidently had him marked, for when Gibb left for another post at the end of 1910, Stanley was made managing director of the Underground Company also. Stanley was to be responsible for shaping London Transport into its unified form and for initiating important developments to the system. He was knighted in 1914, and entered the Government as President of the Board of Trade in December 1916. He returned to the Underground Group as its chairman in August 1919. He was created Baron Ashfield of Southwell in 1920 and was the first chairman of the London Passenger Transport Board when it was created in 1933.

But all this was still well in the future. As from 1st July 1910, the London Electric Railway had been formed to bring the Bakerloo, Piccadilly and Hampstead lines under common management. It sought powers to build an extension of the Hampstead tube southwards from the Strand terminus to a point underneath the District Railway's Charing Cross station on the Embankment. One of the objects was to provide direct interchange between the Bakerloo, District, and Hampstead lines. The work was authorised by an Act of 1911, and a loop line was built with a single platform under Charing Cross (District) station – the present northbound Northern Line platform. It was opened on 6th April 1914. The name of the station on the Embankment became Charing Cross (Embankment) and that of the Strand station Charing Cross (Strand). On 9th May 1915 the names of Charing Cross and Strand were substituted, leading to many years of confusion for passengers bound for Charing Cross main line station, where the nearest Underground connection was now named Strand.

Various measures were taken to avoid the time-consuming and resource-intensive necessity for passengers to buy a ticket each time they travelled. Selling tickets in bulk, in strips or books, was popular on the tube railways but neither system endured. From the 1920s weekly and season tickets (tickets for a month and longer) became available, though it was a few years until they became available at all ticket offices. These were available between any two stations, generally by only one route at a slight discount. These tickets soon became immensely popular with commuters and carried on until zonal fares were introduced in the 1980s.

THE MOST DIRECT ROUTE THROUGH . . LONDON . . FROM ALL POINTS.

The Charing Cross Extension of the Hampstead & Highgate Railway will shortly be open.

There will then be two stations on this line at Charing Cross, the present station will be renamed Charing Cross Strand—and the new one to be called Charing Cross Embankment will be in direct communication with the Bakerloo line and the Metropolitan District Railway. Subways and Escalators will connect these three Railways, and their meeting point will be the busiest in the world.

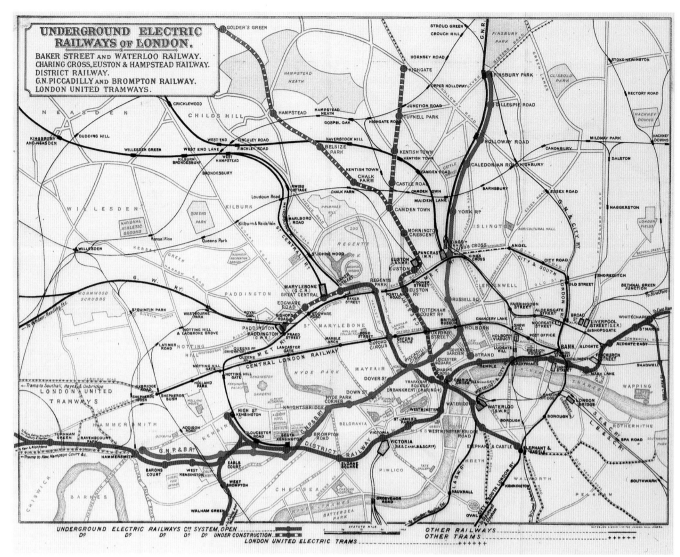

After a major fire on the Paris Underground in 1903 the Board of Trade made strict regulations about the employment of fire-proof materials, and these were applied to the new lines opened after 1904, but there was no imperative for the older railways to comply. A serious fire on the City & South London Railway at Moorgate in July 1908 (and a second fire that year on that company's line) caused a public outcry, magnified by a major conflagration the same year on a Liverpool–Southport electric train which showed just how much destruction was possible. The Board of Trade made several recommendations including the removal of wood at stations underground. All this made the position of pre-1904 tube railways untenable; a programme of enhanced fire protection was followed which brought them close to compliance with the 1904 regulations. In particular the enhanced protection of electrical equipment and removal where possible of underground wooden structures, including wooden platforms, very significantly reduced the fire risk. At the same time a more uniform fire protection regime was adopted for all tube lines including (with some resistance from the operators) fire authority inspection.

After a burst of activity in the first decade of the 20th Century, the first tube extension for four years opened on 28th July 1912. This was the section of the Central London Railway between Bank and Liverpool Street, opened six months before the line became part of the Underground Group. The new station at Liverpool Street was the first Underground station to have escalators from the start. It also boasted improved lighting using lamps with wire filaments that consumed one-quarter of the electricity of the carbon filament lamps used previously and gave lighting that was claimed to be 'the nearest approach to daylight of any incandescent electric lamp on the market'.

Platform and escalator at the new Liverpool Street station of the Central London Railway, opened in 1912. By this time wooden platforms were banned for underground stations but the use of wood in escalators was still felt acceptable. The lighting seen on the escalator was the first of its type installed anywhere in Great Britain. Looking remarkably like fluorescent lighting (not invented until 1935), the frosted glass tubing in fact contained a series of small filament lamps spaced and diffused to give a strip light all the way down. Neon tubular lighting had first been demonstrated at an exhibition in Paris in 1910 but could only produce coloured light.

Bakerloo Extensions

We left the Bakerloo at Edgware Road in 1907 contemplating an extension to Paddington; but by 1909 it was felt that the original proposal would put the station at Paddington in such an unfavourable position that further extension would be impossible, and the scheme was dropped. Later, more ambitious plans were prepared for extending the railway to the north-west, and on 1st December 1913 an extension was opened to Paddington on a route which allowed the tracks to turn northwards, and on 31st January 1915 they had reached Kilburn Park via Warwick Avenue. (Maida Vale station was opened on 6th June the same year.) On 10th May the same year through running over London & North Western Railway's track was introduced to Willesden Junction, the Bakerloo being the first London tube railway to be connected physically, other than by lift, with a true main-line railway. On 16th April 1917 through running was extended to Watford Junction, five years before the LNWR itself began its Euston–Watford electric service. That remained the extent of the Bakerloo Line for more than 20 years.

One of two motor-cars built by Leeds Forge in 1914 for the Bakerloo Watford extension. An interesting new feature on these cars was that of the hand-operated inward-swinging centre doors, which were additional to the traditional gates at the car end.

The rolling stock ordered for the through services to Watford was unusual in that it was a joint design of the London Electric Railway and LNWR and painted in the latter company's livery. Different platform heights on the two railways led to the adoption of a compromise height for the floor level, 4½ inches above that of other tube stock. Delivery of these cars was delayed by war conditions, and for three years use was made of older 'gate' stock to which false floors were added at the entrance to give the required height at platform level. These were augmented by new motor cars built for the CLR extension to Ealing, opening of which was delayed by the Great War. No false floor was fitted in these cars, hence there was a 10 inch gap for passengers to negotiate between platform and car floor.

The stock delivered for the Bakerloo in 1920 followed the lead set by the Central London Railway in 1915 and did away with the passenger gates at the car ends and instead had only inward swinging doors, including one each side at the centre. The doors had strong springs to return them to the closed position after use.

The Watford stock finally arrives. Although ordered in 1914, the 36 motor-cars, along with 12 control trailers and 24 trailers which comprised the LER & LNWR Watford Joint Stock were not delivered until 1920. The stock was built by Metropolitan Carriage Wagon & Finance Company and made up 12 new 6-car trains for the Bakerloo. Its arrival enabled the borrowed CLR motor-cars to be transferred to their rightful home. A system of red and green lamps informed the guard whether the inward swinging doors were closed or open.

Warwick Avenue station opened on 31st January 1915 and is seen here at about the time of the opening to Watford in 1917. The track does not yet have an 'anti-suicide pit' beneath the current return rail. This feature was first introduced at deep-level tube stations with the Morden extension in 1926 and was gradually incorporated into all platform layouts at tube stations, including Warwick Avenue.

Movement on the Met

After 1911 only two underground railways in London remained outside the Underground Group, the short LSWR-owned Waterloo & City Line and the mighty Metropolitan. The Metropolitan Railway strongly held on to its independence, seeing itself as a cut above all the other underground railways. With main line style coaches on most of its services and even a Pullman car in some of its longer-distance trains, it was to some extent justified in so thinking.

With its line extending to the Chilterns and beyond, the Met carried commuters from Buckinghamshire to the City on weekdays and pleasure seekers from London to the country at weekends.

It was not long before the needs of the longer-distance passenger began to be met by an extra pair of tracks to carry fast trains which missed out stations between Baker Street and Wembley Park. The first fast services ran in May 1915, and four-tracking reached Harrow-on-the-Hill in January 1932.

It was in May 1915 that the first edition appeared of an annual guidebook to the Metropolitan's territory. Titled 'Metro-land', the name soon entered the language of Londoners to conjure in the mind an image of an Elysian paradise just up the line from Baker Street. Editions of the book were published until 1932, just before the Metropolitan Railway was taken over by London Transport, and included advertising for housing developments near the route of the line.

In building its line north-west from Baker Street, the Met often had to buy large chunks of land in order to acquire the fairly narrow strip needed by the railway itself. As early as 1880 the Met had sold leases to builders to construct houses neighbouring its station at Willesden Green. By the 1920s and early 1930s, the heyday of Metro-land, many new estates had sprung up both on land that had been purchased by the Metropolitan and on land bought by private developers.

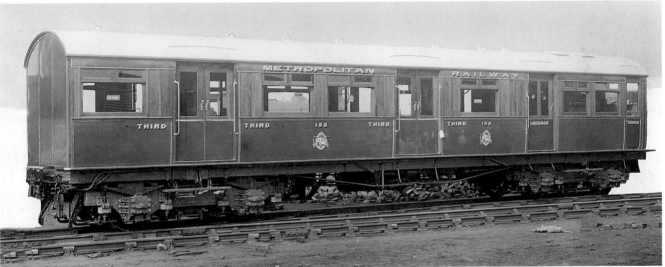

Top **A line-up of trains waiting to take people away from the Wembley Exhibition. A rolling stock shed was built on the right in 1926.**

Centre **In 1925 the Metropolitan ordered two experimental saloon motor-cars from the Metro Carriage. The cars (Nos 198 and 199) were similar to earlier saloon stock in having sliding doors, but they were fitted with new design control equipment from Metropolitan Vickers. The power system was electro-pneumatic, and a mixture of electric and mechanical operation enabled an electrical power saving to be made. They were the last saloon cars to be ordered by the Metropolitan, and on the strength of the trials with their new design of equipment the Company ordered 12 new compartment cars for delivery during 1927. No.198 is seen here when new.**

Left **Neasden station as it appeared in the final year of the Metropolitan Railway, having been renamed from Neasden & Kingsbury in January 1932, when the station was still more or less in its original 1880 condition. Today the two side portions of the original building remain, although the middle section containing the main ticket hall was rebuilt in the 1960s.**

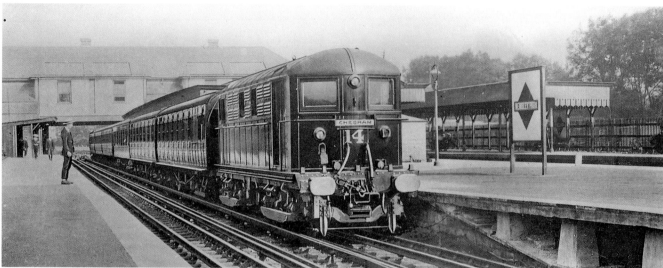

Metropolitan electric locomotives are seen under construction at the Metropolitan-Vickers factory in 1922. Thirteen of the twenty locomotives are visible. No. 14 is seen when new in service with the one Chesham train per day to include a Pullman car. Platform lengthening is evident. Such was the interest in these new locomotives that the model railway manufacturer Hornby produced a miniature version in 1924 complete with three-rail track for boys of all ages. It remained in their catalogue until the late 1930s and is shown below.

During 1922 and 1923 the Metropolitan Railway put into service 20 new electric locomotives, numbered 1–20, in place of the original machines. These new units were built by Metropolitan Vickers Limited at Barrow-in-Furness. They were 39ft 6in long and were mounted on two four-wheeled bogies. Each bogie carried two 300hp nose-suspended motors, four positive current collector shoes – two on each shoe-beam – and two negative shoes – one attached to brackets on each traction motor casing – making eight positive shoes and four negative per locomotive.

There were driving positions at each end of the 'round-nosed' bodies, with the equipment installed in the centre section between communicating gangways down both sides of the locomotive. The equipment included air compressors for Westinghouse brakes of the locomotive itself and exhausters for vacuum brakes fitted to the passenger stock. As the locomotives were equipped for two different braking systems, they carried two 'trip cocks' on each front right-hand shoe beam.

When delivered, the locomotives were finished in the Metropolitan Railway locomotive livery of maroon with black and straw lining, with red solebars, buffer beams and window frames. The fleet name 'Metropolitan' was carried centrally on the sides, flanked by the Metropolitan coat-of-arms.

The locomotives, which weighed 61½ tons and had a tractive effort of some 22,000lb, were designed to accelerate from rest to 25mph in 25 seconds and to be capable of a top speed of 65mph in order to deal with the frequent closely-spaced stops between Aldgate and Baker Street as well as the long non-stop runs on the outer sections of the Metropolitan. They were also designed to start a 265-ton freight train up a 1 in 45 gradient on straight track and to shunt at speeds as low as 2mph.

Former steam-hauled carriages were used. These were teak panelled compartment stock and were very similar to contemporary main-line practice with deep upholstered moquette-covered seating, overhead luggage racks, raised external mouldings with rounded ventilators over the doors of the passenger compartments and strap-operated, droplight windows.

In 1925 the Metropolitan Railway extended its electric services from Harrow to Rickmansworth and opened, jointly with the London & North Eastern Railway, the short branch to Watford. Watford station has always suffered from its poor location in relation to the town centre. The initial train service levels proved to be too optimistic and the LNER's provision of steam trains to Watford from Marylebone and Aylesbury lasted less than a year. A shuttle bus service was operated by the main local bus company between the station and the town centre and this was replaced by a service operated by the Met itself in 1927. This, together with housebuilding near Watford station, improved the fortunes of the branch, but for a station named after an important town it was to become one of the quieter outposts of the Underground.

At that time the Metropolitan Railway had a very mixed fleet of passenger vehicles, much of it 20 or so years old. The inner suburban services were largely provided by the electric multiple-unit saloon type trains and the longer-distance trains (on the Aylesbury service) were of the compartment type with locomotive haulage – electric as far as Rickmansworth and steam beyond.

To provide additional and more powerful motive power, the Metropolitan ordered 12 compartment-type driving motor coaches from the Metropolitan Carriage, Wagon & Finance Co. (later Metro-Cammell Limited), of Birmingham, in 1927. They were generally similar to the 'Dreadnoughts' but had three cab windows at the front.

In 1930, to cope with increased traffic, the Metropolitan bought 30 more motor coaches and 25 trailers from the Birmingham Railway Carriage & Wagon Co. Ltd, and the final order for this stock went to Birmingham in 1931. It consisted of 18 motor coaches, 14 driving trailers, and 33 trailers. Eventually to be known as 'T' stock, these varnished wooden clad trains, together with a 1932-built batch with steel clad bodies, lasted in service until 1962. Twenty-five older trailer coaches which had been built for locomotive haulage were converted at various times between 1927 and 1941 to run with these.

Top **One of twenty third-class saloon motor-coaches built in 1921. The order also included 33 third-class saloon trailers and six first-class driving trailers. The new cars were similar in appearance to stock delivered to the Metropolitan in 1913 and worked mainly on the Circle Line.**

Above **In 1929 the Metropolitan ordered 30 motor coaches and 25 trailers from the Birmingham Railway Carriage & Wagon Co for use on its electric services. This view shows third class motor car No. 229 when new in 1930. The delivery of the new cars, when augmented by existing cars, including the Ashbury trailers, created 13 trains of electric stock for the Metropolitan. The 1930 cars eventually became part of the T-stock from 1940 and many survived until the T-stock was withdrawn in 1961/62.**

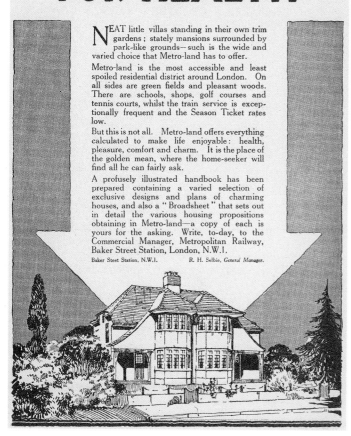

METRO-LAND FOR HEALTH

NEAT little villas standing in their own trim gardens; stately mansions surrounded by park-like grounds—such is the wide and varied choice that Metro-land has to offer.

Metro-land is the most accessible and least spoiled residential district around London. On all sides are green fields and pleasant woods. There are schools, shops, golf courses and tennis courts, whilst the train service is exceptionally frequent and the Season Ticket rates low.

But this is not all. Metro-land offers everything calculated to make life enjoyable: health, pleasure, comfort and charm. It is the place of the golden mean, where the home-seeker will find all he can fairly ask.

A profusely illustrated handbook has been prepared containing a varied selection of exclusive designs and plans of charming houses, and also a "Broadsheet" that sets out in detail the various housing propositions obtaining in Metro-land—a copy of each is yours for the asking. Write, to-day, to the Commercial Manager, Metropolitan Railway, Baker Street Station, London, N.W.1.

Baker Steet Station, N.W.1.   R. H. Selbie, *General Manager*.

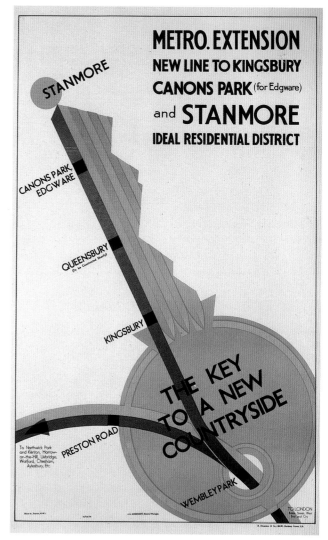

METRO. EXTENSION
NEW LINE TO KINGSBURY
CANONS PARK (for Edgware)
and STANMORE
IDEAL RESIDENTIAL DISTRICT

STANMORE

CANONS PARK, EDGWARE

QUEENSBURY (To be Constructed Shortly)

KINGSBURY

THE KEY TO A NEW COUNTRYSIDE

To Northwick Park and Kenton, Harrow-on-the-Hill, Uxbridge, Watford, Chesham, Aylesbury, Etc.

PRESTON ROAD

WEMBLEY PARK

TO LONDON

The Metropolitan Railway maintained its own distinctive style of publicity until 1933 and sometimes referred to its line as the 'Metro'.

This multiple-unit compartment stock was used on the services from the City and Baker Street to Rickmansworth, Watford. It was also used on the 4½ mile Stanmore branch from its opening on 10th December 1932 until 20th November 1939, when the Bakerloo Line service took over. The special train for the official opening of the Stanmore branch was a unique formation. Three first-class coaches, the Metropolitan directors' saloon, and one of the two Pullman cars were marshalled between two 1930 motor coaches to carry a special party, including the Minister of Transport and the directors of the company, to the ceremony at Stanmore on 9th December 1932.

A train of 'Ashbury' compartment stock converted for electric operation entering Stanmore station on the newly opened extension of the Metropolitan.

Built in the expectation that the branch would take some years to show profit, and with a small subsidy from the Government, the Stanmore branch soon attracted building development around Kingsbury station, but suffered at Canons Park from competition in the form of cheaper fares on the Underground service into London from Edgware. The terminal station, sited just to the east of Stanmore Village, became another relatively quiet outpost but the branch carried sufficient traffic to place further strain on the section of line between Finchley Road and Baker Street.

On 13th November 1933 trains began serving the new Metropolitan station at Northwood Hills. The modest station building, the last designed for the Metropolitan Railway by Charles W. Clark, contained shop units and was dominated by a large canopy over the entrance similar to the one at Kingsbury illustrated above.

Mention has already been made of the four-tracking completed between Finchley Road and Harrow-on-the-Hill by 1932. Unfortunately, to carry four tracks south of Finchley Road to Baker Street, where they would have been most valuable, was out of the question because it would have been so expensive. This section of track became more and more congested, and even the closing of the intermediate stations (Swiss Cottage, Marlborough Road, and St John's Wood) in the morning peak hour did not solve the problem. The Metropolitan therefore proposed to build a deep tube of main-line size, like the GN & City, from a point on the main line between Willesden Green and Kilburn to a junction with the Circle Line on the west side of Edgware Road station. This plan entailed the rebuilding of Edgware Road station. Work started on the station in 1926, and it was given two island platforms with four through platform roads. The new station indicators were prepared, and provision was made for them to announce that the next train would be for Aylesbury and Verney Junction. They were never able to show these destinations, for the line was not built and the bottleneck was not by-passed until the LPTB extended the Bakerloo Line and provided two extra tracks between Baker Street and Finchley Road in November 1939.

Bearing in mind its insular attitude, the Met may not have wanted its Stanmore extension to look like the bold new designs being used for the Piccadilly Line extensions at the same time, but their plain design was probably more influenced by budget considerations on an extension of uncertain profitability. A conservatively designed Kingsbury station is seen in 1933.

Improving the System, 1920–1933

'Millions Has Been Spent on Improving the Underground Railways' – a poster by Gerald Dickson (1926).

On 3rd August 1920 the Central London line was extended the 4¼ miles from Wood Lane to Ealing Broadway. There was just one intermediate station, East Acton. The new line had begun life as the GWR's Ealing & Shepherd's Bush Railway. Originally proposed in 1905, the plans were amended in 1911 to connect the line with the CLR at Wood Lane rather than terminate at Shepherd's Bush Green. It had opened as a GWR freight line as recently as April 1917. The GWR then built a spur from this line to a point to where the Central London could conveniently join up to it from its Wood Lane terminus. The line was then electrified.

The immediate period following the First World War was a difficult one for the nation's economy, and unemployment rose. Inflation had halved the value of money between 1914 and 1918. In 1921 the Government passed the Trade Facilities Act which promised generous financial guarantees for projects which provided employment for large numbers of people. Railway building, being highly labour intensive, provided such employment and in October 1921 Lord Ashfield presented MPs with detailed proposals to extend certain parts of the Underground, including the Hampstead Line to Edgware, using capital guaranteed by the new Act. Eventually the powers were extended by the LER Act (1923) to build an extension of the Hampstead Line from Charing Cross to Kennington, to connect with the CSLR and by a separate Act obtained by the CSLR, to extend that line from Clapham Common to Morden.

By 1922 the pioneering City & South London Railway was in need of modernisation to bring it up to the standards of the other tube railways which had opened since the beginning of the century. The Underground Group had purchased the line in 1913, but the Great War had put on hold any modernisation plans except that new signalling had been installed between 1919 and 1922. Now, the tunnels, which were in various diameters (10ft 2ins, 10ft 6ins and 11ft 6ins) were to be enlarged to the LER standard of 11ft 8ins. Under powers granted in 1913 the line was also to be joined to the Hampstead at Camden Town. Powers had also been obtained to extend the Hampstead from Golders Green to Edgware. Work on both projects began during June 1922. The original intention was to keep much of the CSLR open while work proceeded, although the section from Moorgate Street to Euston was closed temporarily from the night of 8th August, and one station, City Road between Old Street and Angel, was closed permanently. A shield, that allowed trains to pass through it, was specially designed for the tunnel excavation work. A working site was set up at Borough station, which was also closed for the duration. Later Kennington was used as a work site too. On 27th November 1923 there was serious subsidence near Borough station and the line was closed completely until the works finished later the following year. Thus was the unceremonial passing of the original City & South London Railway, with most of its locomotives going for scrap. Many of the wooden carriages found new leases of life as summer houses or workmen's huts.

Two new stations, North Acton and West Acton, opened on the Central London on 5th November 1923. North Acton and West Acton were simple affairs. They were built and owned by the GWR and North Acton offered an interchange with GWR local services. However, the main event in November was saved for Monday the 19th when the Hampstead was extended from Golders Green to Hendon Central. Departing northwards from Golders Green passengers were taken on a ride through rooftops and cuttings and across viaducts to Brent station. From Brent the line continued above ground to Hendon Central. Brent and Hendon Central stations, designed by the Underground's architect Stanley Heaps, had island platforms partly covered by a canopy, and stairways leading down at Brent and up at Hendon Central to the ticket hall and entrance. The ticket halls at both stations were spacious and stylish. Walls were clad in white tile edged in black and green. Black and white 'chess board' non-slip floor tiles had been laid, and each had a passimeter ticket booth. These would now be standard for every new, and many existing, ticket halls. The station facades were in a mock Georgian style with doric columns in portland stone.

The President of the Board of Trade, and local MP, Sir Philip Lloyd-Graeme, officially opened the new extension. The special train used for the ceremony was composed of air-door stock, the motor-cars being converted gate-stock. The trailers used were brand new, and were part of the first delivery of the order for 191 cars for the CSLR modernisation and the Hampstead extension.

From the earliest days of the Metropolitan and District Railways separate tickets were issued from every station to each other, and of each conceivable variety. This not only became unmanageable in terms of space required, but it was quite incompatible with the mounting need to issue tickets ever faster. In the 1920s the process was simplified by grouping all destinations where fares were the same, and this opened the door to widespread issue of tickets by machines, both in ticket offices and by passenger automatic machines. This system lasted until 1948, from when tickets showed just the station of boarding and fare paid. In December 1921 the first automatic ticket machines and 'passimeter' booking office was introduced at Kilburn Park station. The booking clerk in the passimeter booth, which included a gate, issued, dated and cancelled a ticket before releasing the gate to admit the passenger. This rather ugly design was replaced by the polished wood version pictured on the poster on the facing page, though there were variations on the theme and further improvements in appearance. Passimeter booths were eventually to appear at most stations on the system, and only finally disappeared when ticket issuing went fully automatic at the end of the 1980s. A few stations, including Sudbury Town, have preserved examples in situ.

New motor-cars for the CLR Ealing extension on delivery from the Brush factory in 1915. It was to be five years before they entered service on the Central London and they were on loan to the Bakerloo between 1917 and 1920, as already mentioned. These were the first all-enclosed tube cars, doors replacing end gates.

The Coburg Court Hotel harmonises well with the Central London Railway station at Queens Road (now Queensway), which like most tube stations spent its early life as a single-storey structure awaiting such development. Also added since the station was built are the public telephones in this 1914 view.

The Central London Railway extension to Ealing must have had difficulties in attracting the passenger numbers hoped for. On 1st May 1922 its fares to and from Ealing Broadway were reduced. For example, the fare to Oxford Circus came down 24% from 10½d to 8d (still a far cry from the Twopenny Tube of 20 years earlier). The reason given was to avoid anomalies with District Railway fares to central London and mirrored the situation early in the CLR's life when the Metropolitan had had to reduce its fares in the central area to compete.

The District Railway was included in early 1920s plans for expansion of the network. A southerly extension from Wimbledon was proposed over London & South Western Railway tracks to South Morden and Sutton. It appeared on a New Works map that was published at the end of 1922, but work never started on the extension.

A programme which was to continue and accelerate throughout the 1920s and 1930s was the replacement of lifts by escalators at suitable locations. During 1924 escalators were installed at many stations, including Bank (7th May), Shepherd's Bush (5th November), and at many of the rebuilt CSLR stations: Moorgate Street on 3rd July, and at Stockwell, Clapham North and Clapham Common on 1st December, the day the southern section of the rebuilt line was opened. The Clapham Common machine is noteworthy in that it was the first escalator fitted with cleated steps and comb plates, thereby enabling passengers to walk straight on and off it at each landing, rather than at an angle. At some stations the installation of escalators was still not complete so lifts continued to be used for a while. Higher-speed lifts were installed at Angel. One station with lifts which was not to benefit from escalators was South Kentish Town, which closed on 5th June 1924 because of a power shortage resulting from a strike at the Lots Road power station. It had been little used and never reopened. At Oxford Circus, where a new ticket hall had been built beneath Argyll Street, new escalators to the CLR platforms were brought in on 30th June 1925. Escalators to the Bakerloo platforms had been in use since May 1914. Other stations to benefit from moving staircases included Old Street on 19th August 1925 and Tottenham Court Road from 20th September, a month after the opening of a new ticket hall. Faster lifts were installed at Leicester Square in 1925 and at Holborn the following year. Escalators replaced these at both stations within ten years as the general installation of moving stairs wherever possible continued.

Now working on the line for which it had been built, a CLR 1915-built motor car with gate stock trailers on a trip from Ealing to Wood Lane arrives at East Acton soon after the extension was opened in 1920. The area still retained much of a rural character despite being only six miles from Oxford Circus but work on a new housing estate has begun. GWR ownership of the station is shown in the emblem in the seats.

On Easter Sunday 1924, 20th April, the first section of reconstructed CSLR was opened from Moorgate (renamed from Moorgate Street on that day), to Euston, with trains proceeding through new tunnels to join the Hampstead line south of Camden Town. To facilitate this unification one of the most complex junctions on the whole of the Underground, before or since, had been constructed, and it made possible every combination of north–south journey from any one branch to any other. One of the most amazing elements of this job was that it was carried out without disruption to the Hampstead services. The opening of the junction enabled the CSLR trains from Moorgate to run to Golders Green. Two days later work began on joining the CSLR to the Hampstead from the south between Kennington and Charing Cross.

The Hampstead Line reached Edgware on Monday 18th August 1924, when the 3-mile extension from Hendon Central opened. On leaving Hendon, the new line immediately entered twin tunnels excavated beneath the Burroughs and the LMS main line, before emerging into the open and proceeding to Colindale, where a similar station platform layout, ticket hall and entrance building to those at Hendon and Brent had been built. A builders' strike had delayed the completion of the next station, Burnt Oak, which did not open until 27th October, and then only with a temporary booking office. When completed in August 1928 the station façade differed from the other stations in having a simpler design without the doric pillars. Edgware, the terminus station, was an attractive building set on three sides around a small garden flanked by a roadway. The station entrance was at the centre, the east side containing shop units. Doric pillars supported the roof on all three sides. A large ticket hall, similar in style to the others on the new extension was situated at 'street' level. The island platform was reached by stairs. The platform was entirely roofed over, and formed part of the adjacent depot being used at night to park trains. The depot contained four covered inspection pits and four open sidings, sufficient space to accommodate 76 cars. A further platform was added at Edgware in 1932.

Above **Bookmatches promoting travel by Underground.**

Right **A four-car train of standard stock, headed by a 1923 Cammell-Laird built motor car, arrives at Hendon Central soon after the station was opened in this contemporary hand-coloured photograph. A control-trailer is at the far end of the train. The scene above the tunnel portal taking the line towards Edgware was still predominantly rural in 1924.**

At the time much of the area north of Golders Green was still semi-rural, although it was soon to be part of the suburban London explosion of the inter-war period. The Underground Group obviously felt people needed some prompting to move to the area because it produced a series of posters, including one for Edgware, illustrating the delights of suburban living.

On Monday 1st December 1924 the remaining section of the modernised City & South London Railway was opened from Moorgate to Clapham Common. The opening was performed by Lord Ashfield and his daughter the Hon. Marian Stanley. The line was now equipped with four-rail current collection and return, conforming to the rest of the line and the Hampstead, and a through service was begun from Clapham Common to Highgate/Edgware. Not all the stations reopened on 1st December. Both Borough and Kennington, which had become virtual building sites during the works, did not open their doors to passengers again until 23rd February 1925 and 6th July 1925 respectively.

In May 1926, following lack of resolution of a bitter miners' dispute, the Trades Union Congress ordered a national strike of almost all TUC members. Some trades were exempted but these did not include transport. The General Strike began on 4th May with no Underground, tram or LGOC bus services running. The Metropolitan, independent of the Underground, did run some services as did a number of independent bus operators. Some trains also ran on suburban main lines

An immediate appeal was made for volunteers to act as drivers and guards on trains, both on the Underground and on the main lines. In anticipation of the strike, letters had started to go out to retired operating staff of the Metropolitan Railway on 2nd May, asking them if they were prepared to assist if needed. The following day Lord Ashfield, chairman of the Underground Group, sent a letter to all staff appealing for them not to join the strike. The letter either got to most people too late or had very little effect; just 33 station staff and six guards reported for work on 4th May and when it proved impossible on this day to run any services an immediate start was made on training volunteers. Twelve training centres were set up to cope with 250 men a day.

On 5th May limited services were provided on the Bakerloo and Central London lines with trains stopping at certain stations only. The Met, which began the strike day with three trains in service, and others being added as the day progressed, had 15 running on the 5th. The Metropolitan was fortunate in having 30% of its power house and substation staff deciding not to join the strike, an untypically high percentage of workers. In anticipation of the difficulty the volunteers would have getting to and from their work, beds were provided at Neasden works and the substations. Food supplies were laid on and the men were virtually cut off from the outside world for the duration of the strike. The regular staff who carried on working were subsequently rewarded with double pay for the period. Volunteers were paid the rate for the job. It is surprising that with so many volunteers at work running the Underground, there were no serious accidents. The only serious injury reported was sustained by a volunteer driver from Cambridge who was attacked in the cab of a Central London line train and given severe head injuries by pickets. The main line railways were worse affected. A number of collisions occurred and four deaths were reported on the LNER.

Below left Typewritten certificate issued after a volunteer had received the necessary tuition to drive a train. This was not the first time that volunteers had been used to man trains. There had been a strike on the Underground, lasting about ten days, in 1919 but the General Strike was seen as an attack on the British political system and aroused feelings of patriotism amongst the middle classes, many of whom came forward to offer their services.

Below A press photo of a volunteer guard. In the early days of the strike, some newspapers appeared in amateurly printed typewritten form.

METROPOLITAN RAILWAY.
—————————————

This is to certify that the bearer Mr.H.Tighe has been passed

to act as Motorman.

Metropolitan Railway
    Staff Dept.   (signed)   B.Holt.
8.May 1926.   Traffic Manager.
Traffic Manager.

RIGHT AWAY ! A VOLUNTEER GUARD AT WORK
ON THE METROPOLITAN RAILWAY.

By 11th May, the last full day of the strike, eighty of 124 stations owned by the Underground group were open and staff in many other areas of industry had begun to return to work. The workers could not afford a long strike in support of a claim that was not theirs and, following discussions between the government and the TUC, the general stoppage was called off on the early afternoon of the 12th. The railway unions agreed to end the strike on the night of the 13th following undertakings being given regarding reinstatement of the strikers. On the last day of the strike, about one-third of Underground trains were running.

The coal strike continued until October and the repercussions for energy supply meant that full services could not be restored on the Underground until supplies were back to normal. A number of men therefore had to be laid off. Later in May a four-day working week was introduced on the Underground so that those still laid off could be taken on again by redistribution of the available work. This lasted until coal supplies were back to normal.

THE ARCHITECT'S OFFICE
RESOLVES NOT TO BUILD ANY
MORE STATIONS LIKE THIS —

F.H. Stingemore, a draughtsman in the Underground Group's drawing office, frequently produced cartoons for the group's staff magazine. In the January 1927 issue he supplied a series of suggested New Year resolutions, one of which indicates that the white portland stone faced stations on the Morden extension (such as Clapham South, illustrated) were not liked by everyone. At platform level, the Morden extension stations were more traditional in appearance, as shown in the photo of South Wimbledon.

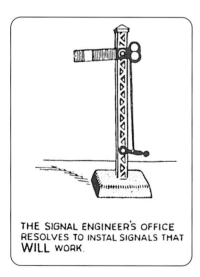

THE SIGNAL ENGINEER'S OFFICE
RESOLVES TO INSTAL SIGNALS THAT
WILL WORK.

Another of the cartoons suggests that signalling problems had been suffered on the new extensions to the system.

On Monday 13th September 1926 two major extensions opened on London's growing tube railway system. South of Clapham Common seven new stations, six being deep underground, serving the 5¼ miles to Morden, welcomed their first passengers. The new stations were the first to demonstrate the impact of a friendship forged in 1915 between Frank Pick and the architect Charles Holden. The seven were Clapham South, Balham, Trinity Road, Tooting Broadway, Colliers Wood, South Wimbledon and, the terminus, Morden. Above ground at least, the station buildings set new standards in design and functionality. Holden was a member of a group called The Design & Industries Association, which promoted the best in industrial design. In 1923, Pick had commissioned Holden, a partner in the firm Adams, Holden & Pearson, to redesign the side entrance and ticket hall of Westminster station. He had also employed him the following year when, as part of the CSLR modernisation, the frontages of several stations including Angel, Old Street, Borough, Stockwell, Oval and Clapham North, were remodelled by the Underground's architect Stanley Heaps under Holden's influence. Work at Bond Street, which acted as a precursor to Holden's work on the Morden extension stations, had involved the construction of various mock-ups in a hall at Earls Court. The finished designs were all in the same mould, but were no less impressive. All were different in profile, depending on whether the site occupied a corner position or was part of a terrace, but they retained the same basic features which included wide entrances, high roofed ticket halls with large frosted windows, one being inset with a prominent red and blue UNDERGROUND bullseye. A canopy, bearing the station name in white on blue enamel panels, ran above all entrances, and to this was fixed one or more tall white poles complete with bullseyes pierced vertically through the centre. The whole façade was finished in white portland stone. Shop units were included in some of the frontages.

The ticket halls were lined in white tile, edged in green and black, a style which extended down to the platforms. All the 'tube' stations were equipped with escalators. At night the stations were floodlit, and searchlights placed on the roofs added to the dramatic effect. At Morden, where the line emerged into the open, there were five platforms beneath an arched canopy. Stairs led to the ticket hall and the station entrance, which was essentially the same style as the others. Outside the station was a large LGOC bus station, and from 27th January 1927 perhaps the most unusual feature, an Underground owned and operated petrol station and garage. It was a very civilised affair with covered accommodation for 500 cars. It was hoped that the car owning population of Surrey would make full use of this facility and use the tube for a quick trip into the West End and City. The garage was staffed by mechanics, who maintained and cleaned the cars to order. Although the Underground Group hailed the garage a success, the idea does not appear to have been extended elsewhere on the system. The new railway passed beneath Morden station forecourt and the main road to Epsom, to run to a large new depot with five car sheds, five maintenance bays and 20 roads for train stabling.

On the same day that the Morden line opened, a 1.62-mile extension to join the CSLR from Kennington to the Hampstead at Charing Cross was opened. From Charing Cross, the Hampstead ran in twin tunnels beneath the River Thames to Waterloo. Here the underground station had been enlarged with a new sub-surface ticket hall and a new bank of three escalators (which were not fully operational until October 1927) leading down to a wide concourse connecting the Hampstead and Bakerloo lines. From Waterloo the line continued to Kennington, the southbound line burrowing beneath the CSLR tunnels just north of the station before running into a new platform adjoining the southbound CSLR line from Elephant & Castle. From Kennington the Hampstead Line branched into two, one spur joining the southbound CSLR tunnel just south of the station platform, the other continuing in a loop to become the northbound Hampstead Line in a platform adjoining the northbound CSLR platform. From here a spur ran to join the loop line just south of the northbound Kennington platform. The new loop line was an effective way of terminating trains at Kennington without the need for the usual reversing procedure and trains from the south could join either the Charing Cross or City branches. There was also a reversing siding for the CSLR trains, which could also be used by trains from the Hampstead Line terminating from the north. The opening ceremony took place at Morden and was performed by J. T. Moore-Brabazon, the Parliamentary Secretary to the Minister of Transport. These extensions created a whole new unified railway, which was to become known as the Morden-Edgware Line.

Another new piece of tube opened on 27th March 1927, but it was not for public use. It ran from the northbound Morden-Edgware to the eastbound Piccadilly tunnels at King's Cross. It had been built to enable Morden-Edgware stock to transfer to Piccadilly tracks for the purpose of visiting the new train overhaul works at Acton.

Stingemore also had some suggestions for increasing advertising revenues, following straphanger adverts in 1925. Advertising on seats, train exteriors and stairs had to wait until the 1990s. Straphanger advertising has also been used in recent times. The train is shown advertising Zebra shoe polish.

On 1st November 1926 the District began a new service from Edgware Road to Putney Bridge using the platforms at Edgware Road which had been built for the aborted extensions from Kilburn and Brondesbury. District operation of the Circle Line ceased the same day. Later in the month the District tracks from Hounslow Central to Hounslow West were doubled.

An unusual piece of equipment was first used at Wood Lane station in 1928. The conversion of the CLR stock to air door meant that the curved platform that had been used in the 'gate' era presented safety problems as the exit doors were now in the centre of the cars. Another platform had to be used but this was not long enough for a six-car train. To increase platform capacity a 35-foot long extension to the terminus platform was constructed for use at busy times. When the platform was in use, it sat over a track leading into Wood Lane depot. When it was swivelled away, the track to the depot could be used. The CLR power station at Wood Lane was closed on 18th March 1928, the line henceforth being fed by the main LER power station at Lots Road.

The Trade Facilities Acts enabled the Underground Group to spend £12.5 million on improving the railway between 1922 and 1928. In 1929 a new piece of legislation superseded it. This was the Development (Loans, Guarantees and Grants) Act, which enabled the Treasury to subsidise expenditure and guarantee the interest on new public utility works. The Underground's Operating Manager J. P. Thomas, no doubt in anticipation of the Act, wrote to Frank Pick in 1928 to list 'The most needful extensions of the Tubes'. In his view these were of the Piccadilly Line north of Finsbury Park, a branch off the City & South London to Brixton and Streatham, the Central London Line to Hackney and Woodford, a brand new tube from Kingsbury to Lewisham via Cricklewood, Marble Arch, Victoria, Oval and Peckham, and an extension of the Bakerloo to Rushey Green via Camberwell and Dulwich. The Group used the provisions of the new Act to fund extensions to the Piccadilly with the construction of a 7½ mile extension from Finsbury Park to Cockfosters, and a 4½ mile extension from Hammersmith to Northfields, parallel with the District.

The northern extension from Finsbury Park was much needed. In rush hours crowds poured out of the tube at Finsbury Park trying to cram onto capacity filled trams and buses heading north toward Manor House and beyond. There had been petitions for a tube extension, and in October 1925 an enquiry, but now the LER could act. In October 1929 it submitted plans for a grant under the new Act. The application was approved in June 1930.

Late in 1928 the new ticket hall at Piccadilly Circus was unveiled. It had been designed by Charles Holden, and work on it had begun in 1924. A vast cavernous cylindrical ticket hall was excavated. Five staircases and subways from the main thoroughfares led to the ticket hall. Wall surfaces were clad in cream marble, and fluted dark red and bronze columns containing light fitments supported a decorative ceiling. Additional lighting was provided by the many display cases, owned by local department stores, which lined the wall space in company with automatic ticket machines and telephone booths. The use of bronze for much of the metal surfaces enhanced the overall appearance of the new hall. The new ticket hall and its escalators to the Bakerloo and Piccadilly platforms were opened by the Mayor of Westminster on 10th December 1928.

Work on the various new extensions was under way as 1930 came to an end, and continued during 1931. By the end of the year the tunnelling was complete. Even before the new services started some rebuilt stations were opened including, on 1st March 1931, the new station building at Ealing Common. It was constructed chiefly of granite and portland stone, and its main feature was a heptagonal tower with a wide canopied entrance to the ticket hall. It was situated in the middle of a single-storey building with shop units. A similar new building at Hounslow West opened on 5th July. These stations represented a development of those built for the Morden extension, and were the work of the Underground's chief architect Stanley Heaps in association with Adams, Holden & Pearson. On 6th July a new temporary station opened at Park Royal, adjacent to Western Avenue, and the old Park Royal & Twyford Abbey station was closed.

A couple of weeks later, on 19th July 1931, the new Sudbury Town station opened. It marked the beginning of a new and undoubtedly the most famous era in the development of the Underground station. Sudbury Town was the result of the continued collaboration between Frank Pick and Charles Holden. In the summer of 1930 the two men had made a trip to Europe to see some of the latest architectural developments in Germany, Denmark, Sweden and Holland. It was believed that by planning stations to be functional, laid out with a specific purpose in mind, and with clean lines and shapes, good design would be created by default. The interpretation of this philosophy for the many stations built for the Piccadilly Line extensions was considerably aided by the use of new materials for the basic structures and traditional red brick and glass for much of the surface cladding and finishing. At Sudbury Town everything was cubic and much was symmetrical. The dominant feature, a majestic box-shaped high-elevated tower, containing the entrance and ticket hall, was constructed of red brick and glass, and was reached across a sweeping forecourt. Space constraints were not a consideration here. It was desirable that the station be visible at night, and full effect was made of internal and external illumination. The huge windows in the tower helped considerably, forming a wall of light against the night sky. And it didn't stop with Sudbury Town, because as 1931 progressed work was proceeding on many new Piccadilly Line extension stations in a similar vein.

The stations built for the Piccadilly Line extensions were on a grand scale making full use of upward space and daylight. Here at Sudbury Town, uplighters fixed to the ticket hall floors also provide a useful publicity site. The wooden passimeter booking office is preserved, out of use, at this listed station today.

While the station work was going on, the job of quadrupling the tracks to carry Piccadilly as well as District trains from Hammersmith to Acton Town and Northfields continued. It included the complete rebuilding of Hammersmith station with a frontage in portland stone and new platform canopies and over-bridges in pre-cast concrete. The tracks were completely relocated to serve two new island platforms, with District trains using the outermost tracks. To the west of Hammersmith, new track was laid on a viaduct, which had formed part of the old Southern Railway line from Richmond to Shepherd's Bush. The old platforms at Ravenscourt Park and Turnham Green could still be utilised for District trains, but a new platform was needed at Stamford Brook to serve the eastbound District. West of Turnham Green the embankment had to be built up and widened, and additional road bridges built to widen the line to Acton Town. Chiswick Park station was completely rebuilt, with new platforms to serve District trains, which would use the two outermost of the four tracks. The new station building consisted of a single story entrance with shop units, dominated by a large high-roofed semi-circular glazed ticket hall with a red brick tower on its western side containing the station name and UNDERGROUND bullseye.

There was much preparation for the opening of the first phase of the Piccadilly Line extensions as 1932 gathered pace. From 8th February some of the District local services from Acton Town to Hounslow West and South Harrow were operated by tube stock. The following week, from 14th February, alterations were made to the District Line services at the western end whereby the service from South Acton to Hounslow was cut back to Acton Town, henceforth becoming a simple shuttle service. The section from Acton Town to South Acton had been double-track, but now it was reduced to single-track only. In the east, in contrast, the District was set to expand, as the LMS, in conjunction with the LER, set about quadrupling the tracks so that District Line trains could run on the 7½ miles from Barking, where the electric service had terminated since 1908, to Upminster.

A new station at Northfields was opened on 19th May 1932, replacing the original Northfields & Little Ealing station. It was in the new Holden style, and consisted of a large box-shaped red brick ticket hall with glazed column sections above a single-storey entrance. There were two island platforms accommodating four tracks.

On Monday 4th July 1932 the Piccadilly Line was extended from Hammersmith to South Harrow and the District service from Acton Town to South Harrow withdrawn. Apart from the new station buildings at Ealing Common and Sudbury Town, work was well advanced on new buildings at Alperton and Sudbury Hill. Again the functionalism style was evident with large box-like ticket halls dominating otherwise single-storey structures which included shop units. At Alperton the top ticket hall tower was adjacent to the platform, the platform canopy rising above even that. A small forecourt added a sweeping effect. Glazing was not as prominent as at Sudbury Town. Similarly at Sudbury Hill the tower was the dominant feature. There was no forecourt, but as with Sudbury Town and Alperton, round bulb lamps atop concrete columns stood guard at the perimeter. The glazed part of the tower contained an open bullseye. The platforms were rebuilt in a complementary style with plenty of glazing and a 'stepped' glass canopy over the staircases. Acton Town, which was not completed until 1933, was basically similar, but had a larger tower with three glazed columns and more shop units.

A stylish feature introduced to Underground stations during the inter-war years were the brass uplighters fixed to the escalator panelling and which in turn reflected light down from the ceilings to the escalators. The uplighters were a feature of new and rebuilt stations in the early thirties.

The District Railway's Sudbury Hill station buildings had been perfectly sufficient for the semi-rural community it had opened in 1903 to serve. But the spreading of suburbia and the prospect of a frequent tube train service meant something larger was needed, Holden's new station of 1932 being the result.

The western extensions were followed on Tuesday 19th July by the first part of the northern extension of the Piccadilly, the 4½ miles from Finsbury Park to Arnos Grove. From Finsbury Park the line proceeded in twin tunnels to Manor House where a first taste of Holden's new underground platform style was to be seen. The whole effect was dominated by biscuit coloured wall tiling inset with decorative metal covers to the ventilation ducting. The platform cross-section was not circular in common with earlier tube stations. The walls were slightly curved up to the circular roof arch and the platforms were illuminated by downlighters fixed beneath the roof vault. The journey to the ticket hall was, of course, by escalator, full use being made of bronze uplighter columns. The general style of the platforms and escalator shafts was to be replicated at the other deep-level stations on the extension. The Manor House ticket hall, which was entirely sub-surface, had a low ceiling and contained a new, more rounded, style of passimeter booth. It lay beneath the busy junction of Seven Sisters Road and Green Lanes and subways linked the ticket hall to the street and to special tramway islands. At Turnpike Lane, a large square ticket hall, adjacent to an even larger ventilation tower created a mini station complex with several shop units. There were plenty of windows in the ticket hall making it light and airy.

An atmospheric night time view of Arnos Grove taken soon after the station opened in 1932. Platform roof lighting takes the eye down through the brilliantly lit interior of a new standard stock motor car and up to the rotunda above the station ticket hall, illuminated from the inside and externally floodlit. How marvellous this must have appeared to the new traveller clutching a return ticket to Leicester Square for a night out in the West End. The new station included car parking facilities, which also appeared at other stations on the Piccadilly extensions where space permitted.

A different approach was used at Wood Green, where the station occupied a site at the corner of Lordship Lane and the High Road. Here the station building was not so tall, being dwarfed slightly by the buildings on either side. Shop units were built into the main structure on either side of the entrance. At Bounds Green, which was less hemmed in by adjacent buildings, an octagonal ticket hall tower was joined to an even taller ventilation tower on its south-eastern corner. The rest of the structure was single-storey with a shallow glazed clerestory section over the escalator shaft. Shop units were also an integral part of the building. The line emerged into the open at Arnos Grove, where two island platforms accommodated three tracks. Trains could terminate here and a fan of sidings to the south of the station enabled some trains to stable. Stairs led from the platforms to a huge ticket hall within a high glazed cylindrical tower, sitting in the middle of a single-storey structure. Columns of glass, alternating with red brickwork, ran the full height of the tower. To the left of the station was a small car park, and a bus pull-in bay separated the station entrance from Bowes Road.

The extension of the District to Upminster in 1932 was over LMS tracks. A train of mixed District stock pauses at Becontree. Until the late 1930s, all trains on the District Line had hand-worked sliding doors and the last of these survived until the 1950s – see also photo on page 152.

On Monday 12th September 1932 District electric trains made their first foray east of Barking, when the line was extended to Upminster. The LMS owned the new infrastructure, which paralleled its own tracks to Southend, and had also built the new stations for the District Line. The aim was to improve capacity and journey times on its own longer distance services by transferring much of the local passenger traffic to the new District Line facility. The first new station on the extension, Upney, had an island platform connected by a long ramp to a modest ticket hall. Becontree, which the LMS had first opened to replace a 1926 'halt' at Gale Street, had separate platforms, the westbound forming an island platform with the down LMS line. Heathway, the stop closest to the giant Ford factory, was in similar style to Upney with an island platform and a ramp. A similar station building was found at Dagenham, where a new station building had replaced the earlier LMS structure. Here the eastbound platform was also a bay platform to enable trains to terminate from east to west, while the westbound platform formed an island with the LMS down line. Hornchurch had a similar street level building to the others on the extension, while the platform layout was similar to Becontree. The terminus station, Upminster, provided interchange with both the LMS Southend service and a spur to the main LNER lines at Romford.

On Saturday 9th January 1933 the Piccadilly Line was extended from Acton Town via South Ealing to Northfields, although the District continued to run a through service to Hounslow West. The new depot at Northfields, with accommodation for 304 cars, was brought into use for the Piccadilly Line at this time.

Although there was no official opening ceremony for the extensions, the Prince of Wales, accompanied by Lord Ashfield, made a tour of the Piccadilly Line's northern extension during February. On Monday 13th March the Piccadilly was extended right through to Hounslow West, the District henceforth running there only during peak periods. On the same day the line was extended the 2.38 miles from Arnos Grove via Southgate to Enfield West. Just prior to Southgate the line entered tunnel again for the short distance to the station platforms which followed the same pattern as those at other deep level stations on the extension. Southgate, at the four-way junction of Chase Side, Chase Road, High Road and Winchmore Hill Road, was a design masterpiece. The station building itself was a single-storey circular structure with a narrower glazed clerestory section on top, from the middle of which protruded a steel column with illuminated circular sections on top which sat a bronze ball. A perimeter road ran around the ticket hall and around that a brick built parade of shops with circular ends to create perfect symmetry with the station. Here was the epitome of 1930s functionalism providing fine, unique, design.

On leaving Southgate the line emerged into the open again to terminate at Enfield West. Here a massive station building had been constructed, which dominated everything in the surrounding area. The ticket hall was the largest on the northern extension, the box-shaped tower containing 14 columns of windows. The single-storey entrance contained a waiting area for bus passengers and a kiosk. Shop units were incorporated into the rest of the structure. The vastness of the ticket hall dwarfed the passimeter and other fittings and made a mockery of the modest island platform which served the trains. A new depot was built to the north of the station to accommodate 250 cars. This was Cockfosters depot, and when it opened the original Piccadilly depot at Lillie Bridge was used to house engineering trains.

1932 was quite a year for the Underground system, with 16½ miles of new route added to the map. Early the following year the map itself went through a dramatic change. In January 1933 the first edition of Henry Beck's diagrammatic map of the Underground was issued. Earlier maps had retained a geographic format, but Beck, a 29 year-old draughtsman with the Underground Group, had designed a diagram layout for the map which had eventually found favour, after an initial rejection by the Group's publicity department. After some tinkering with the design the first edition of the map was ready, and over the years it has told, in its colourful lined form, of the changes in London's Underground network. Beck continued working to perfect the diagram until it was taken over by other hands from 1960. Today it successfully incorporates much more information than was necessary in 1933.

The first poster version of Henry (Harry) Beck's famous diagrammatic Underground map, published in 1933. His first sketch of the idea had been drawn two years earlier during a period of unemployment. His map was rejected by the Underground's publicity department as 'too revolutionary'. Convinced he had a good idea, he submitted it again in 1932, this time successfully.

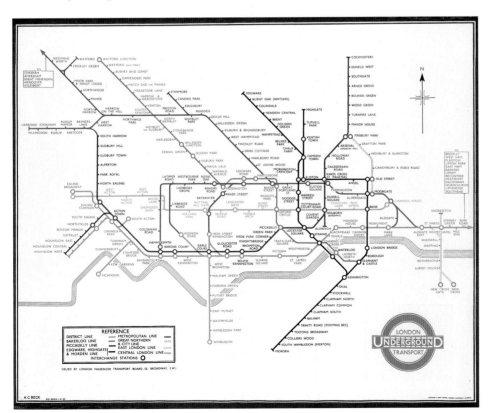

New Trains, New Standards

The 1920s and early 1930s were to witness a huge influx of new rolling stock to the Underground companies. New trains arrived almost every year, and the period brought a much needed refurbishment for others. The stock used to supply the Central London extensions to Ealing Broadway consisted of 24 Brush built motor-cars. They differed from previous deliveries in having swing doors instead of gates, which earned them the distinction of being the first fully enclosed tube cars; they also had elliptical, rather than clerestory, roofs. These cars had been delivered in 1915 and 22 of them had been running on the Bakerloo pending their use on the CLR. They were 47ft 9ins in length and seated 32 passengers. Some CLR trailers had to be modified to run with them because the Brush cars were incompatible with the original CLR fleet.

The District took delivery of 100 new cars between December 1920 and October 1921. They were built by Metro Carriage to a high specification, being constructed principally of steel. They had elliptical roofs and, because they dispensed with the traditional footboards along each side, they were, at 9ft 7ins, eleven inches wider than previous District stock. The bodies were longer too, 50ft 5¼ ins, against the 49ft 6ins of an E class motor-car. There were three sets of hand-worked double-doors on each side, which helped to speed boarding and alighting times at stations. Inside, each car had several vertical grab poles within the circulation areas. These apparently caused congestion and were subsequently removed. The seating capacity was 40 for motor-cars, 44 for control-trailers and 48 for trailers. But the distinctive feature of the F-stock, as the new trains were classified, and the one for which they are best remembered, was the oval shaped windows in each car-end wall, including the cabs. The 100 cars comprised 40 double-ended motor-cars, 12 single cab control-trailers, 48 trailers (12 1st class trailers, and 36 3rd class trailers). The motor-cars were extremely powerful, having four GE 260 traction motors. The F-stock was initially painted in a brownish-red livery, which lasted until later in the 1920s when the cars were painted bright red. The first complete train of F-stock is recorded as running in service during February 1921.

THERE IS MORE ROOM IN THE FRONT OF THE TRAIN

New cars also appeared on the Piccadilly during 1920/21, and in one important respect they were quite revolutionary. There were 40 of them, 20 trailers and 20 control-trailers, and all were built by Cammell Laird of Nottingham. They had one set of large double-doors in the centre of the car separated by a central pillar. The trailers had a single-leaf door at each outer end while the control-trailers had a cab at one end. The cars had distinctive bulging sides and arched roofs with a shallow clerestory running the entire length. The interiors had longitudinal leather seating. The control-trailer cab windows were oval shaped. What made these cars revolutionary were their passenger doors, which were air-operated. Twenty of the Piccadilly's original gate-stock motor-cars were converted to air-door working to run with the new stock, and the first complete air-door tube train entered service on the Piccadilly on 9th December 1921. It was composed of six cars (M–T–CT+CT–T–M) and was staffed by a motorman and two guards, one per cab, each controlling the doors on three cars. Three-car trains could be operated (M–T–CT), and on these occasions one guard only was carried. Because of a delay in successfully converting the necessary number of gate-stock motor-cars to air doors, many of the new cars had to be stored until they could enter service, but by December 1923 all were in use.

On 12th December 1921 the first workshops opened in what was to become the Underground's main overhaul and repair centre, Acton Works. The works occupied a large site adjacent to the LGOC's Chiswick bus building and overhaul works, and a trip on a District train from Chiswick Park to Acton Town afforded a commanding view of both establishments. As built Acton could overhaul 16 cars a week. The target overhaul mileage for a motor-car was 60,000, and that for a trailer 75,000. One of the first tasks undertaken at Acton was a renovation of the F-stock. These trains had proved very powerful, and their ability to move large crowds had quickly created a situation where the older and slower District trains were setting the pace. Motors were removed from some of the double-equipped F-stock motor-cars and trans-ferred to seven of the ten original District Railway electric locomotives, which were rehabilitated before returning to work hauling the daily Southend specials from Ealing Broadway as far as Barking. Passengers had also complained about the stark interiors of the F-stock so they were given a brighter look with new patterned seat moquette replacing the original brown leather, and a green and ivory paint scheme. The green was set to become a feature of most new electric stock built before the mid-1950s.

Rush hour crowds at Piccadilly Circus in 1922. By this time, one entrance at each end of the cars was inadequate and causing delays at stations. Trials with centrally-positioned air operated sliding doors the year before had shown this to be the way forward for the deep-level tube lines. From 1923 all new and modified tube stock had air doors. Power operated doors had been first tried on the District's B stock of 1905 but they were unreliable and hand operation was soon substituted. The subsurface lines had to wait until 1936 for the fitting of air doors on new trains as standard.

The rebuilding of the CSLR, the Edgware extension, together with the proposals for a southern extension of the CSLR, required a large fleet of new trains to provide the service. In 1922 six cars were ordered from various manufacturers to help determine the design for the new stock. A wooden mock-up of a control-trailer was built at Golders Green depot, and the six experimental cars, which were delivered to Lillie Bridge in January 1923, were based on its preferred elements. The six cars, five trailers and one control-trailer were supplied by firms which had built rolling-stock for the LER before. The Gloucester Railway Carriage and Wagon Company supplied the control-trailer, and one trailer. The remaining four trailers came from Leeds Forge, Metropolitan Carriage & Wagon Company, Birmingham Railway Carriage & Wagon Company and Cammell Laird. All the cars seated 44 passengers. Each differed in detail from the others, although they all shared the same basic profile with vertical side panels tapering slightly inwards from below the window line to roof level, and a clerestory roof running the full car length. The exterior livery was crimson for the lower panelling, cream window pillars and door recess panels, black beading and dark red doors. The cab of the control-trailer was crimson. The interior colour scheme varied according to the manufacturer. The cars were also used to test variations in bogie design. Not surprisingly passenger doors were air-operated. The new cars were shown to the press on 3rd February 1923 before entering service on the Piccadilly, running between two gate-stock motor cars specially converted to air-door working. They were transferred to the Hampstead line in August. Public reaction was good and before long orders were placed with Birmingham, Cammell Laird and Metro Carriage for 191 cars to work on the rebuilt CSLR and the extended Hampstead line.

The eventual order, the bulk of which was delivered during 1924, comprised 81 motor-cars, 35 control-trailers and 75 trailers. Cammell Laird built 41 motor-cars, and Metro Carriage 40. The 35 control-trailers were built by Metro Carriage, while 40 trailers came from Cammell Laird and the remaining 35 from Birmingham.

A modern tube trailer car, in this case one of 50 built by Birmingham for the Morden extensions, arrives by conventional if slightly ponderous means at an entrance to Morden depot in August 1925.

The new stock, delivery of which commenced at the end of 1923, was similar in profile and layout to the six 'competition' cars. The principal difference was of fully arched roofs over the passenger doors. The motor-cars bore a resemblance to the previous generation of gate-stock motor-cars in as much as the body frame swept up to expose the motored bogie beneath a compressor and switch compartment which occupied a third of its length. This bogie had two 240-hp motors mounted on it. A central pillar divided the single set of double doors on the motor-cars, a feature not perpetuated on the trailers or control-trailers which had two sets of double-doors on each side. The cab fronts on the motor-cars and control-trailers were identical. The exterior livery was the same as that of the 1922 cars. The motor-cars seated 30, the control-trailers 44 and the trailers 48. Inside, the basic colours were green below window level and cream above, with white ceilings, and mahogany window pillars. All 191 cars had recessed windows, which pulled down for ventilation, and were the first of what eventually became known as the 'standard stock'.

During 1924, following the success of the conversion of the 20 Piccadilly motor-cars to air-door working, it was decided to investigate the feasibility of converting more gate-stock to the system. Two trailers, one from the Hampstead line and one from the Central London were fitted experimentally with air-door equipment. The Hampstead car received a central set of double-doors separated by a pillar, with the gates at each end being replaced by single-leaf air-doors, one of which 'revolved' inwards to stand against the car end wall when open. The CLR car had the gated end platform closed and incorporated into the main saloon. Two single-leaf doors were provided at intervals along each side of the car. This car returned to the Central London where it ran on a normal gate-stock train, the gateman assigned to the car using air-cocks to open the doors. The success of this experiment, as far as the Central London was concerned, enabled plans to be drawn up for a modernisation programme of the CLR fleet, work beginning in 1926.

Despite having built two cars for the 1922 'competition' stock, the Gloucester Carriage and Wagon Company had missed out on an order for the production standard stock. However the Company did receive an order for 50 new motor cars for the District, and the first of these arrived during 1924. The new cars were later given the classification 'G'. Appearance wise they were a step backwards from the F-stock of 1921 in as much as they had straight sides, only two sets of hand-worked double doors on each side, and a clerestory roof running the full 50ft 2in car body length. Basic livery was all red with dark red doors and beading picked out in black. Two new bogie types had been designed for District cars and classified A2 (motored) and K2 (un-motored). The new motor-cars carried an A2 bogie with a K2 at the trailing end. The 50 cars were built to enable older wooden bodied stock to be either withdrawn or converted to trailers. Additional K2 bogies were ordered for the 1905 vintage B-stock motor-cars which were to become trailers (H-stock); by 1925, when all the G-stock had been delivered, 42 of them were in service. These new deliveries enabled the District's pioneering electric A-stock cars to be withdrawn.

During the 1920s, platform name signs began to be standardised on the bar and circle style. The Metropolitan Railway and the East London Railway had diamond backgrounds of differing style as shown here, red for the Met and green for the East London.

On the Central London, eight motor-cars from the 1903 batch were fitted with new motors to enable them to run with the 1917 stock, and eight trailers were converted to control-trailers. The successful trials with air-door cars on the Central London led to a large-scale scheme to convert the entire stock of the line to air-door. Work began in February 1926, and to carry it out the Underground Group activated a hitherto dormant subsidiary, the Union Construction Company (UCC). The powers to build rolling stock had been contained in the original October 1901 registration document of the UCC, which Charles Yerkes had created to complement his railway purchasing adventures at the turn of the century. Part of a disused aircraft factory at Feltham, Middlesex, was taken over and adapted for the work to be carried out. It amounted to a complete renovation of the Central London cars and the finished product was to the same high standard of comfort and design as the new standard stock. The first refurbished 'air-door' CLR train entered service in September 1926 with the last being ready for service in July 1928. While the work was being carried out the CLR borrowed two of the Piccadilly's 1920 air-door stock trains and the Piccadilly received some gate stock from the Hampstead.

During 1924, 127 new cars of standard stock were ordered for the Morden extension. The order comprised 52 motor-cars from Metro Carriage, 25 control-trailers from Cammell Laird, and 50 trailers from Birmingham. They were virtually identical to the 1923 batches and had been ordered as five-car trains. Inward tilting windows in the passenger saloons replaced the pull-down variety fitted to the 1923 batches. In 1925 another batch comprising 120 cars was ordered to enable five-car trains to be made up to six or seven cars. All 48 motor-cars came from Cammell Laird; Metro Carriage built all 67 control-trailers. There were only five trailers in the batch and these came from Metro Carriage.

More standard stock was delivered during 1927, primarily to increase train lengths on the Morden-Edgware. A batch of 112 cars had been ordered from Metro Carriage in 1926. It consisted of 64 motor-cars and 48 trailers. Delivery began in November 1927, and the cars represented the next phase in standard stock development. They retained the same basic profile and layout but were considerably neater in appearance having flush windows and no external beading along the sides. A neater front cab had been designed with the destination plates and code lamps being contained in a panel below the offside cab window, which was reduced in depth as a result. The offside switch compartment cover was now a plain panel instead of the grille, which remained on the nearside. The new cars had bright red doors to match the rest of the panelling. The rear ends were also now all red. Gradually some of these features, including the new destination panel and all-red doors, were applied to the older standard stocks. There was now a constant flow of new trains which would continue until the early 1930s, and which would remove all remaining gate stock on the tube lines, together with many of the oldest surface line cars.

The first of 101 new motor cars for the District entered service in November 1928. They had been ordered in 1927 and were designated 'K' class. They displayed smoother, more rounded, lines than their predecessor the G stock, although they were basically similar in layout. They had two sets of hand operated double-doors on each side.

One of the standard stock trains ordered from Metro Carriage in 1926 and delivered in 1927 and 1928. At this time there was a change in policy regarding 'smoking' and 'non-smoking' cars. From 22nd November 1926, all cars were available to smokers unless marked 'non-smoking'. Hitherto, smoking cars had been specifically marked. This change raised the proportion of 'smoking seats' from 60 to 70 per cent.

The destination plates and code lamps were housed in a panel similar to that developed for the standard tube stock then being built. The clerestory roof was still there, but it curved downwards at each end of the saloon to join the roof line in similar style to the earlier District stock. Four extra seats were fitted into the guard's compartment at the other end of the saloon to the driving cab, but these proved an obstruction and were soon removed. The cars were 49 feet long and all faced east. Thirty-one were owned, on paper at least, by the LMS. All were in service by January 1930, and their arrival coincided with the completion of a further reconfiguration of the District's motive power to provide additional trains and enable some of the earliest motor-cars to be converted to trailers or scrapped.

The rebuilding of the CLR rolling stock was completed in July 1928, and although claimed to be successful the eventual cost had outstripped any advantage in converting more gate-stock to air-door. New rolling stock, embodying all the latest technical advances, was seen as the best option, so the LER decided to utilise the facilities it

had built up at the UCC factory in Feltham to build new standard stock to replace the gate-stock fleet still operating on the Piccadilly. The first batches of home produced trains were delivered in 1929 and consisted of 77 motor-cars, 68 control-trailers and 37 trailers. The UCC cars were similar to the later Metro Carriage batches, but could be distinguished externally by their curved lower side panelling, and internally on motor cars by a redesigned door connecting the saloon with the switch compartment. One of the motor-cars (No.274) had modified ventilation and no central door pillars. The last 20 motors to be delivered did not have central door pillars either. They were used to replace the 20 converted French built motor-cars running with the 1920 Cammell Laird air-door stock. Two of the French cars were converted to double-cab to operate as single cars on the Aldwych shuttle, while the 1920 stock was transferred to the Bakerloo.

One of the CLR's original driving motor coaches plus trailer stands outside Wood Lane depot having had air doors fitted by the UCC Factory at Feltham. The cars also had their interiors fully refurbished to bring them up to the high standard of modern tube stock.

A 1932 press advert publicising commercial advertising on the Underground.

The remaining gate-stock trains running on the Morden-Edgware and the Piccadilly were the next targets for replacement by standard stock. A huge order for 306 cars had been placed with Metro Carriage in 1927 comprising 110 motor-cars, 36 control-trailers, and 160 trailers. Fifty-three more tube cars were ordered from the UCC in 1929 to augment services on the Morden-Edgware, but they actually went to the Piccadilly, allowing some of the Metro Carriage cars to transfer to the Morden-Edgware instead. The 53 UCC cars consisted of 18 motor-cars, 18 control-trailers and 17 trailers. The motor-cars were distinguishable from earlier builds by having raised ventilation inlets, rather than grilles, over the switch compartment. Their arrival, when added to the earlier deliveries from UCC and Metro Carriage, which became the Metropolitan Cammell Carriage & Wagon Company (Metro-Cammell) in 1929 following an amalgamation with Cammell Laird's rail building operation, enabled the last gate-stock train on the Piccadilly to be withdrawn. This was on 7th July 1929, just seven months after the first standard stock train had run on the line.

A few minutes after midnight on 1st January 1930, the very last gate-stock tube train ran on the Underground. The method of entry and exit that had applied from the beginning of tube train operation was now consigned to history. The last gate-stock train ran on the Bakerloo which, in common with the other deep-level tube lines, was now worked entirely with air-door stock. The introduction of air-door stock had, of course, meant the end of the traditional gateman in each car. Initially two guards were carried in each air-door train, one in the trailing end of the driving motor-car and the other in the rear car. There were several reasons for this, safety being the prime consideration. In the 1920s, a system was practised whereby the doors on one half of the train were closed before the doors on the other half to speed boarding times. Two guards were essential for this. Eventually, following the development of an in-train telephone communication system, it was deemed feasible to deploy just one guard per train. Trials began in February 1927 with a train fitted with a driver/guard telephone, and a start was made on converting the whole existing air-door fleet for working by one guard per train the following May, completing in autumn 1928.

Metro-Cammell received orders for more standard stock in 1930 as a replacement for the 1915 Watford stock on the Bakerloo. The order consisted of 22 motor-cars, 20 control-trailers and 20 trailers. These were virtually identical to previous builds, except that the motor-cars had no central door pillar.

Standard stock design moved up a notch in 1930 with the ordering of six experimental cars from the UCC. They were built to test features planned for incorporation in the new fleet of trains needed for the Piccadilly extensions. The six cars consisted of two motor-cars and four trailers. Two of the trailers had wider double-doors (5ft 2in against 4ft 6in), which reduced the number of windows in the centre bay from four to three. The other two trailers had single-leaf air-operated doors at each car end to increase boarding and alighting capacity. Ventilation was modified, dispensing with the air-flow scoops found on standard stock cars hitherto. The guard's door in the motor coaches was also air-operated.

When the District services in the Acton and Hounslow area were revised in February 1932, in preparation for the Piccadilly extensions to Hounslow west and South Harrow, the section to South Acton become a shuttle service. B-class motor-car No.37 was converted to double-cab for use on the shuttle. What made No.37 unusual was that it was the very first driver-only 'train' on the Underground. The doors were converted to air operation and in this form it ran until May 1941, making it the last B-class motor coach in passenger service.

The two hundred and seventy five new cars of standard stock required for the Piccadilly Line extensions embodied some of the features tested on the six experimental UCC cars of 1930, and were the first to be included in a new LER numbering series devised in 1930. The total consisted of 145 motor-cars, all built by Metro-Cammell, and 130 trailers, 90 from Birmingham the company's first standard stock since 1924, and 40 from Gloucester, its first tube cars since the 1922 'competition' stock. Control trailers did not feature this time and would not again. The trailers had two air-operated single-leaf doors at each end. The motor-cars retained the traditional layout, but had slightly tapered cab fronts, which distinguished them from earlier batches. The guard's door was air-operated and could thus be used for entry and exit by passengers when not in use by the guard. The door control panel was built into the end wall so guards could look down the length of the train at station stops.

The additional rolling stock for the Upminster extension turned out to be the last built by the UCC, which by that time had also built the stylish 'Feltham' tramcar

and London's first trolleybuses, the 'Diddlers'. The new District trains, delivered in 1932, were classified L stock and consisted of eight motor-cars and 37 trailers. The motor cars were all west facing and were similar in appearance to the K stock. The only apparent difference was the guard's door, which was now sliding rather than hinged.

By 1929 the Underground Group, spearheaded by Lord Ashfield, was promoting a co-ordination bill in Parliament aimed at creating a unified public transport system for London. A surprise change of government in 1929 stopped the bill in its tracks, along with a similar one being promoted by the London County Council, which controlled much of the Capital's tramways. A further change of government from Labour to National Coalition in 1931 brought in the Liberal Percy Pybus as Minister of Transport. He supported the London Passenger Transport Bill drawn up by Herbert Morrison under the previous Labour administration. Under this proposal a governing Board, under public control but strictly non-political, would plan and operate all bus, tram and Underground railway services within a designated area. The Board would not be subsidised, so services would be self-supporting. After a sometimes difficult passage through Parliament the Bill received Royal Assent on 13th April 1933. The legislation, important though it was, meant little change for the Underground railways, except for the Metropolitan, which lost its independent status and, with some considerable reluctance became, from Saturday 1st July 1933, part of the new London Passenger Transport Board's Underground railway system.

The interior of a new L-stock car built in 1932 for the District showing the partition segregating the enclosed first class compartment from the rest of the car. The practice of labelling certain cars or compartments 'Smoking' has been maintained here after the tube lines had switched to specifying those cars which were 'No Smoking'. The craftsmanship of the staff at UCC's Feltham works is much in evidence.

The LPTB Takes Over

Cockfosters, the first Underground station opened under the reign of the LPTB, early in its life. The roof above the tracks was to be replicated in the design of Uxbridge in 1938.

At midnight on 1st July 1933 the curtain rose on the London Passenger Transport Board and ushered in an all too brief period in which the new organisation was able to build on the past successes of its predecessors at a rapid and impressive pace. From now, our story is of a fully unified system with the Metropolitan Railway brought, reluctantly, into the field. The momentum of growth and service improvements, which had characterised the London Underground in the years before the formation of the LPTB, continued into the new era and the Board was quick to stamp its authority on the proceedings. The legend LONDON TRANSPORT gradually replaced UNDERGROUND on Underground Group trains, and was soon applied to former Metropolitan stock as well, but a short-lived LPTB logo was quickly superseded by a modified version of the bar and circle symbol that had become so well known.

Underground improvements during the rest of 1933 and into 1934 were mostly the fruits of schemes started by the Underground Group, whose top management the new Board inherited. However, the very first new station to be served by Underground trains under London Transport ownership was the LMS-owned South Kenton, shared by Bakerloo Line trains, which opened on 3rd July. On the last day of the same month, the Piccadilly Line north London extension reached Cockfosters. Like the other surface stations on the Piccadilly Line northern extension the platforms were in a shallow cutting, but no attempt was made to create a majestic surface building as had been the case elsewhere. Instead a neat but modest single-storey entrance building led down to the sub-surface ticket hall with its glazed roof and to two island platforms. The middle track sat below a high glazed clerestory roof while the roofs over the two outer tracks were just above car height. Nevertheless, the station, which has hardly altered structurally, provided a stylish terminus to this part of the Piccadilly Line, which had introduced so many excellent station buildings.

The second half of 1933 brought more of the Underground Group's legacy into fruition. On 18th September the remodelled Dover Street station opened. This consisted of a new sub-surface ticket hall, accessible by subway from both sides of Piccadilly and linked by new escalators to the existing platforms, which were now approached from their western end. The old Dover Street station entrance was closed and the station renamed, more appropriately, Green Park, as the 53 acre park lay to the south of one of the new station entrances. A few days later, on the 24th, British Museum station closed, being replaced from the following morning by the new platforms at Holborn affording a direct subway and escalator link with the Piccadilly Line.

The last piece of the Piccadilly Line extension jigsaw fell into place on 23rd October when the line ran on from South Harrow over District tracks to Rayners Lane and then on to Uxbridge, replacing the District Line shuttle service over this section and bringing to an end District operation in north-west London.

Within a few months of taking over from the Underground Group, the LPTB asked general manager J. P. Thomas to look at the possibility of withdrawing first class accommodation on the Metropolitan, District and Great Northern & City Lines. He reported in December 1933 that it was too soon to end it on the Metropolitan and District but that first class could be abolished on the GN&C, the economies outweighing any loss of traffic that might result. The fears of Metropolitan staff and passengers that standards would fall under London Transport ownership were well founded, though it was not until the Second World War provided an excuse that the LPTB felt it could withdraw first class on this and the District.

On 21st January 1934 the shuttle service from Watford to Rickmansworth was withdrawn, and the two double-ended motor coaches used on the service were transferred to the Wembley Park–Stanmore branch where they ran an off-peak shuttle service. They continued to work on the branch until February 1938, when one was withdrawn and the other coupled to a driving trailer and, in this form, continued working on the branch until March 1939 when tube trains took over the shuttle service in advance of the Bakerloo Line extension in November.

New ticket hall at Knightsbridge station in March 1934, one month after being completed. The same programme of work included a new entrance opposite Harrods. This opened on 30th July 1934, enabling the closure of Brompton Road station, 500 yards to the west. A similar large ticket hall at Leicester Square was brought into use the following year. Brompton Road was the last Piccadilly Line station to be closed as a consequence of the 1930s extensions. The closure of Down Street in May 1932 and York Road in September of the same year had enabled faster journey times to be possible in the central area of the much extended Piccadilly Line.

The new station buildings at Boston Manor and Osterley opened on 25th March. They were not quite so lavish as others built for the Piccadilly Line. The entrance halls were of a modest height, with the dominant feature of each station being a red brick tower. At Osterley, which had been built to the west of the old Osterley & Spring Grove station it replaced, a glazed column, which was illuminated at night, sat on top of the tower. Boston Manor differed in as much as the tower was in three basic sections, the main brick structure above which was a smaller tiled section bearing the Underground bullseye. A thin glazed column clung to both sections of the tower and ended above them. Like Osterley this column too was illuminated at night. Both stations had been designed by the Underground's own architect Stanley Heaps.

The 70ft high tower and lighting beacon at Osterley soon became one of the landmarks on the Great West Road. Style, comfort and efficient use of space were the watchwords of the Piccadilly Line extensions both in the design of stations and trains, exemplified by the comfortable and well lit interiors of the standard stock; illustrated is one of 26 motor cars delivered in 1934.

The new South Harrow station building and platforms opened on 5th July 1935. Sited closer to Northolt Road, which the line crossed by a bridge, the complex comprised a smart new station building, adjacent to a new bus station, incorporating a small parade of shops. On the other side of Northolt Road was (and is) a covered market, the entrance to which was given a canopy to match the station entrance opposite. The following March the new Park Royal station opened. It had been designed by the architect Felix Lander who had worked briefly with Charles Holden. The Holden influence was apparent in the finished station, which was dominated by a high red brick tower containing an illuminated Underground bullseye.

On the rolling-stock front 1934 marked a watershed in the evolution of the tube train. The last deliveries of standard stock, 26 motor cars built by Metro-Cammell for the Piccadilly Line, arrived as work progressed on the design of the next generation of tube stock. The 26 new cars (10 A-end and 16 B-end) were virtually identical to the 1931 deliveries except the opening mechanism of the quarter-light windows, which were worked by gravity rather than a spring toggle. The cars were used to strengthen the increasingly popular services on the Piccadilly Line by increasing the remaining six-car trains to seven cars.

Experimentation with a new type of train control system called Metadyne was undertaken during 1934 and into 1935. The system, developed by Metropolitan Vickers, allowed one set of control equipment to operate two motor-cars, and offered regenerative braking, a method by which the energy developed during the braking process is returned to the supply for re-use. It also produced smooth acceleration. Metadyne equipment was installed experimentally on six pre-1910 Metropolitan motor cars, and extensive testing was carried out, with the train even running in passenger service during 1935. The train was repainted red and cream especially for the trial, thereby becoming the first of the former Met stock to receive the standard LER colour scheme. The experiments were deemed successful, and the Board specified Metadyne control for a large part of the new surface stock ordered in August 1936.

All London suburban railways face the problem of providing adequate rolling stock and infrastructure for the two daily peaks, but having a large proportion of their assets standing idle at other times. In the 1930s the Underground lines continued to make some limited savings by running half-length trains in the off-peak, but efforts were made to fill empty seats by widespread advertising, by posters or in newspapers. This tried to persuade the suburb-dwellers to visit central London for shopping, sports and entertainment. Although there were plentiful suburban cinemas, there was a touch of glamour in patronising a West End cinema, where new films could be seen before their general release. The best kind of traffic for the tube flowed in a steady stream. Entertainments, such as football matches, where thousands of patrons wished to arrive and leave at the same time, were expensive to handle because they needed special arrangements, including deploying extra staff on overtime or rest-day working.

Two three-car trains pause next to each other in the Piccadilly Line platforms at the rebuilt Hammersmith station in the 1930s. At the west end of each train is a control trailer, in this case both UCC built examples, fulfilling the function they were built for, enabling the operation of short off-peak trains using only one driving motor car.

LPTB chairman Lord Ashfield and his forward-looking railway chief mechanical engineer William Graff-Baker were looking for a giant leap forward for the next generation of trains on the Underground. One area there was a keenness to see improvement was in noise-reduction inside trains. At this time, track joints, metal brake shoes and opening windows on trains combined to make the travelling experience a very noisy one, especially in tube tunnels. Provision of double glazing and elimination of opening windows would contribute substantially to noise reduction if some form of air conditioning could be designed into new trains. In a one-sentence memo to Graff-Baker dated 27th August 1934, Ashfield states 'I shall be disappointed if we are not the first railway in this country to operate an air-conditioned train'. Graff-Baker replied two days later that he had ordered one set of air-conditioning equipment from the Frigidaire company for fitting to an existing tube car as a trial.

As part of the measures to achieve lower noise levels, the wall and ceiling cavities of one tube car were sprayed with asbestos, as was the underside of the floor. All windows were sealed and double glazed and the ventilators in the roof were closed. The air conditioning equipment, comprising cooling coil, condensor, compressor and fans, enabled cooled air to be drawn-up from underneath one of the cross seats, carried up between the glasses of two of the double-glazed windows and delivered through roof spaces to an adjustable slot in the ceiling running the length of the car.

Interior of standard stock car 7195 as modified for air conditioning, showing the double glazing and the air conditioning unit under the seat.

W. S. GRAFF-BAKER, ESQ.

Chairman.

27th August, 1934.

Private.

I shall be disappointed if we are not the first railway in this country to operate an air conditioned train.

(SD.) ASHFIELD.

Chairman.

Cooled air was delivered via an adjustable slot running the length of the ceiling.

On a trial run on the Morden-Edgware Line, but without passengers, the car was found to be considerably quieter than a normal tube car. This line was 'the worst road for noise' according to Graff-Baker. It was reported that there was no difficulty in carrying out a conversation, whereas in a standard car it was necessary to raise the voice considerably in order to be heard. To test the reduction in temperature, the trial run carried twelve staff plus electric radiators to give out the heat of 40 further passengers. With this non-peak load, the air conditioned car was about 10 degrees Fahrenheit cooler than a non-equipped car with its windows closed.

Graff-Baker reported that the equipment fitted to the trial car was the maximum that could be accommodated without complete reconstruction of the body and that it was, in any case, too expensive to be contemplated for the Underground as a whole. Among his recommendations was to endeavour to develop an alternative and more commercially practicable scheme. Graff-Baker submitted his report to the Board on 22nd January 1935 and just after the evening rush hour on the 28th, Ashfield together with his Vice Chairman Frank Pick and his Traffic Manager J. P. Thomas joined the engineers on the train for a trip from Charing Cross to Golders Green and back to Leicester Square.

Gramophone records were cut on the experimental car, on a standard car and on an otherwise standard car that had had its brake blocks replaced by non-metallic ones. It was found that non-metallic brake blocks made an important contribution to reducing noise. Plans to replace jointed track with welded track would also contribute and by mid-1935 the Underground management were less enthusiastic about the idea of air-conditioning. Operating Manager J. P. Thomas wrote to Vice Chairman Frank Pick on 28th May with a brief report on the state of play. The experimental car had been in passenger service on the Morden-Edgware Line between 25th March and 16th April, except on Sundays and the Easter weekend at the beginning of April. Experience had shown 7195 to be too cool when first entering service but to have a tendency to be stuffy when heavily loaded. The low drumming note made by the car, it was stated, was liable to cause headaches. There would also be a need, Thomas felt, to provide for windows to open automatically in the event of an extended stoppage in a tunnel. These reservations did not, however, prevent two cars of 1935 prototype stock being built with air conditioning for further trials. At the start of the 21st century, air conditioning was again on the agenda but for surface stock only.

Facing page top **A North London electrification scheme map prepared in 1938 showing how with just one short section of new tube tunnel, a whole swathe of north London's steam railways would be absorbed into an enlarged tube network. The aborted extension from Edgware to Bushey Heath was a late addition to the New Works Programme to reach a suitable site for a large new depot.**

Facing page bottom **The London Underground is synonymous with the oft-given entreaty to 'Mind the Gap', an expression so idiosyncratic that it has migrated to logos on clothing and London memorabilia, and to uses well beyond the Underground. The need for the expression arises from difficulties at some Underground stations where because of sharply curved platforms certain entrances to the cars are so far from the platform edge that there is a risk of someone falling into the gap. The worst gaps on the earliest tubes were at Bank and Wood Lane on the Central London Railway, and at Waterloo and Piccadilly Circus on the Bakerloo. These were joined in 1914 by Embankment on the Hampstead Tube and the following year by Paddington on the Bakerloo. It wasn't too much of an issue at first since the cars had entrances at the extreme ends only, and these were in any case staffed. The safety issue seems to have emerged on the introduction of cars with centre doors, and more widespread introduction of air-operated doors where entrances were unsupervised. The first line with curved platforms to get stock of this type was the Bakerloo, where risks were mitigated by locking the centre doors out of use at high risk platforms. In the early 1920s platform edges at curved platforms were painted white and by 1926 the first formal instructions were issued for staff to call out "Mind the Gap – Please". Within a few years some platform edges received painted signs, and in later years even hanging illuminated signs were tried as shown here at Waterloo in 1936. Recorded messages began in the late 1960s when suitable technology became more conveniently available.**

The King's Cross Bridge entrance of the Metropolitan King's Cross Station in 1933, situated at the top of Grays Inn Road opposite the Scala cinema. A new King's Cross station complex was part of the 1935–40 New Works Programme.

Throughout much of 1934, the LPTB, in some instances jointly with the railway companies, had been formulating and developing a massive programme of new works designed to modernise and upgrade the Capital's newly integrated transport system. In June 1935 its plans were laid before Parliament. This was the latest part of a process which had been on-going since the end of the Great War with various planning and advisory committees formulating and investigating the feasibility of schemes designed to tailor transport infrastructure to the needs of a rapidly expanding capital city. The main details of what became known as the New Works Programme, announced on 6th June, were supplemented by another statement in the House on the 18th. The radical and far reaching programme touched upon all aspects of the Board's activities both road and rail. The Underground was to expand both east and west with extensions to the Central London, and to the north with extensions being proposed for both branches of the Morden-Edgware.

Briefly the New Works Programme provided for:

* Extension of the Central London Line west from North Acton along a new extension parallel to the GWR to West Ruislip, and east from Liverpool Street to Leyton, then via LNER tracks to Epping and Ongar.
* Extension of the Morden-Edgware through new tunnels to East Finchley and then via LNER tracks to High Barnet. The LNER line from Finchley Central station (at the time called Finchley) to Edgware was to be taken over and linked to the existing tube at Edgware. The line was to be double-tracked.
* Extension of the Great Northern & City Line, which had been renamed Northern City Line in October 1934, north from its Finsbury Park terminus over LNER tracks via Crouch End to join the new Barnet extension at a high level station at Highgate, then diverting again over the LNER line to Alexandra Palace via Muswell Hill.
* Electrification of the Metropolitan from Rickmansworth to Amersham and Chesham (as already announced).
* Extension of the Bakerloo through new tunnels from Baker Street to Finchley Road (as already announced).

There was uncertainty within the LPTB about electrifying the Central Line extension north of Loughton. J.P. Thomas submitted a memo on 22nd October 1935 recommending the use of diesel railcars on this section. Frank Pick directed that no decision be made until an inspection had been made of an electric battery powered train operating between Dublin and Wicklow. On 20th March of the following year a Great Western Railway diesel railcar was loaned to London Transport for trial running between Aylesbury and Chesham and a proposal was made to operate two similar vehicles in trial passenger service between Chalfont & Latimer and Chesham stations. Authority was requested by J. P. Thomas to purchase two AEC railcars, but nothing more came of this.

The New Works programme also made provision for the complete reconstruction of the stations at Aldgate East, St Paul's and King's Cross among others. It was scheduled for completion in 1940/41. The June 18th statement added the following:

* Extension of the Central London Line from the LNER station at Leytonstone through new tunnels to Newbury Park (LNER) station from where the LNER branch to Woodford would be taken over joining up with the line to Epping.
* Lengthening of Central London Line platforms to take 8-car trains.
* New signalling for the Bakerloo Line.

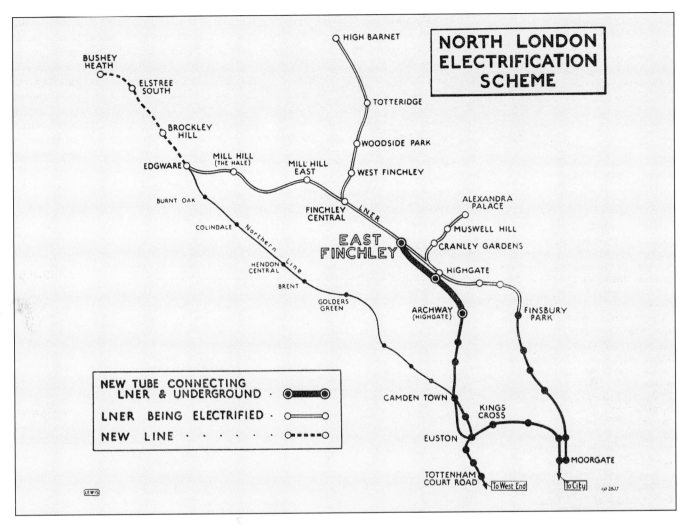

NORTH LONDON ELECTRIFICATION SCHEME

NEW TUBE CONNECTING LNER & UNDERGROUND

LNER BEING ELECTRIFIED

NEW LINE

The remoter parts of the Metropolitan in Buckinghamshire were clearly under threat following the 1933 unification. Services beyond Aylesbury to Verney Junction and Brill had continued to operate, albeit with a declining number of passengers. In May 1935, before a Commons Committee, Frank Pick had questioned the wisdom of an organisation like London Transport running services even as far as Aylesbury let alone to places beyond (Brill is as distant from the centre of London as Brighton). The 50 or so passengers using the Brill branch each day were riding on a service which was losing about £4,000 each year, and this was one of the factors which led the Board, and joint owner and principal service operator the LNER, to close the branch. The last train to Brill ran on the night of 30th November 1935. Earlier in the year the LPTB Board had paid a visit to the branch, travelling from London in the former Metropolitan Railway Rothschild saloon. The coach was withdrawn soon afterwards and mothballed at Neasden depot until 1945 when it was scrapped. It must have seemed an anachronism to Frank Pick and the LPTB Board, or just evidence that the Met's high aspirations felt inappropriate to a metro. On 6th July 1936 there was another retrenchment of the once extensive Metropolitan Railway when the line from Aylesbury to Verney Junction was closed to passenger services.

In the period before closure, the Brill branch of the Metropolitan Line had just four trains per day on Mondays to Fridays and five on Saturdays. It took 1 hour 20 minutes to reach the present-day terminus of Amersham from Brill. This very rural scene, typical of the branch, is at Wood Siding.

Transferred to the LPTB along with the Metropolitan was the Great Northern & City Railway, renamed the Northern City Line in 1934 when this photograph of a 1906 steel bodied trailer car in newly applied Underground livery was taken. Although gate-stock had last run on the rest of the Underground in 1930, it remained on the Northern City until 1939. The sliding door in the centre of the car was operated at the termini only.

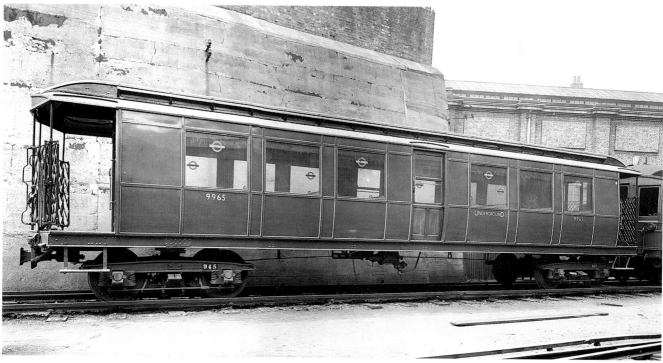

The District Line service to Barking and beyond had been well patronised, especially since the opening of the extension to Upminster. Two additional stations had been built and opened by the LMS for District trains since 1932. Upminster Bridge had opened on 17th December 1934 with Elm Park following on 13th May 1935. There was an urgent need to increase peak hour capacity, at least as far as Barking. Some Hammersmith & City trains had been running as far as East Ham since 30th March 1936, but from 4th May the part of the Hammersmith & City which ran down to New Cross and New Cross Gate daily was diverted to Barking, giving the beleaguered stretch an additional eight trains an hour. The off-peak Hammersmith to New Cross or New Cross Gate service was diverted to terminate at Whitechapel. First class accommodation was abolished on both the Hammersmith & City and the East London Line from the same date.

As mentioned earlier, tube trains began to be fitted with air operated sliding doors from 1923. On the Metropolitan, slam door stock was used, the last variation of this design being delivered in 1932. The District had employed hand operated sliding doors and up to 1936 these were universal on the District Line, the Hammersmith & City Line, the Circle Line and the East London Line. For the first new surface stock trains to be ordered by the London Passenger Transport Board, in 1935, air operated doors were specified which the passenger would open and the guard would close. Moving responsibility for closing the doors to the guard was seen as a way of enabling trains with higher acceleration to be introduced safely. On trains with handworked sliding doors it was not unknown for doors to be left open and for passengers to jump on a train moving out of the platform. There was also the temptation to leave a door or two open while the train was proceeding on its journey in very hot weather.

Nine new trains were delivered for service on the Hammersmith & City Line and District Line during the spring and summer of 1936 and were known as M and N classes, being built by the BRCW and Metro-Cammell respectively. Apart from the fitting of air-door equipment to part of the order, they were similar to the UCC-built L stock of 1932 and were the last trains on the Underground to be built with clerestory roofs. Most of the M class entered service on 4th May 1936 in time for the extra peak train service to Barking. In August, as the N stock was being delivered, London Transport placed an order for 58 two-car units of an advanced design to replace 30-year-old hand worked door stock on the Hammersmith and City.

M-stock motor car No. 4392, built for the Hammersmith & City section of the Metropolitan Line, is seen here when new in May 1936. This car was one of the very last on the Underground to be fitted with hand-operated passenger doors. It displays the unusual positioning of the side panelling transfers, with the stock number in the position usually occupied by the London Transport transfer and the addition of a line identification transfer, a short-lived mid-1930s idea.

The provisions of the New Works Programme had not been set in stone and between 1936 and 1939 other measures were proposed for addition to the main Programme, and these were authorised under various Acts of Parliament. One of these, put forward in 1937, was an extension of the Central London Line from West Ruislip the 2¾ miles to Denham. There was also the provision for the extension of the Morden-Edgware from Edgware to Aldenham, and the building of a train depot at Aldenham to accommodate 500 cars. Other 1937 powers authorised by Acts of Parliament included the reconstruction of Amersham station, and also Highbury, Marylebone, Monument, Liverpool Street and Notting Hill Gate.

A significant event took place on 8th April 1937 with the entry into service on the Piccadilly Line of the first all new design of tube train for 15 years. Early in 1933, some experiments had been carried out using standard stock cars to test streamline aerodynamics, new air conditioning equipment, and automatic and mechanical couplers. These pioneering tests apart, the main feature of the new train and the greatest departure from former practice was the position of the electrical equipment which was placed entirely beneath the car floors instead of in a separate compartment inside the motor-cars, thereby freeing-up more space for passenger seating. The first train, comprising six motor-cars, was delivered from Metro-Cammell to London Transport at the end of 1936. It was followed during 1937 by 18 other cars built principally to the same specification but with different traction equipment. By having each car motored, acceleration surpassed anything that had gone before. Each car was 52ft 6ins long. There were two sets of air-operated double doors and a single-leaf door on each side. Roofs were elliptical. The windows were flush fitting and there was a total absence of panel beading below roof level. The first two cars were air-conditioned and had double-glazed windows throughout, while the others had conventional opening windows fitted.

The handsome lines of the 1935 tube-stock brought to the tube the concept of streamlining, which was then in vogue on anything from express steam locomotives to saloon cars. The new trains followed closely the designer's original thoughts, manifested in a 1934 mock-up (illustrated facing page top). The bay fronted cab restricted passenger capacity in the driving coach saloon thereby failing to maximise fully the advantages gained in placing electrical equipment below floor level.

But the most dramatic feature of the first 18 cars was the streamlined cab ends. In the mid-1930s streamlining was very much in vogue and all the Big Four railway companies had dabbled with streamlined steam locomotives to varying degrees. The cabs on the 1935 tube stock, as it came to be called, were bay-fronted with the side cab doors set at an angle within the bay. The bay contained a front cab door and two side windows, separated from the side doors by thick pillars inset with a panel containing the train running number. In the front cab door were five square code lights and the train destination screen. The cab was topped with a domed roof containing a 'v' shaped air-inlet ventilator. The exterior livery was red below the window and cream above, the livery wrapping right around the cab. Side doors were all red. The driver's position in the cab was central, with 'joystick' controls replacing the conventional handles. Inside, the two outermost bays were fitted with longitudinal seating while the centre bay seating was transverse. The new motor-cars seated 40, against 30 in a standard-stock motor-car.

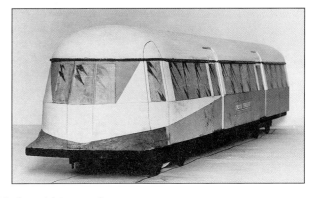

One of the six-car trains differed in as much as it had a more conventional cab design and layout. Gone was any attempt at streamlining. The cab was flat-ended and shallower than the streamlined cabs, allowing for two additional seats in the passenger saloon. The code lights and destination screen were in the conventional position under the offside front window. All 24 had been delivered by the end of October 1937 and the last train, made up of the three flat-fronted sets, entered service on the Piccadilly Line early in 1938 by which time a huge fleet of new tube trains, sufficient to tackle the additional service authorised under the New Works Programme, was on order.

Underground trains ran over almost the entire system through the night of 11th/12th May 1937 to carry passengers on the occasion of the Coronation of King George VI. This was the first time there had been all-night running since the Diamond Jubilee of Queen Victoria in 1897, when a central London section of the steam services operated. It was to be another 62 years before all-night services ran again, on New Year's Eve 1999.

Since the Hampstead Tube and the City & South London Railway had been combined in 1924 the title used for the line had been Morden-Edgware. With the planned extensions beyond Edgware and new branches, it was desirable to find a new name. From what must have been a record number of suggestions for an Underground line name, a shortlist of nine was circulated to 23 principal officers of the Board early in 1937. Their order of preference for a new name was:

1. North South Line	4. Northern Line	7. Greater London Line
2. North and South Line	5. Cross Town Line	8. Interborough Line
3. Norsouth Line	6. City Line	9. City West Line

The Board, however, considered the first three names unsuitable and so chose Northern Line, reflecting the extension over former Great Northern Railway branches. The new name was officially introduced from 28th August 1937. On the same date the Central London Line was renamed Central Line.

A newly delivered Gloucester built O-stock driving motor car at Northfields depot in 1937. The two-car sets which made up a six-car train were permanently coupled as each shared one set of Metadyne control equipment.

1937 proved to be a key year in rolling-stock development. On 1st September the first train of the new generation of surface stock entered service when four cars of O stock started work on the District Line. These were the first of the order placed in 1936 and, like the experimental tube trains introduced in April, they embodied many new features. The stock was built jointly by Birmingham Railway Carriage & Wagon Company and the Gloucester Railway Carriage & Wagon Company and differed remarkably from anything that had gone before. Gone for good was the clerestory roof. In its place an elliptical roof, and gently sloping car sides which ended by flaring outwards at the base. Cabs retained the post-1927 layout for the code lights and destination plates, which in this case were built into the car bodywork and not on a separate panel. The livery was all red. Large windows created a bright, airy interior. The new stock made full use of the Metadyne control system, which had been the subject of experiments between 1934 and 1936. The cars used in the experiments were scrapped in June 1937.

The O stock was built primarily to replace the 1906 stock working on the Hammersmith & City Line, which it began to do from 1st December 1937. London Transport also wished to replace older trains on the Metropolitan's Uxbridge service as well as some of the older cars still working on the District. Following on from the O stock order the Board ordered two further batches of cars from Birmingham and Gloucester. A further 159 Metadyne controlled cars (106 motors and 53 trailers) for the Uxbridge line, to be known as P stock, plus 25 motor-cars and 183 trailers of Q stock for the District. The Q stock did not have Metadyne control as it was expected to work with older stock in mixed formation trains. Bodywise, both the P and Q stocks were to be of similar design to the O stock. The Board also ordered 58 trailers from Gloucester to make the O stock units up to three-cars. These were delivered between June and October 1938.

A unique experiment began on the Northern Line on 8th November 1937 when a nine-car train operated between Colindale and Kennington. The Northern Line had been suffering from severe overcrowding in the peaks, and passenger protests, including train sit-ins when trains had been terminated earlier than scheduled, had taken place. The nine-car train was an attempt to ease the situation a little by increasing train capacity by 240 seats (or 29%). Some signalling and track alteration was needed, and the original proposals for the experiment required a number of platforms to be lengthened, but in the event only platforms at Edgware, Burnt Oak, Colindale, Hendon Central, Brent and Golders Green were adapted. All nine cars were available at these stations with the two rear cars being designated Tottenham Court Road only. At stations between Hampstead and Goodge Street these cars remained in the tunnel while the front seven were in the platform as normal. At Tottenham Court Road the front two cars would stop in the tunnel allowing passengers in the two rear cars to alight. At stops between Leicester Square and Kennington the two rear cars, now empty, would remain in the tunnel.

The longest trains ever to run in passenger service on tube lines were the nine-car trains on the Northern Line. When the experiment began in November 1937, the platform lengthening at Edgware had not been completed so the train ran from Golders Green to Kennington, back to Colindale, south again to Kennington and back to Hampstead to stable in Golders Green depot until the evening peak. Then it re-entered service at Hampstead, travelled to Kennington, reversed and returned to Colindale. The extended platform at Edgware was available from 7th February 1938 when it was incorporated into the nine-car service pattern. The Board deemed the experiment an unqualified success and seriously considered extending the principle to other lines should the need arise. But for the moment the Northern Line was to be the focus of the experiment, which was set to expand. By the end of February 1938 four nine-car trains were running on the Charing Cross branch in the peaks. The formation of the nine-car trains, which were composed of standard stock, was M–T–M+T–T–T+M–T–M. The guard could be positioned in either the third or seventh car.

The first use of a continuous name frieze on platforms was at Tottenham Court Road in 1937. Tunnel platforms on the rest of the Underground soon followed, most like here using paper labels for a time before enamel plates replaced them.

A NAME AS LONG AS A TUBE STATION

ON EVERY STATION!

If you want to get out at Tottenham Court-road tube station to-night there is no chance of your missing it.

A continuous strip with TOTTENHAM COURT-ROAD in nine-inch letters appears all along the wall at the back of each platform.

At present the inscription is on paper; but it is to be made permanent.

It Means Speed

The same policy is to be followed immediately at Euston. Warren-street, Goodge - street. Leicester - square, Strand, Charing Cross and Waterloo; and in the near future every tube station will have its name displayed in the same way.

District Railway stations, too, are to have more name plates.

The many letters from people complaining that they have gone past their tube stations have caused the Transport Board to adopt the continuous frieze plan.

It is believed a gain in speed will result, as people will alight more quickly. A few seconds saved at every station may mean the addition of another train in a peak hour.

Facing page Original interior of a 1938 tube-stock driving motor-car showing the efficient but welcoming interior with details such as the shovel-shaped glass lamp shades which survived until the 1960s.

If 1937 had been a year for innovation and frantic activity then 1938 was to be even more so. On 24th January the last six-car train of 1935 prototype tube stock entered service on the Piccadilly Line. This was the one with the non-streamlined flat-ended cab, and it was this design that LT had decided was the most suitable for the large order of new tube trains, delivery of which was to start later in 1938. Drivers had disliked the cab layout of the streamlined cars, and being bay-fronted they wasted some of the valuable space the new stock was designed to save.

By the early months of 1938 work was well under way on the extensions to the Northern Line, where the proposed name for the new northern terminus, Aldenham, was changed in favour of Bushey Heath, and the Central Line. Here, the introduction of frequent and faster services on what was to become an urban railway several times its present length, meant some adaptation to the existing infrastructure on the line. Tunnels had to be enlarged to take standard stock, the existing 3-rail system had to be converted to standard 4-rail, bull-head rail had to replace outdated bridge rail, and platforms needed lengthening to take eight-car trains. The latter was to prove a problem at Shepherd's Bush where space in a disused crossover tunnel had to be utilised and this is still apparent today. The LPTB obtained powers during 1938 to build a new station at Wood Lane and increase the size of the car depot there to allow longer trains to be stabled. In June the GWR and LT tracks between the North Acton and Wood Lane junctions were segregated to separate electric and steam services in readiness for the introduction of tube services to Ruislip and beyond.

The 1930s modernisation of the Piccadilly Line continued into 1938, reaching a conclusion at the end of the year. On 26th June the reconstructed Ruislip Manor station opened. Again red brick and large glazed areas were strongly featured in the Adams, Holden & Pearson design. The ticket hall was situated beneath the tracks which continued across an overbridge and was reached by entrances on either side of the bridge. As with other stations on the branch, shop units were included.

On 30th June the first train of 1938 tube stock entered service on the Northern Line. The stock was a culmination of many months of experimentation and testing of the 1935 prototypes. The first train consisted of seven cars comprising a three and a four-car unit. The three-car unit was simply M–T–M; the trailer being of a standard layout, with two sets of double doors each side and two single-leaf doors at each end. The four-car unit was arranged M–T–NDM–M. The NDM (Non-driving motor-car) was a new feature on the Underground. Although it had the same body shell as a trailer car, in a way it was the opposite of the control trailer principle, having no cab, but equipped with motors to give the train more power. The motor-car of 1938 stock was basically similar in appearance to the fourth 1935 experimental train, except that there were four windows at the outer ends of the saloon, instead of three. Livery was all red, except for window pillars which were picked out in cream. The destination screen depth had been increased to allow for three lines of destination information plates to be accommodated, reflecting the complicated patterns of service of some of the planned New Works extensions. Other features included passenger operated push-button doors. Inside, white ceilings, polished wood window frames and deep-cushioned seating made the new trains very comfortable to travel in. The motor-cars seated 42, the NDMs and trailers 40.

There had been much deliberation as to which lines should benefit from the new fleet of trains and between 1936 and 1938 the estimated number changed several times depending on the lines which were to receive the new trains, and the length of the train to be operated. Eventually it was decided that the new trains should be allocated to the Northern Line, including enough stock to provide some nine-car trains for peak hours, the Bakerloo plus a small number for the Central and Piccadilly. Even then the plans changed as a result of the onset of the Second World War. However, what can be recorded is that eventually the new 1938 stock, delivery of which was not fully complete until after the War, comprised 644 motor-cars and 206 NDMs (built by Metro-Cammell), and 271 trailers (built by the Birmingham Railway Carriage and Wagon Company). The plans for new stock and the transfer of standard stock had released 58 trailers of 1927 standard stock, which could not be allocated. These were converted to run with the 1938 stock which was being built for the Bakerloo Line.

The LNER 'owned' 160 cars of 1938 tube cars by virtue of the Northern Line now operating over lines formerly owned by the Company. This arrangement, which was similar to the one where the LMS owned 10% of the District Line stock as a result of the joint running between Bow Curve and Barking/Upminster, ended with the nationalisation of the railways on 1st January 1948. From October 1938 there was sufficient spare standard stock available for a start to be made on transferring it to the Central Line to replace the line's original 1903 electric stock.

The flatter front-end style of the production 1938 tube-stock driving motor cars made the best use of space for features such as destination display screen, train running number and illuminated destination code.

On 8th August 1938 the new Rayners Lane station opened. Despite rapid housing growth during the early 1930s, the Rayners Lane station buildings had been pretty primitive, and had included a wooden ticket office. It was not until 1936 that designs for a new station were in hand. The design of the station buildings was by Reginald Uren under the auspices of Adams, Holden & Pearson. The style reflected the Holden designs of the early 1930s with a large high roofed ticket hall of red brick with glazed columns on the sides and frontage from above canopy level to the roof. The rear of the ticket hall, which overlooked the platform, was 75% glazed and was quite impressive. The ticket hall had entrances at either side.

By late summer the Hammersmith & City Line was operated almost entirely by O stock trains, although some of the old joint Met saloon stock was kept available for service until 1942. The M stock was part of a train refurbishment programme to prepare the District Line for the arrival of the Q stock in 1939. It involved converting all motor-cars, and some trailers, built after 1923 to air-door working and the fitting of electro-pneumatic braking. The older B, C, D and E classes were not suitable for conversion to work with the Q stock, but many were retained and kept their hand-operated doors. The B stock was gradually withdrawn on arrival of the new Q stock, their place on the East London Line being taken by C, D and E cars which now formed part of a 'new' H stock, the 'H' referring to cars with hand-worked doors, and worked in trains with some of the newer trailers not converted to air door working which also formed part of the H stock. Some older District motor-cars were converted to trailers during 1938.

At the time the new trains were entering service, first class compartments were still provided on the Metropolitan and District Line trains, but there was some campaigning for its abolition because of overcrowding. A relaxation had already been introduced on the District which caused some confusion and annoyance to both first and third class passengers (there was no second class). This allowed third class passengers to sit in first class areas if they were east of Charing Cross and third class accommodation was full, but west of Charing Cross they could only stand in first class if third class was full.

Met steam compartment stock at Aylesbury in May 1936 when First Class accommodation was still on offer. The more comfortable seating was retained in the first class compartments when separate classes were abolished, so they were always the first to fill up. The carpets fitted in first class were, however, removed.

Another long-gone feature of the Underground are slam door coaches. These were all inherited from the Metropolitan Railway and they provided the majority of rolling stock on the Metropolitan Line until the early 1960s. In September 1938, alterations in track layout between Finchley Road and Wembley Park meant that passengers needed to be warned, with the aid of 5,000 posters at stations and on trains, that at Willesden Green, Kilburn and Finchley Road stations they would in future need to get out of the trains on the opposite side. There was no change at Neasden, Dollis Hill and West Hampstead. The slogan for the poster campaign was 'Please Look First'. The work was in preparation for Bakerloo services to Stanmore.

In the midst of all the expansion, stock renewal and general service improvements came crisis. In Europe Germany had, since 1934, been under a dictatorship hell bent on regaining territory lost in the Great War. Until the autumn of 1938 this goal had been achieved without much force, and Germany was now in a very powerful position. The vexed question of ceding the Sudetenland area of Czechoslovakia, and its largely German population, back to Germany brought Europe closer to war than at any time since 1918, and for several days in September and October 1938 the threat seemed very real. Modern warfare meant bombing raids from the air, and although the Underground was relatively protected in its subterranean world, a bomb penetrating the tunnels which lay beneath the Thames could flood much of the system in minutes. On the evening of 27th September, with tension in Europe running high and last ditch attempts being made in Munich to avert war by the main countries involved, including Britain, the Northern and Bakerloo service stopped before normal finishing time for work to start on plugging the Charing Cross tunnels with concrete. The service beneath the Thames remained suspended until 8th October when the crisis passed and the tunnels were reopened. But minds had now been focused on what could happen to the vulnerable parts of the Underground in the future, and plans for a more permanent safety strategy were soon being formulated.

If the Munich Crisis had shown that LT could react quickly to possible danger, the opening of a new station at Aldgate East showed how a major engineering task could be carried out with military precision and with the minimum of inconvenience to travellers. The new station was necessary to facilitate more efficient train working at the junction between the District and Hammersmith & City Lines which lay just to the west of the existing platforms. The new station was built literally a few feet east of the old one. Over one weekend the old platforms, which had been supported on stilts, were dismantled enabling the new platforms, which were decorated in the cream coloured tiling used throughout the 1930s, to be available for use from the first train on 31st October.

The last major event in this eventful year took place on 4th December. This was the opening of the new Uxbridge station in the High Street, and the closure of the old station in Belmont Road. The platform was in similar style to the one at Cockfosters, while the large ticket hall led through to the High Street where the station frontage formed part of a parade of shops. Although not as immediately imposing as some of the other stations built for the Piccadilly Line, Uxbridge did sport some fine stained glass windows above the entrance, by the artist Ervin Bossanyi.

The new Aldgate East station as it appeared when it opened in October 1938. There is little evidence of the intricate work that had taken place to get the station built and opened without disrupting the train service or street traffic above. This included the diversion of water and gas mains, and electricity cabling, along with sewers, in addition to the construction of the new platforms and the eventual lowering of the tracks. A short distance to the east lay St Mary's station which, as it would be even closer to the new platforms at Aldgate East, closed on 30th April 1938.

This view of a half-closed floodgate shows a wedge on the right hand rail used to seal the gap (caused by the rail) when the gate was closed, and the ramp (lifted) to carry the negative pick-up shoes clear of the lower metal sill. The gates were normally slid electrically but could be operated by hand if necessary.

The former Metropolitan Railway terminus at Uxbridge was moved in 1938 to a better location in the High Street, the main shopping centre. This pleasingly rural scene shows the old station at Belmont Road.

Despite the ever-looming threat of war, 1939 proved to be a very busy year for the Underground, not least in the first fruits of the New Works Programme, which were to become evident. On 1st January five new escalators were brought into use at St Paul's. These had been first proposed in 1931, but it had taken the New Works Programme to make them happen. The following day the first 1938 stock train entered service on the Bakerloo Line. The first of the order from Gloucester for 25 Q stock motor-cars entered service in March, and all were in stock by July. They were practically identical to the O stock except that they had through-car ventilation at roof level. The guard's position had moved back to the more traditional location in the passenger saloon. The cab side doors had recessed windows instead of the flush fitted ones on the O stock, and the comfortable high-back transverse seats of the O stock, and earlier District stock, gave way to seating which finished at window level. As it was intended to run the Q stock with older cars, Ward coupling was fitted at each end. Since 1937, most new Underground stock had been equipped with automatic 'Wedglock' couplers.

The rest of the Q stock order was for 181 trailers. All were built by Gloucester and the first had entered service in November 1938. The new Q stock was first worked as complete trains on the Metropolitan Line in March 1939. The P stock entered service in July and had been built principally to replace the Ashbury bogie stock and saloon stock on the Metropolitan Line. Following augmentation of the initial order for 53 three-car sets the P stock eventually consisted of 146 motor cars and 55 trailers.

As delivered the trailers of the O, P and Q stocks were either 1st/3rd class composites or 3rd class only. The P stock cars were similar to the Q stock, but the trains had Metadyne control as the O stock. Delivery of the P stock continued into 1941, by which time the O, P and Q stocks were providing much of the motive power on the Hammersmith & City, District and Metropolitan lines. The interiors, with their deep cushioned seats and polished wood and chrome, were rather luxurious to be referred to as third class, but there were only two classes on the Underground. First class passengers, until it was abolished soon after the stock was delivered, were however more likely to get seats, and occupied a compartment separated by a door from the rest of the passengers (see photo on page 111). Following abolition of first class, these partition doors were removed.

Wooden bodied Great Northern & City stock at Finsbury Park shortly before replacement by standard tube stock in May 1939.

On 27th March, in advance of the opening of the Bakerloo extension from Baker Street to Finchley Road, tube trains took over the running of the Wembley Park to Stanmore branch of the Metropolitan Line, and on 15th May standard stock displaced from the Northern Line replaced the original GN&CR gate stock on the Northern City, the last gate stock on the Underground system. On 10th June the last of the original CLR stock ran in normal service on the Central Line. The line was now worked entirely by standard stock. A special commemorative run of the last original CLR train was made on 12th July.

A large new circular ticket hall opened at King's Cross on 18th June 1939, but work on a subway linking the ticket hall to St Pancras LMS station was not complete until 1941. The following day (19th June) the first 1938 stock train in nine-car formation entered service on the Northern Line. The operation of these long trains, which involved the complication of all doors in the end cars remaining closed at stations that could not accommodate the full length, was abandoned during the war and the cars released were used in the formation of extra trains.

On 3rd July the first stage of the Northern Line extension north from Highgate was opened. In preparation, Highgate station had been renamed Archway (Highgate) on 11th June. The two-mile extension would eventually include a new below ground station at Highgate, but this would not open until 1941. Trains went from Archway (Highgate) direct to East Finchley (LNER) station, which had been completely reconstructed to a design by Adams, Holden & Pearson. Red brick predominated on the exterior buildings, which included a large glazed section inset with the LT bullseye and LNER symbol. The platforms were more interesting. The four tracks served two island platforms. The station offices straddled all four tracks and were linked to the platforms by spiral staircases, the outer walls of which were glazed. One prominent feature of the station was a statue of an archer, bow and arrow pointing towards London, by the sculptor Eric Aumonier.

Since the Munich Crisis of 1938, the political situation in Europe had deteriorated. Germany invaded Czechoslovakia in March 1939, and by August was turning its attention to former German territory along the Danzig corridor in Poland. Great Britain had promised to come to Poland's aid in the event of any aggression. On 1st September the Germans invaded Poland, and at 11am on Sunday 3rd September 1939 Britain declared war on Germany.

On 15th May 1939 Princess Elizabeth (later to become Queen Elizabeth II) and Princess Margaret made their first journey on the Underground. They travelled with a Lady-in-Waiting and their governess from St James's Park to Tottenham Court Road and back. Queen Elizabeth returned to the Underground in 1969 and 1977 to open the Victoria Line and the Heathrow extension of the Piccadilly Line.

The first stage of the Northern Line extensions over LNER tracks in suburban north London was the extension from Archway to East Finchley, opened on 3rd July 1939. A 1938 stock train enters East Finchley where an impressive station building awaits completion.

The Underground at War

Piccadilly Circus at war. In the background a wooden shroud protects Eros, while a brick and corrugated-iron entrance has been built around the subway staircase leading down to the station from the south west corner of Piccadilly. Such structures were designed to provide some protection against bomb blast and restrict the flow of incoming people in the event of panic during air raids.

For many the real effects of being at war had begun on 1st September 1939. On that day a blackout was imposed, and the services of London Transport and the main line railways came under Government control using powers contained in the Defence Regulations (1939). Under the Railway Control Order (1939), the Minister of Transport appointed a Railway Executive Committee. The Committee had been 'on call' since the Munich crisis a year earlier and now came into full flower.

But London Transport had moved onto a war footing some days before. On 27th August the Bakerloo Line was closed south of Piccadilly Circus so that the job of installing the floodgates at Charing Cross and Waterloo could be completed. Work on the Northern Line floodgates between these two stations was also well advanced, but on 1st September the service was suspended between Strand and Kennington and the tunnels on the north side of the Thames plugged with concrete, as they had been in 1938. Similar emergency anti-flooding measures were undertaken at other vulnerable locations, including ticket halls and subways, in lieu of permanent flood gates being installed, and many stations were closed while the work proceeded. The section of Northern Line between Moorgate and London Bridge was closed from 7th September 1939 and did not reopen until May 1940.

The war brought a sudden end to many features of the Underground's operation. The running of nine-car trains on the Northern Line ceased soon after the war began because the plugging of the tunnels at Charing Cross meant there was no suitable location to reverse them. On 16th September the peak hour GWR service to Liverpool Street and Aldgate, which was Metropolitan loco hauled from Bishop's Road (Paddington), was withdrawn. It was followed by the withdrawal of the through Ealing Broadway to Southend District service from 1st October. This meant the end of the line for the seven former District Railway electric locomotives (Nos L1–L7), which were later scrapped. On 7th October Pullman cars ran for the last time on the Metropolitan. On 20th November the Hammersmith & City peak hour service to New Cross and New Cross Gate was withdrawn and trains diverted to Whitechapel and Barking. Between October and November all the Q stock which had been working on the Metropolitan was transferred to the District, as new P stock continued to arrive for service on the Met.

In a way 1939 ended on a high note for the Underground with the opening on 25th November of the Bakerloo Line extension from Baker Street to Finchley Road and through Bakerloo services to Stanmore. Tunnelling for the two and a quarter mile extension to Finchley Road had been completed in November 1937. The Metropolitan stations at Lords, which had been renamed from St John's Wood in June 1939, and Marlborough Road closed on the night of 19th November. In their place were new Bakerloo stations at St John's Wood and Swiss Cottage. St John's Wood was designed by the Underground's architect Stanley Heaps, and its main feature was a red brick cylindrical ticket hall and a wide entrance. The platforms were finished in the now standard cream tile rising about ten feet from the platform floor. Edging tiling was in brown and advertising border tiling was black. The station name was in a tiled frieze. The roof vault was painted plaster. The trackside wall was tiled down to track level. The style set the pattern for the platforms at Swiss Cottage, where the only difference was the edging tiling which was in pale green, and for most other deep level tube stations opened in the later 1940s. For a while Swiss Cottage was served by both the Bakerloo and Metropolitan Lines, but the Met platforms were closed on 17th August 1940.

The new extension broke surface immediately south of Finchley Road coming up between the Metropolitan tracks and between two island platforms, one of which was new. Modifications were made to other stations between Finchley Road and Wembley Park, which from 20th November were served by Bakerloo trains all day and by Metropolitan trains on the Rayners Lane to Aldgate service in peak hours. The latter service survived until 9th December 1940, after which the Bakerloo had the stations between Finchley Road and Wembley Park to itself, all Metropolitan trains henceforth running non-stop between these stations. Two fly-unders had been built to the south and north of Wembley Park station. The first segregated trains coming into service from Neasden depot, while the other enabled Bakerloo trains to join and leave the Stanmore branch without crossing Metropolitan Line tracks. Neasden depot, which had been rebuilt in 1938 to a design by Stanley Heaps, was now the main maintenance and stabling depot for the Metropolitan and Bakerloo lines, leaving London Road, Queens Park and Croxley Green purely for Bakerloo train stabling. By the time the new service began the timetable allowed for 27 six-car trains of 1938 stock and 17 six-car trains of standard stock to operate on the Bakerloo.

After a week of getting accustomed to a new atmosphere, the people of London spent their first wartime week-end more enjoyably than any of them could have foreseen at the outset of war. Great numbers spent much of the week-end outside their homes. The continuing brilliance of the weather on Saturday combined with the extensive ban on football matches, theatres and cinemas, tempted many to a new discovery of London. Some visited scenes and places they had not inspected for years past, if ever before. The parks were filled. Hyde Park, with people sitting in deck-chairs in the sunshine, was as tranquil as at any September week-end. But all had gasmasks with them.

The Times, 11 September 1939

The almost complete lack of people around the new St John's Wood station could mean that it has yet to open for business. But its opening cannot be far off as publicity has been fixed to the exterior poster sites.

The period spanning the first eleven months of the war came to be known as the 'phoney' war, for apart from the obvious inconveniences like the blackout and rationing, life carried on much as normal for those not called-up for service. The long-feared bombing raids did not materialise. Nevertheless, as a precaution, sheets of anti blast netting were fixed to train saloon windows, giving very poor visibility, and interior lighting levels were much reduced. Later an improved type of protective window netting containing a diamond shaped 'clear' section was supplied so train passengers could see station names more clearly. On 1st February 1940 first class accommodation on the District and Metropolitan (Uxbridge) service was withdrawn. It now only remained on the Aylesbury and Watford branches of the Metropolitan Line, which became standard class only from 6th October 1941.

By the early months of 1940, activity on the New Works Programme had slowed right down and some projects, like the Northern Line extension from Edgware to Bushey Heath and Finsbury Park to Alexandra Palace, as well as the quadrupling of the Metropolitan tracks from Harrow to Rickmansworth, had already been put on ice. However, work on the Northern Line extension to High Barnet continued, and on 14th April tube trains ran on the 5.38 miles north from East Finchley for the first time. The intermediate stations were Finchley Central, renamed from Finchley (Church End), West Finchley, Woodside Park, and Totteridge & Whetstone. These stations remained very much as they had been during GNR and LNER days apart from the addition of the Underground branding. It was now possible to travel by tube train from High Barnet in Hertfordshire to Morden in Surrey, a distance of 22½ miles. This journey included the longest continuous tunnel in the world at the time, 17¼ miles via Bank from East Finchley to Morden. A new depot and sidings were built at Highgate Woods on the site of a former LNER carriage depot and sidings.

Frank Pick, the LPTB Vice Chairman, retired from the Board on 17th May 1940. His contribution to London's transport both in his service with the Board and its predecessor the Underground Group was immeasurable. He was truly the architect of much that by that time was making London Transport the envy of world transport operators. He joined the Information department of the Ministry of Transport, but sadly died suddenly in November 1941 at the age of 66. London Transport also had to do without the services of many of its key staff because of the war, including W.S. Graff-Baker, the Underground's Chief Mechanical Engineer who was appointed Director of Tank Production and Chief Architect Stanley Heaps who became Director of Construction (Aircraft Production).

By the spring of 1940 construction work on the Central Line extensions was beginning to wind down, although the LNER completed the new Loughton station buildings including a new ticket office and platforms, and these opened on 28th April. Most of the tunnelling had been completed but the track laying was still not complete. Work on this was suspended on 24th May with all work on the extension being stopped the following month. By then the standard 4-rail current system had been fully installed on the operational part of the line.

Delivery of new tube (1938 stock) and surface (P and Q stocks) trains continued but at a much-reduced rate. As there was little prospect of the Central Line extensions opening for some time the standard stock displaced from the Northern and Bakerloo lines was placed in store, much of it in the open, at depots around the system.

Frank Pick (1875–1941), who set the style of so much that was good about London's Underground in the early decades of the twentieth century.

The war of necessity changed the appearance of trains both inside and out. Train windows were covered in anti-blast protective mesh and interior lighting was replaced by bulbs of much lower wattage supplemented by small reading lights installed just below the advert panels.

The 'phoney war' ended with a jolt on 15th August 1940 with a bomb at Croydon Aerodrome. Spasmodic raids continued throughout August, but these were just a precursor to the full-scale onslaught from the air, which began on the afternoon of Saturday 7th September and continued relentlessly until the early weeks of 1941. On the night of 7th September, as the first heavy night-time raids began, people began to descend on deep level Underground stations in droves. Young, old, babes-in-arms, everyone made for the safety of the tube in a survival instinct which cared not one jot for the official notices proclaiming that tube stations were not to be used as air-raid shelters. Most deep-level stations were invaded, some people even making the perilous journey from parts of London not on the tube system to enjoy their relative safety. As dusk gathered they booked short journey tickets and, when services finished for the day, refused to leave the safe havens created by deep-level stations. They slept anywhere they could find a space, some found rest on stationary escalators and some, incredibly, even slept on the track. The situation continued for several nights with people arriving early, carrying everything they would need to survive a night below ground: bedding, deck-chairs, food and drink. Staff and police were kept busy moving people between stations to avoid overcrowding at those in more populous areas. After a few weeks it was estimated that 175,000 people were taking nightly cover in deep-level tube stations. Some kind of control and organisation was urgently needed, and Mr J.P. Thomas, the former General Manager of the Underground, was brought out of his retirement to help London Transport bring some order to things.

Refugees from the bombing take shelter in Elephant & Castle station. An empty train is stabled in the platform overnight, a practice continued at this location still, owing to insufficient depot capacity.

In November bunk beds were installed at Lambeth North station and by the end of 1941 22,000 bunk beds were available at 79 stations. Shelterers could even obtain season tickets to ensure a regular place. The lack of a deep level water supply meant only chemical toilet closets could be provided. One station used for shelter was Aldwych; the shuttle service to this station had been suspended from 21st September 1940, the opportunity being taken also to use parts of the station to provide a safe haven for numerous works of art from the British Museum.

Special four-car refreshment trains were introduced from November 6th 1940, to save those sheltering taking food and drink down into the tube. The shelterers were expected to bring their own mugs. The trains ran during the midday period, making their deliveries for the next night and collecting the previous night's 'empties'. They were allowed only 30 seconds at each station to unload their wares. By 26th November almost all stations being used as shelters were being served by the Refreshment Specials.

But although it had the advantage of being below ground level the Underground was still vulnerable to devastation and disruption should a bomb manage to penetrate the right target. The following list gives an indication of just how much loss of life and damage occurred on the Underground in the few weeks to the end of 1940.

7th September – Plaistow station damaged by bomb. Serious damage to rolling stock.

11th September – Wapping station destroyed by a firebomb.

24th September – Bomb at Tottenham Court Road station – One person killed.

12th October – Trafalgar Square station bombed – 7 shelterers killed

13th October – Bomb penetrated platform at Bounds Green – 19 shelterers killed.

14th October – Balham station hit by bomb, which exploded underground – 68 shelterers killed. Bomb at Camden Town station – One person killed.

16th October – King's Cross (Met and Circle) closed following bomb damage

12th November – Sloane Square station hit by bomb – 79 passengers in train injured.

The modernisation of Sloane Square had only been completed on 27th March 1940, now it would all have to be done again. Escalators had been installed, Sloane Square then being the only wholly sub-surface station to have them. There were countless other incidents which caused disruption for varying periods. What is easy to record is that, for each one, staff worked very hard to restore services as quickly as possible although often this took some time. In the case of Balham the service was not restored until 12th January 1941.

Two more casualties of the air raids were the Edgware Road to Addison Road via Uxbridge Road Metropolitan service, and the service operated by the LNWR from Willesden Junction to Earl's Court Underground Station. Both ceased on 19th October 1940 because of bomb damage at Uxbridge Road station.

By October 1940 the situation was so serious that the Government was drawing up plans for a network of deep level shelters in London, many on the Underground system. The Government itself was making use of the Underground, or at least a former part of it, because the War Cabinet sometimes met at a specially converted facility at the closed Down Street station, used normally by the Railway Executive Committee.

Although not part of the LT system at the time, the Southern Railway's Waterloo & City Line reached the end of a modernisation programme during October 1940 with the introduction of a fleet of new trains and new signalling.

On 29th December 1940 a firebomb struck the open-air part of Moorgate station destroying a six-car train of O and P stock. Also damaged beyond repair was an ex-CSLR electric locomotive, which had been on display at the station. Several other surface stock cars were destroyed or badly damaged during the early months of air-raids, but rather than send them all for scrap LT engineers salvaged two, a P stock motor-car, which had been damaged in a raid on Neasden depot, and Q stock trailer car, damaged in the Plaistow bomb blast. The two were literally cut in half and the two undamaged ends joined together to create a new motor car which was numbered 14233. The engineers were justly proud of their achievement, which would have put a used car dealer behind bars had it been tried with motor vehicles, and 14233 subsequently carried a special poster describing the work. 14233 still exists, as it was selected for preservation by the Buckinghamshire Railway Society when the bulk of the O/P stock was withdrawn.

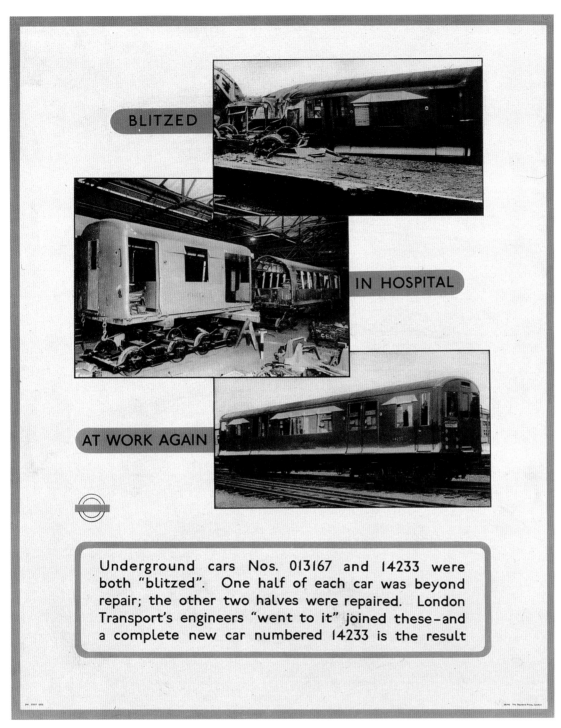

BLITZED

IN HOSPITAL

AT WORK AGAIN

Underground cars Nos. 013167 and 14233 were both "blitzed". One half of each car was beyond repair; the other two halves were repaired. London Transport's engineers "went to it" joined these – and a complete new car numbered 14233 is the result

At the end of 1940, after only two stages had been completed and opened, building work on the various Northern Line extensions was suspended. All references to them were removed from the Underground map at the same time. On 19th January 1941 the new Highgate station opened. It was not finished, and at its opening passengers had to walk up a flight of stairs from the ticket hall to the street, a climb regulars would have to endure until one of the planned escalators was installed in 1957. The platforms at Highgate, the design and decoration of which followed those at St John's Wood and Swiss Cottage on the Bakerloo, could accommodate nine-car trains, but these had ceased operating at the start of the war and were destined never to resume. As plans stood, Highgate was to be a key interchange on the fully fledged Northern Line, serving trains which had come from the Bank and Charing Cross branches at deep level, and trains which had come from the extended Northern City Line north of Finsbury Park en route to Alexandra Palace at surface level. A new station interchange complex had been designed and almost completed when the work was stopped.

A cut-away artist's impression of how the completed Highgate station might have looked, although the artist, D. Macpherson, has chosen to keep the surface platforms in the hands of LNER trains rather than the planned Northern Line services to Alexandra Palace. A sculpture of Dick Whittington and his cat was planned for the main Archway Road entrance, but the legend's return to Highgate was never to be realised.

Facing page top The very plain back entrance to Highgate station with the high level platform canopy visible behind it. A more elaborate building was designed just before the war but never built.

Facing page bottom **Sloane Square** station was modernised at the beginning of the war with the provision of escalators, unique in connecting a Circle Line platform to street level. This end of the station, including the street level building, was destroyed by a bomb on 12th November 1940.

ENTRANCE FROM ARCHWAY ROAD
ESCALATORS Opening Later

THE WOODMAN

PLATFORM OF LNER

ENTRANCE FROM SHEPHERDS HILL

TICKET OFFICE

TICKET HALL

STAIRWAY TO LNER

ENTRANCE FROM PRIORY GARDENS & WOOD LANE

ESCALATOR TO NORTHERN LINE

SOUTHBOUND PLATFORM OF NORTHERN LINE

NORTHBOUND PLATFORM OF NORTHERN LINE

Billy Brown of London Town was a cartoon tube traveller who was never afraid to tell unreasonable passengers how their misdeeds were a hindrance to good travelling habits. It is hard to imagine what sort of reaction such self-righteous messages would have on today's tube passengers; the reaction was not entirely favourable in wartime.

Facing page The devastation at Bank station in January 1941 after a bomb destroyed the ticket hall and escalators to the Central Line, killing 56 people. In February, when all the debris had been cleared, a Bailey Bridge was erected over the crater to carry road traffic. The station reopened on 17th March 1941, and one escalator to the Central Line, intended for installation at Highgate station, was in use by December. One more was added in 1944 'borrowed' from Chancery Lane, and the final one entered service in August 1947.

The bombing continued into 1941. On 11th January, Bank station received a direct hit when a bomb exploded in an escalator machine room, collapsing the main ticket hall, killing 56 people on the station and injuring 69. The huge crater, which it left, had to be covered with a Bailey Bridge for use by road traffic at the busy junction. The station was closed for two months.

In a quick reversal of fortune the LNER steam service from Finsbury Park to East Finchley was withdrawn on 3rd March and the service to Alexandra Palace was cut back to rush hours only in the following year.

The new King's Cross (Metropolitan and Circle) station opened on 14th March. The platforms were some 250 yards to the west of the old station, which had been closed since 16th October 1940 as a result of bomb damage. The new Metropolitan platforms were in single tunnels connected by a large concourse built within the old running tunnel. Cream coloured tiling, complemented by pale green edging tiling was used to decorate the new platforms. At the eastern end a staircase linked the concourse to a subway running beneath Euston Road connecting the Metropolitan platforms to the Northern and Piccadilly lines ticket hall.

On 10th May the section of District from St James's Park to Victoria was temporarily closed following a bomb. On the same day a train of P stock was damaged by a blast at Baker Street and one of its cars was damaged beyond repair.

Another section of the extended Northern Line opened on 18th May. This was the short 0.89-mile spur from Finchley Central to Mill Hill East, and it was opened in advance of the main extension to Edgware primarily to serve the Inglis Barracks at Mill Hill. The LNER steam service had been withdrawn one week after the start of the war for the electrification work to be carried out. The line was single track, as it had been in steam days. A service from Mill Hill East to Morden via Charing Cross was operated until 19:00 on Mondays to Saturdays. After this time and all day on Sundays two 2-car shuttle trains plied back and forth between Finchley Central and Mill Hill East. Until May 1942 these shuttles were made up of standard stock, the last to run in service on the Northern Line. The station at Mill Hill East was the original GNR structure and little alteration was needed for it to begin its life as a tube station.

Plessey workers busy on war work in a Central Line platform tunnel at Wanstead or Gants Hill.

During 1941 and into 1942 feverish activity had been under way in the newly completed tunnels between Wanstead and Gants Hill, not to get them ready for Central Line trains, but to install a fully equipped factory to help Britain's war effort. The factory, which was built by The Plessey Company, had become operational in March 1942. It employed around 2,000 people working in shifts to enable it to function 24 hours a day, turning out aircraft components and other vital pieces of equipment. Proper lighting was installed and track beds were concreted over to create 300,000 square feet of floor space. A miniature railway relayed components from section to section along the two-mile long shop floor.

During the war London Transport received on loan many buses from provincial operators to help overcome losses from air raids. Later it was able to return the compliment to other bus operators. In 1942 LT also loaned four 6-car trains, which included 22 cars of withdrawn Hammersmith & City stock, to the Mersey Railway, the loans remaining in their new home until 1945.

The air raids abated somewhat later in 1941, and by July only 28,000 people a night were seeking refuge in deep level tube stations in contrast to the 88,000 who had being doing so in January. Air raids were few and far between in 1942 when only around 5,000 people a night were using the tubes for night-time shelter. In 1943 the raids intensified and the deep level stations were in demand once more. Such was the case on the night of 3rd March 1943 when the air-raid sirens shrilled a warning of a raid in east London and people made for the safety of the as yet unopened Bethnal Green station on the Central Line eastern extension. Bethnal Green Council had 10,000 designated spaces at Bethnal Green for shelterers, and fear that bombs were about to rain down following the sound of anti-aircraft rockets caused the masses of people entering the station to suddenly surge forward onto those already descending the stairs. A woman fell close to the bottom step causing those behind to trip and fall also. Soon many hundreds had fallen on top of those at the bottom of the stairs, while the crush of people trying to get into the station continued. In the mêlée 173 people died of suffocation, 146 of them women and children. This was by far the most shocking and tragic incident to occur on the Underground during the war, and news of it was deliberately kept from the nation until January 1945, although an Inquiry was launched immediately. In the wake of the tragedy lighting levels at some stations used as shelters were improved. In March 1993, on the 50th anniversary of the tragedy, a commemorative plaque was unveiled at Bethnal Green station by the Mayor of Tower Hamlets Council.

From 3rd May 1943 LT trains, in the form of two northbound and one southbound working, ran beyond Aylesbury to Quainton Road once again to augment the LNER service. This arrangement survived until May 1948, a few months into the British Railways era.

In the midst of the strife and horror of war, plans for the return to peace were being made. A strategy for London's future, The County of London Plan, was published in 1943 and one of its recommendations would, a quarter of a century and much planning and debate later, become the Victoria Line.

As far back as October 1940, the Government had decided that a system of deep level shelters should be built in case of intensive bombing. The Board, as agents for the Minister of Home Security, was to build eight shelters with total sleeping accommodation for 64,000 people. Originally it was decided to have ten shelters each consisting of two parallel 1,400 ft tunnels, 16ft 6in in diameter. The sites were chosen so that the tunnels could form part of a possible express underground railway in the future. There were five sites south of the river – at Clapham South, Clapham Common, Clapham North, Stockwell and Oval, and five further north, at St Paul's, Chancery Lane, Goodge Street, Camden Town and Belsize Park. The shelter at Oval had to be abandoned because there was too much water in the ground. The one at St Paul's was not built because it was feared that damage may be caused to the foundations of the Cathedral. Each of the eight shelters built had two decks for sleeping reached by separate spiral staircases in the access shafts. For a long time they were used for military purposes – one became U.S. General Eisenhower's HQ before D-day – but five of them were opened to the public for a while when the flying bomb attacks started.

The Underground again suffered during the 'doodle bug' and V2 rocket era of 1944 and early 1945, although, fortunately, not on the scale it had during bombing raids of the early 1940s. The war in Europe finally ended in May 1945, and in its Annual Report for the year the Board paid tribute to its staff and passengers:

'The heroism and endurance displayed by Londoners had their counterpart in the qualities displayed by all sections of the Board's staff, who loyally co-operated, frequently under conditions of great personal danger, in maintaining the services upon which the war effort of Londoners so vitally depended. Only with the determination, forbearance and good humour of passengers and staff alike could the Board have accomplished their task under the conditions of war.'

Inside one of the deep level air raid shelters built along the route of the Northern Line between 1941 and 1943. This one is next to Clapham South station and shows longitudinal and traverse bunks within a 16ft 6ins tunnel. A shelter was also built at Chancery Lane on the Central Line.

The Post War Era, 1945–1959

The fluorescent lighting at Piccadilly Circus doesn't seem to have done much to cheer up the passengers, but it has made the platform brighter. Of interest in this early post war view is a line diagram poster fixed to the trackside ceiling vault, another experiment but not one pursued.

During the war, a disused part of Piccadilly Circus station was used for safe storage of paintings from the Tate Gallery. The photograph below shows the works of art being taken out of their temporary home in February 1946.

After the euphoria of VE Day the remnants and reminders of the war gradually disappeared from the Underground system. Among the first to go were the bunk beds, canteen points and chemical toilets used by the shelterers, together with the thousands of pieces of protective window mesh from the trains. In October, in bright contrast to the years of drabness, fluorescent lighting strips illuminated the westbound Piccadilly Line platform at Piccadilly Circus. Strip lighting had been first tried out experimentally on a District Line car in October 1944. Later the whole of Piccadilly Circus station was equipped with the new lighting, as were the new stations on the first extensions opened after the war, those of the Central Line, and over the years it became commonplace over the entire Underground.

The tube slowly returned to normal. Escalators, which had been stopped in off-peak periods during the war to save power, now ran all day again, and train services were gradually restored to pre-war levels. Work planned under the New Works Programme restarted. Although the original £35–£40 million cost of the programme had risen to more than £50 million, the Government was anxious that work on the Central Line extensions resumed as soon as possible. Plessey's tunnel factory was dismantled and the concrete flooring broken-out. All this took five months. In April 1946 work began to get the Central Line extension's rolling-stock fleet ready. Around 340 cars of standard stock displaced from the Bakerloo and Northern lines had been stored during the war, much of it out in the open, and the elements had taken their toll. All rust-prone areas, electrical wiring, rubber mouldings and some panelling needed replacement, and some 300 cars had been completely rebuilt by the end of 1947. The renewal of the train fleet in the late 1930s was showing dividends and, during 1947, London Transport was able to claim an 18% increase in the average speed of its train service since 1933.

The Piccadilly Line Aldwych branch reopened on 1st July 1946 after its wartime closure. Two months later, on 1st September, Mark Lane District Line station was renamed Tower Hill, and Queen's Road, on the Central, became Queensway. Right at the end of the year, on 19th December, Addison Road station was renamed Kensington (Olympia) to highlight its proximity to the Olympia exhibition centre.

On Tuesday 3rd December 1946 the Minister of Transport, Alfred Barnes, opened the first of the extensions designed to transform the Central Line from a seven mile long inner urban tube railway to a suburban railway comprising more than 50 route miles. The first step towards this was the 5.19 mile extension from Liverpool Street to Stratford with intermediate stations at Bethnal Green and Mile End. Bethnal Green had no surface buildings and entry to the ticket hall was by way of three subways from the junction of Bethnal Green Road and Burdett Road. The platforms followed the same general design and layout as those on the Bakerloo extension. One new feature was that of clocks with red and blue LT bullseyes on the face in place of numerals. These appeared at many of the stations on the new extension. From Bethnal Green the new tube proceeded to Mile End where it rose to join the District Line platforms. These had been transformed into two island platforms to give quick cross-platform interchange.

From Mile End the line dived again to proceed through the one and three-quarter mile tunnel, then the longest between any two stations on the Underground, to Stratford. Excavation was difficult on this stretch which passed beneath the River Lee and through the east London marshes, and compressed air had to be used. At some locations the tunnel roof came within a few feet of gravel and mud from the river-bed. The ground had to be chemically treated to allow the necessary excavation. Pipes were driven down into the mud from pontoons anchored in mid stream to enable the necessary ground preparation to be carried out. The treatment caused the river-bed to become hardened over the tunnel excavations. More problems were encountered at the point where the LNER bridge crossed Carpenters Road. Here the tube tunnels rose to join the main line above ground at Stratford and at this level compressed air could not be used. The bridge foundations had to be strengthened and the road beneath was dug out to make a trench, which was lined with steel and filled with concrete through which the new tunnels were drilled. Nearer the surface the cut and cover tunnelling method was used. The line broke surface just west of Stratford terminating at a new island platform which afforded cross-platform interchange with the eastbound LNER suburban services. Trains then proceeded east to reverse close to Leyton station before returning to a new westbound island platform at Stratford where interchange with the LNER local services to Liverpool Street was possible. Following the opening of the new extension, the peak hour service now required 40 trains against 27 at the end of 1945.

The next steps in the Central Line's eastward march took place on Monday 5th May 1947 when it was extended the two and a quarter miles to Leytonstone. From Stratford the line proceeded in twin tunnels to the former GER/LNER station at Leyton. Trains emerged from the tunnels and rose to the surface in a cutting west of Leyton before arriving in the platforms. A crossover just west of the station had been used to reverse trains during the period the service terminated at Stratford. This was removed when the extension to Leytonstone opened. Little alteration was necessary at Leyton but at Leytonstone, the next station, single storey entrances were built on both sides of the railway with subways down to a new ticket hall built beneath the tracks. An extra bay platform for westbound trains was also provided. Church Lane was diverted through a new underpass beneath the railway just west of the station. The Central Line required eight additional peak hour six-car trains following the opening to Leytonstone. The through steam service from Liverpool Street ceased with the extension to Leytonstone, steam trains from Ongar and Epping teminating now at Leytonstone.

On June 28th, Mr Barnes officially opened the first western extension of the Central Line. This was the 3.9 miles from North Acton to Greenford with intermediate stations at Hanger Lane and Perivale. All the western Central Line extensions were above ground. The stations were, at the time, still under GWR ownership, and none of the planned station buildings were complete by opening day. The ticket hall at Hanger Lane was finished in January 1949, by which time it, and several other stations on the new western extension, had passed to LT ownership. A large cylindrical ticket-hall dominated the structure only half of which was above ground level, as passengers reached the ticket office by stairs. Perivale station, designed by GWR architect Brian Lewis, had a glazed concrete frontage, with shop units built into its main structure. At Greenford could be found one of the oddities of the Underground. Passengers travelled *up* by escalator to reach the platforms. The station entrance was built next to the bridge viaduct. The extension opened to passengers on Monday 30th June 1947, and from that date the peak hour train requirement for the Central Line rose to 52.

Fluorescent lighting was first experimentally fitted to R stock Underground car No. 8784 in 1944. It became standard in new train deliveries from 1949 (R47 surface stock) and 1956 for tube stock.

The official opening by the Minister of Transport of the Central Line extension from Liverpool Street to Stratford on 3rd December 1946. Passenger services started the next day.

A tantalising taste of modernity was brought briefly to the Metropolitan Line by cars 17000 and 20000. Car 17000 is shown as rebuilt in 1949 and carrying its new number 17001.
Below is an interior view of car 20000 as originally built with double-seating either side of the gangway. The car line map was placed at right angles to the gangway as on the A-stock of 1960, which was a development of these experimental cars. The other car started off with semi-compartments but was soon refitted with an offset gangway with three seats on one side and two on the other, the form eventually adopted by the production stock.

The design for the rolling stock to run on the proposed electrified Metropolitan services to Amersham and Chesham had been occupying the engineers and designers at Acton since 1939. LT wanted to retain compartment style seating but incorporate sliding doors into the new stock. Some static mock-ups were constructed at Acton Works, and eventually two experimental cars were built there. One (No.17000) retained a compartment style layout, providing 57 seats. The car was divided into three sections, with a corridor running along one side. There were three sets of air-operated double doors on each side. The car entered passenger service on the Metropolitan in January 1946. In June 1947 another experimental car (No.20000) entered service. It had a centre gangway and seated 56. Both 17000 and 20000 had fluorescent lighting. In 1949 No.17000 was renumbered 17001 and rebuilt with a centre gangway flanked by banks of triple seating on one side and double seating on the other, as research had shown that passengers were not keen on the original seating arrangement and that it slowed boarding and alighting. The revised layout was to set the pattern for the trains that would eventually be built for the electrified Amersham services more than a decade later. Both cars had to run in a train of slam-door T stock, as a second guard was required to operate the doors, and in 1953, having served their intended purpose, the cars were withdrawn. They were broken up two years later. P stock began working on the Circle Line from 17th February 1947, allowing a start to be made on withdrawal of some of the 1913/1921 Circle stock.

Seven more stations, and seven route miles, were added to the Central Line map on 14th December 1947. Transport Minister Barnes, who by this time must have been seriously thinking about buying a season ticket for the Central Line, officially opened the extensions from Leytonstone to Newbury Park and Woodford. Three of the new stations, Wanstead, Redbridge and Gants Hill, had been designed by Charles Holden, his last for the Underground. Unlike the stations on the western end of the line, all those in the east were complete by opening day. The Minister was accompanied again by Lord Ashfield, undertaking one of his last engagements as Chairman of the LPTB. He had resigned on 31st October in advance of the nationalisation of the undertaking, and accepted a seat on the Board of the new British Transport Commission (BTC), which was to oversee the Country's newly nationalised transport, including railways, road haulage, and waterways.

Showpiece of the new extension was Gants Hill. What it lacked in surface buildings it amply made up for below ground. The station was built beneath a busy roundabout linking five major roads. The ticket hall, which lay directly beneath the roundabout, was reached by a network of subways from seven points around the circus. Three escalators led from the small, low-roofed, ticket hall down to a huge vaulted roof concourse leading to the platforms at either side. The influence of the Moscow Metro, which a party of LT engineers had visited in 1935, was unmistakable. The whole station, including the subways, was clad in cream tile edged in orange.

Contrasting views of White City station when new, illustrating how the large windows in the ticket hall help make the building more prominent at night than during the day. An additional ticket office for use when White City Stadium was in use can be seen to the left of the main entrance in the daylight view. Inside, an expansive glazed roof straddled two wide island platforms, which gave White City three running tracks. The new station was built west of the old Wood Lane station, which closed on the night of 22nd November 1947. But for years afterwards an eastbound train journey from White City, which passed through the old station, would reveal enamel station nameplates still in place.

The Central Line has come to suburban Essex. Some fairly relaxed looking office workers board a train at Wanstead in the early days of the new extension. This modern tube tunnel platform contrasted greatly with the inherited open-air platforms on the extension, which were left largely untouched from Victorian days. Loughton was a notable exception: here a modern concrete design with flowing curves replaced the original Victorian platform buildings in a scheme carried out by the LNER. Most of the open-air platforms on the eastern stretch of the Central Line remain in Victorian style to this day.

The huge vaulted-roof concourse at Gants Hill, seen soon after the completion of building work at the station. Stylish wooden seats still await installation in the centre of the concourse. Praise for new stations on the eastern extension of the Central Line came from the Architects' Journal in June 1949, which said that here was one of the few places where high quality new buildings could be seen in London.

On Friday 12th December 1947, an ornamental gate waits to be swung clear of the inaugural train taking the Minister of Transport, LPTB chairman Lord Ashfield and other dignitaries to Newbury Park and back to a reception at Gants Hill where seven more stations on the Central Line eastern extension would be declared open. Public service began on the following Sunday. From Gants Hill the new line headed south east, then curved north to join the former GER/LNER Ilford to Woodford loop line at Newbury Park, a tunnel distance of one and a half miles. The LNER service via Newbury Park to Woodford had ceased on 29th November 1947, being replaced by a special bus service, which was adjusted at the opening of each new section until the whole loop extension was served by tube trains.

Probably the most momentous event of 1947 took place in the very last second of the year when at the stroke of midnight the LPTB ended its fourteen and a half year existence. The reign of the 'big four' railway companies ended that night also. On 1st January 1948, with the setting up of the British Transport Commission, the new London Transport Executive (LTE) took control of most former 'big four' interests in the Underground system. This included the Northern Line from East Finchley to High Barnet (LNER), the GWR-owned section of the Central from White City to Ealing and Greenford (except for Ealing Broadway station), the East London Line, which had been owned by the Southern Railway, the Hammersmith & City Line from Hammersmith to Westbourne Park (part owned by the GWR) and the Whitechapel and Bow Railway (part owned by the LMS). The new Chairman of LTE was former LPTB Board member Lord Latham.

The opening of the Central Line extensions continued with Newbury Park to Hainault on 31st May 1948, Hainault to Woodford, Woodford to Loughton and Greenford to West Ruislip on 21st November. Steam trains had continued to serve the stations between Woodford and Ongar prior to 21st November, but these were cut back to Loughton when the electric trains reached there and further cut back to Epping on 25th September 1949 when the Central Line extensions were completed. On this date, the Epping to Ongar section also transferred to London Transport ownership. It remained steam operated as a separate part of the Central Line until electrification in 1957. Two new depots serviced the extended Central Line, one at West Ruislip and the other at Hainault. Both had been completed in 1939 and were used during the war as a manufacturing base for anti-aircraft guns.

Meanwhile, early in 1949, a Working Party of the BTC considering the issues raised by the 1943 County of London Plan recommended that planning and feasibility studies be carried out on a deep level tube line linking north east London with King's Cross, Euston and Victoria. This was later to become the Victoria Line, of which more shall be said later.

When the Central Line extensions were completed on 25th September 1949 and all sections now electrified with the exception of Epping to Ongar, the question remained about the future form of traction on this six-mile single-track section. For the time being, operation continued with steam locomotives and carriages hired from the Eastern Region of BR. In 1952 it was decided to investigate the possibility of converting this short part of the Central Line to diesel operation with diesel railcars. An AEC three-car lightweight diesel railcar set was loaned to London Transport by ACV Sales Ltd in the second half of June 1952. In May and June 1952 the three-car train had been used for trials on BR services between Marylebone and Princes Risborough and between Finsbury Park and Alexandra Palace. Between 16th June and 27th June it spent ten days on the Epping–Ongar service, carrying a total of 3,659 passengers during that time. Whilst the riding of the train was reported to be smooth on straight sections of track, the rigid wheelbase caused a tugging sensation on curves. There was also considerable bumping and side-play when going through points and crossings. There were also some passenger complaints about insufficient knee room between seats. The operating manager reported that running diesel railcars on the Epping–Ongar section would be practicable and economical but that electrification could now be completed by using otherwise spare 1935 stock trains and at lower cost than at first envisaged. Electrification took place five years later. The operating manager did not rule out purchase of diesel railcars, suggesting them again (as in 1936) for the Chalfont–Chesham shuttle and as a last ditch possible solution for Finsbury Park to Alexandra Palace service.

The AEC lightweight diesel railcar tried out on the Central Line's Epping–Ongar service in June 1952.

Epping, on the edge of rural Essex, seems an unlikely setting for a tube train. The steam locomotive and its two carriages on the adjacent platform, waiting to take passengers on the single line to Ongar, seem much more at home. Tube trains and steam trains could be seen side by side at Epping for eight years, from September 1949 until tube trains replaced steam in November 1957.

The first new trains of the post-war era arrived in 1949. The District Line's C, D and E (H stock) hand-worked door trains, over thirty of which were still in service at the beginning of the post-war period, were in need of replacement. The trailer cars for the O, P and Q stocks had been built to allow for conversion to motor-cars if required, and it was decided to design a train which utilised these cars for the driving motors with new cars forming the rest of the train. The new cars would all be motorised NDMs, although only one axle per bogie would be motorised, and orders for an initial batch of 143 cars were placed with Birmingham (89 cars) and Gloucester (54). Eighty-two Q38 trailers were to be converted to motor-cars, complete with cabs, by Gloucester to make up complete six or eight car trains. Thus was born the R stock, the driving motors being classified R38 and the trailers R47, the year they were ordered. Delivery of the R stock began in November 1949. The profile of the new stock was practically identical to the O and P stocks. The new cars could be identified by having just two separate windows in the centre bay instead of four. External livery was all red with grey roofs. Internally the new stock followed the style set by the O, P, and Q stocks in having large areas of polished wood panelling. The R stock was the first on the Underground to be fitted with fluorescent lighting from new.

The R stock construction programme had to be carefully planned to allow for numbers of Q38 trailers to be taken out of service for conversion to motor-cars. The first phase of the programme allowed for 31 new trains which, apart from releasing more Q38 trailers for conversion to R38 motor-cars for use in the second stage of the programme, enabled the transfer of the F stock to the Metropolitan Line. It also allowed the P stock trains that had been running on the District to return to the Metropolitan. With the remainder, a start was made on replacing the H stock.

A mixed train of Q stock typical of those that operated on the District between 1938 and 1971.

A warm day finds this train of H stock at East Putney, with a former District Railway C-class motor car leading. The passengers' practice of keeping open the hand-worked doors in warm weather would give the Railway Inspectorate apoplexy in today's safety critical environment. The last hand-worked door stock was withdrawn from the Olympia service in 1957.

The first train of R stock entered service on the District Line on 17th April 1950, and in June the first train of F stock was transferred from the District to the Metropolitan for use on the Uxbridge service. By December enough F stock had made the move to allow some P stock to be transferred from the Uxbridge service to the Circle Line to replace the wooden electric stock, some dating from 1905. The last of these trains ran on 31st December 1950.

By this time the Bakerloo was worked entirely with 1938 tube stock, the last standard stock on the line having been withdrawn in May 1949 for transfer to the Central to help increase the number of eight-car trains on that line. The original intention had been to operate the Bakerloo with a mixture of standard stock and 1938 tube stock, but enough 1938 stock had been available for the Bakerloo because of the suspension of work on the Northern Line extensions for which they had been ordered and built. By the late 1940s there seemed little prospect of work on these extensions resuming, at least for the present, so the Bakerloo was able to keep its own 1938 train fleet, which was augmented by new 1938 stock cars stored during the war pending the completion of the Northern Line extensions. It was also estimated that planned service increases on the Northern and Piccadilly lines, as well as restocking the Northern City Line with 1938 stock, would require an extra 127 cars. Plans were drawn up for both the purchase of new cars, and the conversion of the 1935 streamlined motor-cars to trailers.

Not all these proposals reached fruition. Plans for service increases on the Northern and Piccadilly lines were dropped, and the Northern City would have to wait another sixteen years for its 1938 stock. However, by now there was also the prospect of extra trains being required for the extension of the Bakerloo from Elephant & Castle to Camberwell with perhaps a continuation to Herne Hill. An extension beyond Elephant & Castle had been first suggested in the 1920s, and was one of the options considered by the 1944 Railway (London Plan) Committee, which reported in 1948. The Report suggested many schemes to improve the London railway network, especially by linking up established routes north and south of the Thames.

It was originally estimated that an additional 98 cars would be needed for the Bakerloo if the Camberwell extension went ahead. This was reduced to 89 following the abandonment of the service augmentation plans, and amended again when LT decided not to introduce 'block' trains, i.e. trains that could not be operated as separate halves if required during off-peak periods. Three different types of car (motor, non-driving motor and trailer) were required to make up a train of 1938 stock and careful thought had to be given to the eventual configuration of train formation and services they would work on. This had been the case with the now abandoned nine-car train proposals for the Northern Line. It was now decided to rebuild and convert the 18 streamlined motor-cars of 1935 stock, unused since the beginning of the war, to trailers, and purchase new cars to make up the required train formations. To this end 21 new trailers and 71 new uncoupling non-driving motor-cars (UNDM) of 1949 tube stock were eventually ordered, and twenty-two 1938 NDMs were converted to UNDMs to fit in with the new configuration. The 1949 cars were almost identical to their 1938 counterparts. All were built by the Birmingham Railway Carriage and Wagon Company.

The UNDMs were designed to replace the need for a motor car at the coupled end of a three-car set in a seven-car train, and, despite having no cab, they could be used to drive a train being shunted in a depot. In June 1950, four-car off-peak trains were introduced on the Bakerloo Line, as well as on many other Underground lines, so shunting became an operational feature. Following delivery of the 1949 tube stock, which began in November 1951, the 1938 stock was marshalled to provide 184 seven-car trains, 15 of which were to be transferred, over a two year period, to the Piccadilly Line. By this time the Camberwell extension had been deferred due to financial constraints so the move to the Piccadilly, which had originally been deemed temporary, could now be more permanent.

It is worth noting that in 1951 there had been plans for a wholly new fleet of 100 seven-car trains for the Piccadilly Line. The new trains were code-named 1952 stock, and they were to have been a development of the 1938 stock. In 1949, 1938 stock car 10306 was experimentally rebuilt at Acton Works with some new features which would have graced the 1952 stock had it ever got under the ground. These included sliding door and saloon windows continuing up into the roof-line. It would be many years before these features would find their way onto production tube trains.

A section of the interior of 1938 stock car 10306, showing the curved window panels in the doors and window frames, the latter a feature not seen again on a tube train until 1986.

As the 1950s gathered pace, it was obvious that the inter-war expansion of London into the surrounding countryside had peaked, and in November 1950 London Transport announced that the Northern Line extensions beyond Edgware and Elstree to Bushey Heath could not be justified. The giant Aldenham depot, which was practically complete, was to become London Transport's Bus Overhaul Works, and it functioned in this role until 1987. The building was finally demolished in 1996. The door to the possible extension of the Northern from Mill Hill East via Mill Hill (The Hale) to Edgware was kept ajar, but only just. One change on the Northern during 1950 was the renaming of Trinity Road to Tooting Bec (on 1st October). On 25th September Moor Park and Sandy Lodge station on the Metropolitan was renamed Moor Park.

By the end of 1951 work was under way on the second phase of the R stock programme for the District Line. Post-war shortages of steel had caused LT to consider the use of aluminium as an alternative material for carriage panelling. During the war LT engineers had worked with aluminium in aircraft construction, and it seemed appropriate to consider its use again in the light of the steel shortage. An order for 90 new aluminium bodied cars of R stock (six motor-cars and 84 NDMs) was placed with Metro-Cammell in 1949 with Gloucester undertaking the work of converting 49 more Q38 trailers to motor-cars. The new order provided for an increase of three trains on the District Line during the peaks. The overall District services once all the R stock had been delivered would then be 30 eight-car and 12 six-car trains of R stock, 14 eight-car and 28 six-car trains of Q stock and three 4-car trains of pre-1915 H stock for the Olympia service.

The new carriages were classified R49 and very similar in appearance to the previous deliveries of R stock. LT was anxious to see if any cost savings emerged by operating the lighter aluminium cars. Although the building contract specified that the new stock be painted in the traditional red, it occurred to the engineers that even more weight would be saved by not painting the car exteriors; aluminium alloy being anti-corrosive did not require traditional painting. In August 1951 two motor-cars, one 1938 tube stock and a P stock, were each fitted with aluminium alloy body panels, part polished, part sanded. After undergoing trials for several weeks without any apparent adverse effects it was decided to ask Metro-Cammell to leave one completed R49 car unpainted. The car (No.23567) was delivered in April 1952 and entered service two months later. Public reaction was favourable and LT asked Metro-Cammell to deliver sufficient unpainted cars to enable a complete 'silver' train, including two unpainted R49 motor-cars, to be made up. The only relief to the expanse of silver-coloured alloy was a red band beneath the window line which continued around the front of the train cabs. The train entered service on the District Line on 19th January 1953.

A complete train of aluminium bodied R-stock, all built by Metro-Cammell and headed by an R49 driving motor car, poses for the camera when new in 1953.

As the new trains were entering service on the District a major rehabilitation of the F stock was nearing completion. The work began soon after the F stock was transferred to the Metropolitan with the first cars being dealt with in September 1951. Aluminium alloy doors replaced the original wood and steel doors. The cars were rewired, repanelled where necessary, better lighting and new seating were installed, and passenger door control was fitted. The programme was completed in December 1953 and contributed to the F stock being fit for a further ten years.

The entry into service of the final car in the second phase of the R stock programme took place in March 1953. This, combined with the completion of the F stock rehabilitation programme enabled the replacement of the East London Line's H stock (formerly C, D, and E classes) by four-car trains of the F stock from 7th December. This left just a handful of H stock cars to operate the Olympia service, which ran only when exhibitions were held in the centre. In May the three trains comprising 1935 stock were transferred away from the Central Line to work on the Aldwych branch of the Piccadilly.

While the operational railway was being maintained, planning was proceeding on the route options for the new line from north east London via Finsbury Park, King's Cross, Euston and the West End to Victoria. In February 1954 the possibility that the new line should run beyond Victoria to Fulham Broadway and over District tracks to Wimbledon was being addressed. By now the Government had agreed to LT sponsoring a private member's bill for approval of the scheme in Parliament. In November 1954, the Minister of Transport gave his consent to the inclusion of enabling powers for the construction of Route C of the 1944 Railway (London Plan), in the BTC's Private Bill to be introduced in the 1955 session of Parliament. The route was an amalgam of two of the original optioned routes, C and D, which would bring the tube to north-east London. The new tube would now run to Walthamstow instead of Edmonton as originally planned. The line would also interchange with the Northern City Line at Highbury. When the BTC Act allowing the new line to be built received Royal Assent the following year the new line was being openly referred to as the Victoria Line. The name came out of a meeting early in 1955. Paul Garbutt recalls that ideas like Viking Line (Victoria/King's Cross) and Walvic Line had been floated. Other suggestions included Mayfair Line and West End Line, but Victoria Line 'sounded just right'.

In June 1955, following problems with the Metadyne control system used on the P stock trains working on the Circle Line, London Transport decided to replace it with the more reliable Pneumatic Camshaft Mechanism (PCM) control equipment used in the 1938 tube stock. The first train so fitted was ready for service in April 1956, and initial results showed an improvement in train reliability. Gradually the rest of the O/P fleet lost its Metadyne control in favour of PCM equipment, a process that took until 1965 to complete.

Another link with the past was lost in November 1955 when the sidings and goods hoist at Whitechapel on the East London Line were taken out of use, and the following March the British Railways line from Ilford to Newbury Park, on the Central Line, was disconnected. By the mid-1950s the age of steam on Britain's main line railways was under sentence of death, but LT still had use for steam locomotives on shunting and permanent way duties, especially at the giant Neasden depot. Replacements for the ageing fleet of steam locos was debated, and because of their limited use LT decided to buy some ex-GWR 0–6–0 pannier tanks from British Railways rather than invest in diesel shunters. Between 1956 and 1963 twelve 0–6–0 PTs were acquired from BR and painted into LT maroon.

The single-track steam service between Epping and Ongar, operated by BR, latterly using ex-GER F5 2–4–2 and N7 0–6–2 tank locos, was finally replaced by a tube train service on 18th November 1957 using the 1935 flat-ended experimental stock cars transferred back from the Piccadilly Line. They had been used on the Central Line previously, between October 1950 and May 1954. The Aldwych shuttle then reverted to two-car standard stock formation. For three years between 1957 and 1960 a three-car train of 1938 tube stock ran on the Ongar branch, the one and only time a complete train of this stock operated on the Central Line.

The oldest standard stock was now approaching its thirty-fifth birthday and was thus becoming due for replacement. A new design was on the drawing board. 'New' maybe a generous description because the design was, to the layman, aluminium bodied 1938 stock without the domed cab roof. In 1956 three prototype trains were ordered, one each from Metro-Cammell, Birmingham and Gloucester, to test the concepts of the new design.

The refurbishment of the F stock in the early 1950s did little to alter the appearance of these handsome trains as this view taken near the end of the life of the stock shows. The last F Stock full length train ran on the Uxbridge branch of the Met on 15th March 1963. Four-car trains of F stock continued on the East London Line until 7th September.

The Metro-Cammell 'silver' train arrives at Hammersmith, no doubt to some admiring looks from intending passengers.

The first production train of 1959 tube stock is posed for publicity photographs shortly before entering service in December 1959. It would take four and a half years for the 1959/1962 tube stocks to displace the remaining standard stock on the Central and Piccadilly Lines.

The prototype trains comprised seven cars (M–T–NDM–M+M–T–M). The Gloucester train had thick beading below the saloon windows, a feature not seen on a tube train since 1925. The most outstanding feature of all three, and the one which caught the headlines, was their unpainted 'silver' finish, LT having now decided to build all future rolling-stock of aluminium alloy panelling which was to be left unpainted. A destination indicator box was positioned above the front cab door, and roof mounted door operation indicator lights alerted the guard to any doors which had not closed properly at stations. Internally things were a little different from the 1938 styling. Transverse seating in the centre bays faced the corresponding opposite seat. The red and grey moquette was in a pattern of straight lines and used alongside blue-grey paintwork. Ceilings were white and along the length of each ran dual strip lighting, which made the car interiors extremely bright. The interior colour scheme and the use of fluorescent lighting transformed the insides from the homely feel of 1938 tube stock to a colder, office-like environment.

The Metro-Cammell train entered service on the Piccadilly Line on 9th September 1957, with the Gloucester train following on 7th October. Piccadilly Line passengers had to wait until 14th April 1958 to sample the Birmingham train. Eventually the bulk contract for the replacement of the standard stock on the Piccadilly Line was awarded to Metro-Cammell. Orders were also placed in 1958 with Cravens Ltd of Sheffield for twelve prototype motor cars for a new Central Line fleet, and 31 new eight-car trains to replace the loco-hauled and T stock trains on the Metropolitan.

On 28th July 1958 there was a fire on a Central Line train at Holland Park. One person later died from the effect of fumes. The fire started in some electrical wiring. At the inquiry held into the incident, concern was expressed that some vital safety features were rendered inoperable if the guard had to leave his post and isolated the passenger-open door circuit, as he was instructed to do. It was therefore decided to discontinue the passenger door opening facility, and in March 1959 it was removed from all the lines on which it was still being used.

The first train of the batch of 76 seven-car aluminium bodied tube trains ordered from Metro-Cammell entered service on the Piccadilly Line on 14th December 1959. This was the start of the 1959 tube stock programme. Under it, all the Piccadilly Line's standard stock would be replaced, and some of the newer 1927-1934 cars transferred to the Central to replace the 1923–26 vintage standard stock. Spare cars would be used to make up the remaining seven-car trains on the Central to eight cars. The new trains differed very little from the Metro-Cammell 1956 prototype, but the deep seat cushions of the 1956 prototypes were replaced by shallower ones. The raw unpainted livery remained, relieved only by a dove grey roof. This was changed to gloss black early on in the production run. Meanwhile it was still London Transport's intention to develop a bespoke train fleet for the Central Line.

On 1st March 1959 the rebuilt Notting Hill Gate station opened with its new escalator connection to the Central Line platforms, affording, for the first time, an interchange between the Central and District & Circle Lines. A new ticket hall served all lines. The previous day the South Acton shuttle service to and from Acton Town last ran, and the two double-ended G stock cars were taken out of service. For the time being this was the end of one-man operation on the Underground.

The need to provide some extra trains for the District Line, as well as increasing the length of Circle Line trains from five to six cars, set the planners' minds working in the late 1950s. The option eventually decided upon involved converting seventeen Q38 trailers to O/P trailers to increase the length of Circle Line trains to six cars, and converting a further seven Q38 trailers into R38 motor-cars to run with 13 new aluminium bodied NDMs (R59 stock) ordered from Metro-Cammell to the 1949 pattern. They were delivered between July and September 1959. All were left unpainted, and the newly converted R38 motor cars were painted silver to match. The seven Q38 trailers were converted to R38 motor cars at Acton Works.

During 1956/57 five other R stock cars had been painted silver to match the original unpainted car No.23567, creating two 'silver' trains on the District. Following the arrival of the R59 cars, and the conversion of the Q38 trailers to motors, there were, technically, three more. All the R59 stock was in service by the end of October 1959.

A Brand New Line

In January 1960 work began on two experimental tunnels between Finsbury Park and South Tottenham. The tunnels would join up at Manor House, and the principal purpose in building them was to test the use of 'drum digger' rotary shields in tunnel excavation. The drum digger consisted of two drums, with the leading end of the outer drum bevelled to form a cutting edge. A smaller drum rotating within the outer drum had cutting teeth, which cut into the area in front of the space between the inner and outer drums. Hydraulic rams drove the digger forward, the spoil being discharged into skips for removal. The drum digger could excavate more than 60 feet a day, more than the conventional Greathead shield used on most tube tunnel excavation hitherto. The mile long tunnel would be able to form part of the finished Victoria Line, if its construction got the final go-ahead. Work on the tunnel was completed in July 1961. The drum digger method enabled the tunnel to be excavated faster than if a Greathead shield had been used. Later the tunnel was used for noise and ventilation tests. The BTC Act (1960) authorised the construction of tunnels south of Victoria to allow for further extensions to be built.

In April 1960 two 7-car trains of 1959 tube stock, which had been used for staff training, entered passenger service on the Central Line, to be followed on 25th July by the line's first eight-car silver train. Originally the plan had been to restock the Piccadilly with 1959 trains and transfer the best of its standard stock to the Central to replace cars of 1923–26 vintage. The arrival of the prototypes for the new fleet of trains LT planned for the Central was still some months off. Now came a change of plan brought about largely by the electrification of the BR (Eastern Region) services out of Liverpool Street, bringing with it the prospect of more traffic on the Central Line. Capacity had to be increased urgently, and an allocation of the last 57 trains of the Piccadilly's 1959 stock order to the Central Line was seen as a quick solution. As the trains would contain three-car units, an order for an additional 57 NDMs of 1959 tube stock to make the Central Line trains up to eight-car (M–T–NDM–M+M–T–NDM–M) formation was placed with Metro-Cammell, and the first three-car unit containing additionally one of the new NDMs entered service in May 1961.

To give the Central Line its own fleet of modern rolling stock, an order for 84½ new trains similar to the 1959 stock was placed with the Birmingham Railway Carriage & Wagon Co. (338 motor-cars and 112 NDMs), and the BR works at Derby (169 trailers). These (the 1962 stock) would run on the Central Line enabling the 1959 stock, minus the 57 additional NDMs, to return to the Piccadilly. In the meantime, from February 1960, cars from the 1931/34 Piccadilly stock, released by the delivery of 1959 stock, were transferred to the Central, the first time they had strayed from their home line.

Some elements of the pre-war New Works Programme took time to reach fruition. Work on the four-tracking of the Metropolitan Line from Harrow to Rickmansworth, and the onward electrification to Amersham and Chesham, suspended during the war, did not resume until 1959. The immense task of lengthening and widening 17 bridges, and laying new tracks, all within a distance of six and a half miles, continued during 1960. The electrification to Amersham and Chesham was completed first, and on 15th August 1960 the first electric train, composed of T stock, ran under test to Amersham. The work had included the installation of new signalling, electricity substations and a new signal cabin at Amersham, where a new platform and footbridge were also being built.

On Monday 12th September 1960 the steam era on the Metropolitan began slipping away with the operation of the last steam-hauled train on the Chesham branch. The quaint Ashbury coaches used on the push-pull service for over 60 years were withdrawn, four of them (Nos 368, 387, 394 and 412), happily in the new age of railway preservation, finding a new home on the Bluebell Railway in Sussex. The steam service to Aylesbury, operated by British Railways (London Midland Region) on LT's behalf, continued. Looking ahead to future train services on the Metropolitan, LT ordered a further 216 cars from Cravens, making up 27 eight-car trains, to replace the F and P stocks on the Uxbridge branch.

Casualties of the electrification of the Metropolitan's Chesham branch were the six compartment coaches dating from 1898–1900 which regularly worked on the branch. Apart from the four which found a new home with the Bluebell Railway, another, No. 519, can be seen at London's Transport Museum. The one which failed to find a new home was No. 513, seen here in the sunshine outside Neasden Depot.

A view of Cravens tube motor coach which, coming only a few months after the entry into service of the first 1959 tube stock train, represented a radical departure in design from what was, appearance-wise, a progression of 1938 tube stock. Double glazing of the passenger saloon windows was among its new features.

The first of the twelve prototype motor-cars originally intended to test concepts for the new Central Line fleet arrived from Cravens in June 1960. After evaluation and testing the first train went into service on Wednesday 9th November. London Transport now intended to use the cars as a test bed for the next generation of tube train. The 1960 tube stock embodied many new features. Each bogie was equipped with two traction motors connected in permanent series, removing the need for an NDM. The motor-cars could couple to any other motor-car of the same type regardless of whether it was A or D end in either direction, a useful feature on the Central Line with the Hainault loop necessitating standard coupling units being kept facing the same direction.

The new cars had three bays on each side each containing two large 'double' windows instead of the usual four. These windows were double glazed. Above these were ventilation apertures. To ventilate the car interiors, passengers pulled down flaps above each window. These flaps contained the Central Line route diagram. The aluminium body panels tapered inwards from waist level on both sides of the cars, and at the front end. The cab had a domed roof containing a destination indicator box. The three eight-car trains created by the twelve new motor-cars offered an interesting contrast in styles. Instead of building twelve new trailers to run with them, twelve standard stock trailers (four built by MCW in 1927, and eight by BRCW and GRCW dating from 1931), were refurbished, including the installation of fluorescent lighting. All were painted silver to closely match the new motor-cars in unpainted aluminium.

This mock-up of the interior of 1960 stock shows how LT designers evaluated both longitudinal and transverse seating. The ventilation flaps carrying the car line diagram can be seen above the large side double-glazed windows.

Four-tracking of the Metropolitan Line between Harrow and Northwood Hills was completed on 11th September 1961; earlier in the year, on 15th January, the rebuilt Northwood station came into partial use. It had been built on a steel and reinforced concrete raft, allowing the four tracks to pass beneath. The new building was not finally completed until 1962. Work continued at the next stop up the line, Moor Park, where a new station building and island platform came into use on 23rd April. The station exterior was clad in cedarwood and had mosaic tiling and plate glass entrance doors. Plastic, aluminium and glass were used in the construction of the ticket office. Use of the new facilities at Moor Park was made possible by the diversion of the track between Northwood and Watford South junction. The whole quadruple tracking programme for the Metropolitan Line was complete by 17th June 1962. Other works on the Metropolitan provided an additional bay platform at Chesham, and new substations at Chalfont and Chorleywood. Platforms were lengthened to take eight-car trains, and some station car parks were enlarged.

In June 1961 the first new train for the Metropolitan main line service in almost thirty years entered service. It was the first of 248 cars of A60 stock, 124 motors and 124 trailers, built (like the 1960 prototype tube stock) by Cravens, to make 31 eight car trains with the aim of displacing the loco-hauled and T stock trains working north of Harrow-on-the-Hill. The profile of the A60 stock, 'A' for Amersham, was very similar to the experimental cars of 1947 described earlier, but exterior panelling was unpainted aluminium. Inside, the seating layout was similar to the final configuration installed on experimental car 17001. All seating was transverse with double seats on one side of the gangway and treble on the other. Motor-cars seated 54 and trailers 58. Luggage racks were fitted. The basic interior colour schemes were grey and maroon. Each axle on the motor-cars was motored. By September 1961, enough A60 stock had been delivered to allow the last of the Metropolitan Vickers electric locomotives, which had been running on the Metropolitan since 1922, to bid farewell. The last ran in passenger service on 9th September, the same day that through services from Baker Street to Aylesbury were withdrawn. After this all Aylesbury trains ran from Marylebone. Following the withdrawal of the electric locos, the A stock began replacing the T stock in use on the Watford service.

Deliveries of the A60 stock gave way to the second order, identical in design but classified A62 stock and comprising 108 motor-cars and 108 trailers. By 15th March sufficient quantities of new A stock had arrived to enable the last of the 1920 F stock trains working on the Uxbridge branch to be withdrawn, leaving just five 4-car trains of F stock on the East London Line. P stock was also being displaced from the Metropolitan by the new trains and, once conversion to PCM control had taken place, these found their way to the District Line allowing a start to be made on the withdrawal of the oldest cars of Q stock. All the A62 stock was in service by 13th December 1963.

Modernisation of the Metropolitan Line north of Harrow-on-the-Hill was completed on 18th June 1962. The whole project had taken four years and cost £4.5 million. For a time slam door trains continued to run on the Metropolitan in the form of the T-stock seen in the photograph of a guard giving the starting signal, but on Friday 5th October 1962 the last one made its final journey to Watford. Two escaped the scrap men to become electric sleet locomotives in LT's works fleet. When they were finally disposed of in 1987 they were purchased for preservation, and today reside at the Spa Valley Railway in Tunbridge Wells. The second photo shows the A stock in service and commemorative trains of T stock at Neasden for the Met Centenary celebrations in 1963.

Early in 1962 LT announced that closed circuit television was to be installed at Holborn to help monitor passenger flows during rush hours. The system was to be a feature of station control on the Victoria Line, and it came into trial use at Holborn in November 1962. Today it is used at every Underground station and depot.

In May 1962 the last unit of 1959 stock entered service on the Central Line preceded on 12th April by the first train of 1962 stock. The new trains were practically identical to the 1959 stock. The motor-cars and NDMs were built by Metro-Cammell, the order having been transferred from Birmingham because the company had asked to be released from its contract. BR built the trailers at its Derby Works. The 1959 NDMs were already numbered in the 1962 series, and were added to their respective units as they were delivered. The arrival of the 1962 stock enabled the 1959 trains to migrate to their rightful home on the Piccadilly Line and the scrapping of standard stock to continue. Delivery continued until June 1964. All 1962 stock was composed of four-car units apart from the last one, a three-car unit (M–T–M) delivered to the Piccadilly in 1964 for use on the Aldwych shuttle service. The 1962 stock, like the 1959 and A stock before it, was made ready for service at Ruislip depot. Replacement of standard stock continued relentlessly, the last example on the Central Line main services running on 20th December 1962. Standard stock on the Central Line was then confined to the shuttle services, the last finally bidding farewell to the line in early 1963.

On 20th August 1962 the Government finally gave its approval to the building of the Victoria Line, at a cost of £56 million. All the years of debate, route planning, trial excavation and tunnelling could now bear fruit. As soon as the go ahead was received, a contract for exploratory work at Oxford Circus was let, with a further seven major engineering contracts coming within the first six months. It was envisaged that forty working sites would be in use, and that fourteen major contracts would be let for the whole project. At the time it was estimated that the Victoria Line would take five and a half years to complete, being fully open in 1968. Work began on 20th September 1962 on the task of rebuilding and enlarging the busy station at Oxford Circus, which was to take the full duration of the whole line building project.

Work on the new line quickly gathered pace. On 12th December tests began with a two-car unit of R stock fitted for Automatic Train Operation (ATO) which was to be an important feature of Victoria Line trains. ATO enabled the train, controlled by an operator, to drive itself, taking instructions from pulses received from the track. The system fitted to the R stock unit (Nos 22681–23580) was in two basic parts, one controlling normal running and braking, and the other, emergency braking. A train running on the ATO principle would 'know' if the line ahead was clear, as well as when to stop, and start, by the coded signals picked up through the track. A stretch of track between Acton Town and South Ealing was used to test the system, which was soon working satisfactorily. On 8th April 1963 trials of ATO in passenger service began on the District Line between Stamford Brook and Ravenscourt Park (eastbound), car 22682 replacing 22681 as the test vehicle.

The London Transport Executive came to the end of the line on 31st December 1962, as did the British Transport Commission. The Transport Act (1962) abolished the Commission and divided its activities between four new Boards reporting directly to the Minister of Transport. One of these was the London Transport Board (LTB), which took over the management of London Transport. Board members were appointed by the Minister of Transport. Chairman of the new Board was Mr A.B.B. Valentine, who had been Chairman of the LTE since 1959, when he had replaced John Elliot. Mr Elliot had succeeded LTE's first Chairman, Lord Latham, in 1953.

Early in 1964, while the infrastructure for the Victoria Line was taking shape, experimentation work on other aspects of the new line's operation was proceeding. One new feature was automated ticket issuing and collection, and some important trials were undertaken to test different types of fare collection methods. As with the first automatic train experiments a year earlier, the western end of the District Line, nearest to the signalling centre, was chosen for the tests. The first was carried out at Ravenscourt Park, Stamford Brook and Chiswick Park, beginning on 5th January 1964 at Stamford Brook. Passengers were issued with a special yellow ticket of the normal size, magnetically coded. The ticket was placed in a slot in a special barrier. In a split second the barrier 'read' the ticket and opened the barrier gate. The ticket could then be retrieved from a slot. LT engineers had designed the equipment, and it was estimated that 30 people could pass through the gate each minute. This first experiment was followed on 15th March by the second stage when a different type of entry gate, designed by the American Advanced Data System Corporation was put on trial at Chiswick Park. It was a four-door gate controlled by light beams. The first two gates opened when a valid ticket was placed in the slot. Would-be passengers stepped on a pressure pad breaking a beam of light, which closed the first two gates and opened the second two allowing the passenger through. The advantage of this system was that, providing the correct number of valid tickets were inserted, several passengers could pass through the gates before they closed. In April the third gate experiments began at Ravenscourt Park. Here a tripod, or milk-stool, gate was installed, working on the same inward principle as the other experiments.

The contract to build the Victoria Line train fleet was placed on 10th March 1964. The £2.25 million order for 244 cars (122 motors and 122 trailers) went to Metro-Cammell. On 5th April the Underground scored another world first when a full-scale service trial of automatic train operation began on the Central Line's Hainault to Woodford branch. The 1960 Cravens tube stock was converted into five 4-car automatic sets (M–T–T–M). The sixth four-car Cravens set, which had been used as a test best for the ATO equipment, was subsequently used as a track recording train. LT intended to operate the Victoria Line with eight-car trains made up of two four-car sets. Later in 1964 experiments were carried out with driver public address on a 1960 stock train.

One of the first major engineering tasks of the Victoria Line project took place over the 1963 August Bank Holiday. This was the erection of a huge steel umbrella over the busy Oxford Circus road junction to enable the reconstruction of the station below, including the building of a new ticket hall, without disrupting the flow of one of London's busiest thoroughfares. During a 65 hour period, 245 steel sections were slotted together to create the umbrella which weighed almost 700 tons. The structure, which increased the height of the road by 3ft 6ins, had to be strong and durable as it needed to withstand constant use for more than three years. By the end of 1963 there were over thirty construction sites in use.

The automatic train principle was similar to that already tried on the District Line. Upon the train operator pressing two 'start' buttons, the train would move off, accelerating to normal speed until it reached either the next station or a signal at danger. It would then come to a halt. The system ensures that if something happened to the train operator the train would, at least, reach the next station. It was all controlled by two separate systems, one for signalling and the other the automatic driving command. Both systems were worked by electric currents offering codes through the running rails which 'told' the train what to do. Any break in the coded instruction caused the train to brake and come to a halt. Six insulated relay rooms were installed at stations along the Hainault to Woodford line. The system was thoroughly tested and closely monitored before LT was able to decide on how best to adopt ATO on the Victoria Line.

During 1964 a start was made on giving the painted R stock a silver white livery to help staff distinguish it from the CP stock which was now running on the District Line and which retained the traditional red livery. A white painted R-stock train heads east towards Upminster. The off-white livery did little to enhance the appearance of these graceful trains, but it was closer in appearance to the unpainted units of R-stock than the red originally carried. Behind it can be seen one of the Underground's electrical substations.

While the Victoria Line dominated activity on the Underground in the mid-1960s other things were happening too. In March 1964 LT announced plans to relocate Tower Hill station, further east. On the other side of the City work was well advanced on redeveloping the Barbican site, roughly the area between Moorgate and Aldersgate (Barbican) stations. The whole area had suffered badly from bombing during the war and a huge regeneration scheme to include high level housing, shops and entertainment facilities was planned. This was to have an effect on the Circle and Metropolitan lines for between spring 1964 and December 1966 the existing railway, including the City 'Widened' lines used by BR suburban trains, had to be moved and 'straightened'. Much of this stretch had been in the open, but it was now covered over. To cushion the noise from the new buildings to be built overhead, a technique was used whereby more than 1,000 concrete beams resting upon rubber blocks formed the track bed in an attempt to cushion vibration. The £2.5 million scheme was funded by the Corporation of London. At the end of 1964 work was under way on the £1 million modernisation of London Bridge station, including the installation of escalators to replace the lifts.

Rationalisation of the District Line's Q stock took place in 1964, including the scrapping of the ex-Q23 motor-cars which had been running as trailers since 1959. Q stock on the East London Line, which had replaced F stock just over a year before, was replaced by six-car trains of CP stock on 12th October. This too turned out to be a short-lived arrangement. New Cross depot could not accommodate the required number of six-car trains and this resulted in a reduction in peak hour service. The six-car trains were also longer than some of the East London Line platforms, necessitating the disabling of end doors at Wapping and Rotherhithe. On 17th May 1965 everything was back to normal when four-car Q stock trains returned to the line. A timetable change from 10th October 1964 allowed for the withdrawal of the District Line's peak hour service to Hounslow. The stabling of District trains at Northfields depot ceased as well as Piccadilly Line trains at Ealing Common.

After 3rd October 1964 the Northern City Line service was withdrawn permanently between Drayton Park and Finsbury Park and replaced by a bus service which ran until the Victoria Line opened. This was so engineers could begin work on incorporating sections of the tunnels into the Victoria and Piccadilly lines to give easy cross-platform interchange between the two at Finsbury Park. At the same time the older standard stock which had been used in two and six-car formations on the line since 1939 was replaced by newer 1931/34 stock from the Piccadilly to form seven four-car trains. Some of the displaced standard stock, with other examples withdrawn from the Piccadilly Line, was made ready for a new lease of life on the Isle of Wight where, working for BR, they ran for over 20 more years.

By early 1965 the first stage of a £12 million modernisation for the giant Lots Road power station was nearing completion. It was part of a total overhaul of power supply and distribution for the Underground, which included work at substations across the system. The power station at Lots Road continued to supply electricity for London's Underground until 2002. Since then power has been taken from the National Grid, and the listed building at Lots Road has been put to other uses.

From 14th June 1965 the Bakerloo service from Queen's Park to Watford Junction was reduced to peak hours only. This came at a time when there was much debate over new Underground links following a study by the Passenger Transport Planning Committee for London, a joint committee involving LT and BR. Three main proposals, shown in the map below, emerged from the study. The Committee believed these projects would help relieve crowded sections of the Underground and suburban railways, especially in the Waterloo and south east London areas. The Committee also recommended that consideration be given to an Underground link with Heathrow Airport, the first stage of which opened ten years later.

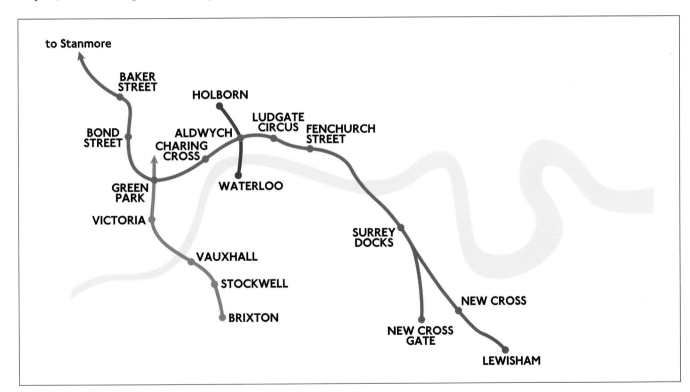

Construction of the Victoria Line had been progressing steadily during 1965 and by the end of the year all the major civil engineering contracts had been placed. Work was in progress at every location on the line map. Civil engineering work for the new Northumberland Park depot was completed. At most key stations on the route the excavation of escalator shafts, concourse tunnels and low level passageways was well under way.

In March 1966 the Government gave approval for the extension of the Victoria Line to Brixton, with intermediate stations at Vauxhall and Stockwell. This enabled LT to begin preparatory work and purchase components like tunnel segments at a time when bulk orders were being made for similar components and equipment. Full powers for the Brixton extension were granted on 4th August 1967. A further 12 trains of 1967 stock were ordered from Metro-Cammell for use on the extended line.

Proposals by the Passenger Transport Planning Committee for London for the Fleet Line and for extensions to the Aldwych shuttle of the Piccadilly and the Victoria Line to Brixton.

The automated ticketing experiments which began in 1964 continued into 1966. A new ticket office opened at Hammersmith (District and Piccadilly) station in July. It had been designed to have ticket windows on either side of the gates, although the gates were not finally installed until mid-1967. When the gates were in position they assured that passengers who had travelled past their intended destination could not leave the railway without paying an excess fare. Upon paying an excess fare, they received a ticket to activate the 'exit' gate. In fact, during the first three days the exit gates were operational 4,000 excess fare tickets were issued. Other features at Hammersmith included a machine which issued a multitude of different tickets. It had been designed by London Transport and could issue specially coded tickets for twenty different fare values, giving change in the process. A bank note change machine was also installed. It dispensed 2 shilling (10p) pieces in exchange for £1 and 10 shilling (50p) notes. All ticket machines at Hammersmith had been adapted to accept 2 shilling pieces. All these innovations made Hammersmith the first Underground station with fully automated ticketing issuing.

Automatic fare collection was to transform ticketing over the next 25 years. In place of (in most cases) a single ticket collector, banks of automatic barriers almost eliminated the queues that sometimes occurred on exit and fraudulent travel was reduced. After its full-scale introduction on the Victoria Line it was not until the late 1980s that a system-wide automatic fare collection began to be put in place.

The Northern City Line received a fleet of 'new' trains from 3rd November 1966. Service cuts had released sufficient 1938 stock trains from the Northern, Piccadilly and Bakerloo lines to replace the last standard stock trains still running on LT metals. The last four-car standard stock train ran on the Northern City during the morning peak on 3rd November. All that now remained of this once huge fleet were the remaining converted trailers on the Bakerloo, the last of these surviving until 1973, and the converted trailers running with the 1935 and 1960 stocks, plus several examples still in use as works trains. The 1935 stock was withdrawn from passenger service on 7th December 1966.

Automatic Fare Collection equipment at the rebuilt Hammersmith ticket hall. The ticket barriers are recognisably the ancestors of today's but the ticket issuing machines have been completely transformed by new technology.

The new Tower Hill station opened for business on 5th February 1967, the old station having closed after the last train passed through in the early hours of the same day. Grey tiling was used to clad the ticket hall and platform walls, giving passengers a foretaste of what was to come at the new Victoria Line stations. The new Tower Hill was not completely finished, as work then had to begin on diverting the existing westbound line. This would serve a new outer platform in the new station and then continue westwards through the space occupied by the westbound platform of the old Tower Hill station, as this lay directly in its path. The middle platform at the new station, which served as a temporary westbound platform while the work continued, could then be used to reverse the peak hour trains which formerly terminated at Mansion House and do much to relieve peak hour congestion at Tower Hill. This aspect of the work was finally completed in January 1968. The new station also afforded a more convenient interchange with Fenchurch Street BR station.

An idea that thankfully did not catch on was fibreglass seating, tried out on Circle Line car 014082 in 1967. Passengers were asked what they thought, and the fact that more than 30 years later trains are still fitted with fabric covered cushion seating may give a clue to the response. Glass fibre was however used in the seating for the new trains built for the Victoria Line, but only for the armrests. The first new train was delivered on 27th September 1967 and resembled the 1960 tube stock, but with the modifications first seen in the cab end mock-up of 1965. Side windows were double-glazed, ventilation being provided by pull-down panels above each window. The panel held the car line map. The exterior panelling contained the legend UNDERGROUND instead of LONDON TRANSPORT. The motor-cars seated 40, sixteen on transverse seating, whereas the trailers, with only longitudinal seating, seated 36. The interior colour scheme was basically grey, relieved only by a dark-red cab connecting door. Seat moquette was a mixture of black, grey and red. The sliding doors had their windows extending into the curved section at the top, to give standing passengers a clear view of the station names, an idea first tried out on 1938 stock car 10306 in 1950. Illuminated advertisement panels were fitted. The trains were fully equipped for ATO, which was similar in principle to that under experimentation on the Central Line's Hainault branch. Coils, which received the coded signals needed to drive and stop the train, were fitted to the front bogie of each motor car. The trains could be driven manually, but at reduced speed, if required, so the train operators had to be qualified for driving normal tube stock. By the end of the year the original 1967 tube stock order for 224 cars had been augmented by a further 72 to take account of the requirements of the Brixton extension, the first quarter mile tunnelling for which had been completed by the end of 1967.

One event at the end of 1967 was to have far reaching consequences for the Underground and the whole of London Transport. On 15th December the Government announced that the Greater London Council (GLC) would be assuming control of LT by virtue of becoming the statutory transport planning authority for London, with powers to appoint members of a London Transport Executive (LTE). The GLC would control policy and finance without being involved in day-to-day operation, which would be the responsibility of the new LTE. This brought back a level of control between London Transport and the Government, absent since 1st January 1963 when the London Transport Board had been set up, reporting directly to the Minister of Transport.

The post-war era witnessed the gradual decline of the steam locomotive on Britain's railways. It may, therefore, have come as a surprise to many that, following withdrawal of the last steam locomotive on British Railways in 1968, one of the few places they could still be seen at work, especially during the small hours, was the London Underground. They were used principally within Neasden depot and on permanent way duties around the system. On 4th June 1971 the last steam hauled train loaded with waste materials left Lillie Bridge depot at 00:15 and trundled to Neasden. It was hauled by an ex-GWR pannier tank engine purchased by LT in 1961 and numbered L90. A special commemorative run took place on Sunday 6th June when loco L94 hauled a special train on a return trip to Moorgate from Neasden where a special depot event was held. Several years before the final curtain fell, former GWR 0-6-0 Pannier Tank locomotive No. L93 steams its way through Stamford Brook station carrying out the purpose for which it was purchased from British Railways by LT in October 1958.

Another event to affect the Underground took place early in 1968, when the Lots Road power station ceased generating power at 33⅓ cycles per second, and switched to a 50 c.p.s current system using oil fired burners and new high capacity turbines. This was the standard throughout the country, but Lots Road had been using the 33⅓ system since it opened in 1905. The conversion enabled LT to close the former Metropolitan Railway Generating Station at Neasden which, when it finally closed in the early hours of 21st July 1968, was the last power station in the country still to be generating at 33⅓ c.p.s. After Neasden's closure power for the Underground came from Lots Road and the former LCC Tramway power station at Greenwich. Neasden's wooden cooling towers, which had dominated the local skyline, were demolished during August. The power station, except for two chimneys, had been completely demolished by the end of 1968.

The first train of 1967 stock went into trial service on the Hainault–Woodford section of the Central Line on 21st February 1968. It was intended that each new four-car unit would be tried out on this line before being transferred to Northumberland Park depot in readiness for the opening of the Victoria Line later in the year. The arrangement whereby some 1967 stock worked on the Hainault–Woodford branch continued until May 1984. New stock for other lines was on order during 1968. In May LT announced a £3.5 million order with Metro-Cammell for 212 new cars for the Hammersmith & City and Circle lines. The new trains would ultimately replace the aged Q stock by enabling the transfer of the CO/CP stock to the District. It was intended to retain Q38 stock on the East London Line.

Over Easter 1968 (12th–15th April), the Oxford Circus umbrella bridge was dismantled and removed. The station was closed to all except interchange passengers over that weekend. On 28th June the Government approved plans to add a new station at Pimlico to the already agreed Brixton extension. A study by LT had concluded that the station would generate considerable benefit by reducing road traffic in the area.

Twenty-five years after it was first mooted, and six since it finally received Government authority, the first stage of the £90 million Victoria Line opened on Sunday 1st September 1968 without, it seems, any form of official ceremony. The first stage was the 5½ mile section from Walthamstow Central to Highbury & Islington. The whole line was under ground. At Walthamstow Central, where the British Rail station formed the surface building to the new Victoria Line terminus, the line terminated in two separate deep-level platforms, linked to the BR platforms by two escalators and then by stairway to the ticket hall and to a new Bus Station. All the platforms on the Victoria Line were designed and built to the same basic

The first unit of 1967 tube stock is seen at Woodford station when new, while making a test run on the Central Line's Woodford–Hainault loop.

pattern, the only distinguishing feature for each station being a tiled motif set into the recess wall behind the platform seating. Wall tiling on both platform and trackside walls was grey, broken on the platform side by the station name frieze which was in the new Victoria Line identity pale blue colour. The general feeling of the line was of an efficient but somewhat clinical environment.

From Walthamstow Central, the new line proceeded to the new Blackhorse Road station situated on the opposite side of Blackhorse Road to the BR station. No physical interchange existed between the two. The spacious new ticket hall, designed by LT's own architects, was one of the few notable public surface buildings to be constructed for the Victoria Line. On its external wall a motif of a black horse, in fibre glass and cast iron backed with blue mosaic, brought relief to the otherwise glass dominated box-like structure.

At Tottenham Hale the line interchanged with the BR (Eastern Region) services to Bishops Stortford and Cambridge. The interchange was facilitated by two escalators. Between Tottenham Hale and the next station, Seven Sisters, the tracks from the new Northumberland Park depot joined the line. The depot was sited to the east of the BR line, over a mile from the junction with the actual Victoria Line. The main depot building was 900 feet long and could accommodate 22 eight-car trains. There was also a maintenance depot with nine inspection pits, an administration block and a workshop where major maintenance work was carried out.

Seven Sisters was a terminus station for short working trains from the south, and a third platform was provided for trains reversing or going into the depot. Seven Sisters also provided another interchange with BR Eastern Region services. Sub-surface ticket halls were built at both ends of the station, both linked to the platforms by escalators. Almost two miles further on at Finsbury Park, yet another connection with Eastern Region was made, but more importantly there was direct cross-platform interchange with the Piccadilly Line made possible by use of the former Northern City Line platforms.

Controlling train movement on the new line was a £70 million control centre at Cobourg Street, Euston. It was designed so it could be expanded to provide centralised control for the Northern Line as well. A Traffic Controller and Train Regulators monitored the service. A large illuminated diagram of the whole Victoria Line route showed the regulators the position of trains on the line. They could also view any platform by means of a CCTV network, make announcements to passengers, and they could speak to any Victoria Line train driver by means of carrier-wave telephones. Northern Line control was 'plugged in' to Cobourg Street, a project completed during the early 1970s.

Stage One of the Victoria Line opened from Walthamstow as far as Highbury in September 1968. The headlights of the 1967-stock train reflect on the bare walls of Seven Sisters station soon after opening.

On 7th March 1969, Her Majesty the Queen opened the section of the Victoria Line between Warren Street and Victoria with a small ceremony at her local station, Green Park.

The second stage of the new line opened on Sunday 1st December 1968. This was the two and a half-mile section from Highbury & Islington to Warren Street, with intermediate stations at King's Cross and Euston. At King's Cross the Victoria Line interchanged with the Northern and Piccadilly lines, but there was no same level interchange with either. Two new escalators connected the much enlarged Northern and Piccadilly ticket hall with a new concourse and the new Victoria Line platforms. A subway and staircase at concourse level connected the new line with the Northern and Piccadilly Line concourse.

At Euston, as with King's Cross, the new line provided BR passengers arriving at this important terminus with another tube alternative to the busy Northern Line branches. Here a complex tunnelling operation had been necessary, as it was the intention to provide a cross-platform interchange between the Victoria Line and the Northern Line Bank branch. As a result three new platforms were required because the existing Bank branch platform was of the original CSLR island type and could only therefore be used in one direction. It became southbound only with the northbound tracks being filled in to create a wider southbound platform. A new southbound Victoria Line platform was built adjacent to it to allow cross platform interchange. Two new northbound platforms, one for the northbound Victoria Line and the other for the Northern Line Bank branch were constructed, with cross-platform interchange between them. The rebuilt Underground station was now fully operational with its new ticket hall and the four pairs of new escalators going to and from the platforms.

Finally at Warren Street there was yet another interchange with the Northern Line, this time with only the Charing Cross branch. It was not an easy interchange as it involved two escalators and a staircase. Warren Street's existing ticket office had been equipped with tripod gates since July 1968, and it was this type, along with the four-door type, that had been adopted for the new stations on the Victoria Line, although not all stations were equipped by the time the line opened. The four-door gates could operate in either direction and could thus be adapted to suit peak time passenger flows. Tripod gates required less space and were useful in ticket halls like Warren Street where space was limited. On the same day, 1st December, Aldersgate & Barbican was renamed Barbican, to reflect the new development which had sprung up around its immediate area.

1969 was the year the Victoria Line reached the station from which it took its name. At 11.00 on Friday 7th March, Her Majesty the Queen officially opened the line, starting the proceedings at Green Park where the Queen entered the cab of car 3052 and pressed the start buttons to move the train off towards Oxford Circus. After touring Oxford Circus station she returned by train to Victoria. Much was made in the media of the difficulty the Queen had at Green Park in purchasing a 6d (2½p) ticket from the automatic machine, which at first rejected the royal coin. At Victoria she unveiled a plaque to commemorate the opening. At 15.00 on the afternoon of 7th March the new section opened to the public. The journey from Victoria to Walthamstow took 24 minutes.

Three new interchanges opened that day. At Oxford Circus, the Victoria Line interchanged with the Central and Bakerloo lines, with same level interchange being afforded with the latter. At Green Park, a passageway provided what was a lengthy interchange with the Piccadilly. At Victoria, the terminus station, two escalators connected the new line with the Circle and District lines, and a further three took passengers up to a large new ticket hall, a short flight of stairs away from the main line station. Beyond Victoria, two sidings that could stable two trains overnight had been built, and beyond that work was continuing on the extension to Brixton. By the end of 1968, 90% of the tunnelling had been completed, and work was under way on the station tunnels at Vauxhall, Stockwell and Brixton. The Greathead shield was used for tunnelling the Brixton extension. Although slower than the drum digger, it was easier to control through the gravel encountered south of the Thames. Much of the gravel was waterlogged, and the work had to be carried out using compressed air. At Vauxhall the sodden ground was frozen with chilled brine to enable the escalator shaft to be excavated.

LT's publicity machine went into overdrive for the opening of the Victoria Line. Posters, leaflets, a commemorative book, a special GPO postmark, a series of films describing its building and even a TV commercial were produced. The commercial was one of the first to feature a technique now commonplace on TV with a slot at the start and end of commercial breaks emphasising the short time it now took to get from Victoria to Oxford Circus by the new line.

Facing page Platform tile patterns on the Victoria Line on opening. The pattern at Oxford Circus was later covered over by a new design.

TILE MOTIFS ON THE VICTORIA LINE

by Julia Black
An adaptation of a William Morris design. He was born and worked for a time in Walthamstow where a museum displays examples of his work.

by Hans Unger
The black horse also appears as a sculpture, by David McFall, on the exterior of the station.

by Edward Bawden
The name is derived from a ferry over the river Lea in earlier times. The word 'hale' is said to be a corruption of 'haul'; or perhaps 'hail'.

by Hans Unger
The seven sisters were seven trees which gave a name to the locality.

by Tom Eckersley
The crossed pistols refer to the duelling that took place here when this was outside the edge of London.

by Edward Bawden
The high bury, manor or castle, was destroyed at the time of the Peasants' Revolt (1381).

by Tom Eckersley
A literal design based on a cross and crowns. The King concerned (if there ever was one) is not identified.

by Tom Eckersley
A reminder of the Doric Arch which stood on the station site.

by Crosby/Fletcher/Forbes
A maze or Warren as a pun on the name. A solution is possible for the traveller with time to spare.

by Hans Unger
A device to incorporate the circle of the circus with the linking of the Bakerloo, Central and Victoria Lines.

by Hans Unger
A bird's eye view of the trees in the park against the green background of the grass.

by Edward Bawden
The great Queen herself, from a silhouette by Benjamin Pearce. A plaque in the ticket hall records the visit of Queen Elizabeth to open the Victoria Line in March 1969.

The downside to 1969 was a lengthy dispute at LT's Acton overhaul works. It began towards the end of September and involved the promotion of semi-skilled workers in posts to which LT were recruiting from outside. The dispute dragged on until a formula acceptable to all sides was found. Work at Acton resumed on 22nd December, but the damage to train maintenance schedules was considerable. The 1938 tube stock was particularly badly affected and services soon began to suffer as a result. Soon the Northern Line was 30 trains below strength out of a normal schedule of 96 peak hour trains. The 'misery line' tag, for so many years the media's pet name for the Northern Line, first appeared about this time, and stuck. Lift and escalator component overhaul was also affected resulting in many machines being temporarily taken out of service.

So ended the 1960s, which had seen the first completely new tube railway in London for more than half a century come into being. Out with the old decade went the London Transport Board, for on 1st January 1970 the GLC took control of a new London Transport Executive, which had an operating area roughly similar to the GLC boundary. LT's country bus services, the bulk of which ran outside the Greater London area now passed to the National Bus Company in the guise of London Country Bus Services Ltd, but the parts of the Underground that ran outside this area, the Central Line east of Woodford, and the Metropolitan Line west of Northwood, remained part of the Underground network.

In April 1970, the first unit of the Hammersmith & City and Circle Line replacement stock, coded C69 (C for Circle) arrived from Metro-Cammell. The car bodies were to a new design, having four sets of double-doors on each side to facilitate quicker boarding and alighting. Windows were double-glazed and the cars were fitted with air-suspension. The seating between each set of double-doors was transverse; longitudinal seating was provided at the car ends. The interior colour scheme was similar to the 1967 tube stock, being predominantly blue/grey. The cars seated 32, and the seats themselves were covered in a blue/green moquette. Illuminated advertisement panels were fitted to the cross-car partitions. The stock was formed of two-car units, motor and trailer, and a typical six-car train was formed M–T+T–M+T–M. The guard occupied the rear cab where the door control equipment was situated. One interesting feature of the new trains was the provision for future conversion to automatic control. The first entered service on 28th September 1970 allowing the gradual displacement of CO/CP trains to the District where a start was then made on withdrawing the Q stock.

New C69 stock train under test at King's Cross early one morning in 1970. The entry into service of these trains indirectly enabled the withdrawal of rolling stock on the District that dated back to the 1920s.

In May 1970 LT unveiled plans for the new Fleet Line. The route was similar to the original plan announced in 1965. It was an ambitious scheme which LT planners believed could trigger development worth £100 million by opening up areas for housing and commercial development, particularly in south-east London. The estimated cost of the line in 1970 was £80–£90 million. At the same time support was growing for an extension of the Piccadilly Line from Hounslow West to Heathrow Airport with an intermediate station at Hatton Cross. The estimated cost of the extension was £19 million. LT asked the GLC for authority to buy 540 new tube cars for the Piccadilly Line. With the extension to Heathrow in mind, the cars would have space for luggage. Later in the year an order for 30 new seven-car trains (210 cars) for the Northern Line was placed with Metro-Cammell. They were to make the first inroads into the huge fleet of 1938 tube stock trains.

In July 1970 the GLC approved the construction of the Heathrow extension, subject to 75% of the necessary funding coming from the Government; the Council would fund the remaining 25%. In the event the Government declined to fund the 75% hoped for, claiming that as the indications were the extension would pay its way, it would be inappropriate to contribute. London Transport therefore secured a loan for the remaining sum, with the intention of repaying it from the revenue earned by the new extension. The Government agreed to contribute 25% in 1972. Excavation work began on the three and a half-mile extension on 28th April 1971, ceremonially begun by Sir Desmond Plummer, Leader of the GLC.

HRH Princess Alexandra officially opened the Brixton extension of the Victoria Line on Friday 23rd July 1971. The Princess unveiled a plaque at Brixton before making a return trip to see the progress being made on Pimlico station, which had started after work on the main extension had begun. The stations on the extension were in the same style as those on the original Victoria Line. Passing through the still being built station at Pimlico, the first stop on the new extension was Vauxhall, where there was an interchange with the BR (Southern) station. The platforms, which were in the same style as others on the Victoria Line, had a motif depicting an ornamental trellis from the Vauxhall Gardens, which had closed in 1859. At the next station, Stockwell, there was interchange with the Northern Line. Here it was even possible to provide cross-platform interchange because the Northern Line platforms at Stockwell had been built outside the running tunnels. The wall motif consisted of blue zigzag lines. The original ticket hall was enlarged and a new escalator installed in readiness for the Victoria Line.

Brixton, the southern terminus, was a modest affair, especially considering that it would have a vital role as a huge railhead for people reaching the tube from a wide area. The ticket hall was reached by steps from the entrance in Brixton Road. Two escalators took passengers to and from the now familiar style platform. Perhaps inspiration had deserted the designers of the station motif. In tile on the platform walls was simply a ton of bricks, a visual pun on the name Brixton. A new tunnel extension further south provided overnight stabling for two trains. During 1970 five new covered sidings had been added to Northumberland Park depot in readiness for the additional trains ordered for the extension to Brixton.

As so often in this narrative a new development is tempered by a farewell, in this case the District Line's Q stock, the last of which ran in passenger service on the evening of Friday 24th September 1971. It had been the intention to retain the Q38 stock to operate in four-car formation on the East London Line, and two such trains had run in service on the line during 1971. However sufficient spare CO/CP stock was found to be available, these working in five-car formation, and the last Q stock train ran on the East London on the morning of 17th September. Fortunately some cars of Q stock were preserved, and one can still be seen at London's Transport Museum. Back on the District, on 4th October 1971, a start was made to standardise train length from six or eight-car to seven-car in order to reduce time-consuming coupling and uncoupling operations which were already affecting service reliability.

By the end of 1971, 969 new tube cars were either being built or on order. In addition to the 210 for the Northern Line, (1972 Mark I stock), a further order for 231 cars of the same type (1972 Mark II stock) had been placed, ultimately for the Fleet Line but initially to work on the Northern. The remaining 528 cars would form 88 six-car trains for the Piccadilly Line to commence delivery in 1973 (1973 tube stock), orders for which were placed with Metro-Cammell in 1971. Their arrival would enable the 1959 stock to transfer to the Northern Line to replace the last of the line's 1938 tube stock. A mock up of the cab and front section of a 1973 stock motor car was built at Acton Works in 1971.

VICTORIA LINE

The picture completed
BRIXTON EXTENSION NOW OPEN

The 1971 extension to Brixton was the first new part of the Underground to open in south London since 1926.

Triumphs and Tragedies

On 14th September 1972 the final piece in the Victoria Line jigsaw fell into place when the new Pimlico station opened. The tiled station entrance led to a sub-surface ticket hall and thence by escalators to the platforms. The tile motif, set into the wall behind the platform seats consisted of yellow dots on a white background, a reflection of the modern art in the nearby Tate Gallery.

In February 1972 work began on building the Fleet Line, the first excavations being in the Trafalgar Square and Strand area. The intention was to use these tunnels as sidings until a decision was reached on the future extension of the line. During the spring contracts were placed for 2¾ miles of tunnel between Baker Street and Strand. In April work began on a reconstruction of Bond Street station with an enlarged ticket hall, a new concourse and the excavation of two new escalator shafts. A 600 tonne steel umbrella was erected at the junction of Oxford Street and Davies Street to enable work on the new ticket hall to be carried out beneath without disrupting road traffic. A scheme to reconstruct Strand station with a large new ticket hall and the provision of three escalators to replace the lifts was approved by the GLC. Eventually it was to link up with Trafalgar Square to create a whole new station complex to be called Charing Cross. During the 1973 Easter Holiday an umbrella bridge was erected across the forecourt of Charing Cross (BR) station to allow for the building of the large ticket hall planned for the new Charing Cross station complex. A further development was the complete closure of Strand station from 17th June 1973 in preparation for the opening of the new Charing Cross station complex, when the intention was to rename the existing Charing Cross station Embankment.

The first of the 1972 (MkI) trains entered service on the Northern Line on 26th June 1972. They were very similar to the 1967 tube stock, except that the three-car unit make-up included an UNDM. The whole 210-car order comprised 90 motor-cars, 90 trailers and 30 UNDMs, and a typical seven-car train consisted of M–T–T–M+UNDM–T–M. The UNDMs used some equipment taken from withdrawn 1938/49 stock UNDMs. The new trains were fitted with guard's control equipment at the end of the motor-car saloon. The new trains arrived at a time when Acton Works was beginning the task of giving heavy overhauls to 238 cars of 1938 tube stock for the reduced Bakerloo service which would operate after the Fleet Line opened. The cars were painted externally in a lighter 'bus' red livery, which was henceforth applied to most red LT rolling stock on overhaul. By the time the last 1972 (MkI) train was delivered to the Northern Line in February 1973, inroads were being made into the 1938 stock, many of which were taken for scrap.

In February 1973 the Ministry of Transport and the GLC set up a London Rail Study to look at the problems facing London's railways before the turn of the century and to make recommendations. The Study published a report the following year, which forecast that over £2 billion would need to be spent during the period on the existing rail network and new services, if London's railways were to play their part in meeting the future needs of the Capital. As far as the Underground was concerned, the report recommended the extension of the Fleet Line from Strand via Fenchurch Street and Docklands, then earmarked for redevelopment, and on to Woolwich and Thamesmead, where a huge new residential development was being built. It also suggested a line from Chelsea to Hackney which, by adding the Wimbledon branch of the District and the Leytonstone to Hainault branch of the Central Line, would create a new south-west–north-east tube line. This idea had been first mooted by LT in January 1970. Among the other proposals was a deep level 'CrossRail' link from east to west to create a line from Shenfield in Essex to Aylesbury/Reading. This would be operated by British Rail. Despite considerable debate and planning over more than twenty-five years, the last two schemes remain so far unbuilt.

In July 1973 a useful link between Ruislip Depot and the Metropolitan and Piccadilly lines between Ruislip and Ickenham was established. It would prove valuable in transferring new stock from Metro-Cammell in Birmingham, which was usually delivered to Ruislip Depot by rail. On 19th November the first train of 1972 (MkII) stock entered service on the Northern Line. The distinguishing feature was the passenger doors, which were painted red, the first splash of colour on train bodywork for more than 15 years. A red 'roundel', the new name for the traditional bullseye, now replaced the UNDERGROUND fleet name. The subtle difference of the 'roundel' was in the thickness of the cross-bar, which was more in proportion with that of the circle. This contrasted with the bullseye, whose crossbar was heavier. Mechanically, the stock was similar to the Mark I version, except that provision was made for possible conversion to ATO. Internally, grey-blue moquette and blue armrests were fitted to the seats, instead of the red and grey scheme found on the Mark I stock. LT subsequently announced its intention to paint all the doors of its silver stock red, but the plan never materialised.

At the end of 1972 work was well advanced on the Piccadilly Line extension to Heathrow. At Hounslow West, a new below-ground island platform was being built by the cut-and-cover method to replace the surface terminus platforms. Island platforms were also provided at Hatton Cross and Heathrow Central and the construction site for the latter had a fairly accurate representation of 1973 tube stock on its hoardings.

An interesting event took place on 13th January 1974, when the CO/CP surface stock on the East London Line was replaced by five 4-car trains of 1938 tube stock from the Bakerloo. At the time the move to tube stock was intended to be permanent because LT announced plans to raise the track height at platforms to reduce the depth between platform and train step. The COP stock was needed to relieve train shortages on the District Line caused by fractured wheel problems. The 'new' East London Line trains carried special car line maps, as well as notices warning passengers to beware of the steeper step to enter the cars.

The first of the 1973 tube stock trains for the Piccadilly Line arrived at West Ruislip from Metro-Cammell on 16th August 1974. The cars were longer than older tube stocks, being 57ft 4ins (motor cars) and 58ft (trailers), against 52ft 9ins and 52ft 5ins for the motor cars and trailers of the 1972 stocks. Externally they resembled the 1967/1972 stocks apart from a slightly different cab profile. The lower section of the cab was painted red, the only relief from the predominant external silver. The cars were formed into six-car trains for operation on the Piccadilly Line, the usual composition being M–T–UNDM+UNDM–T–M. Some units were three-car (M–T–M) with automatic couplers. These units were to ensure suffcient six-car trains were available for service in the event of a three-car unit containing an UNDM requiring maintenance. The stock was built for eventual one-person operation (OPO), but initially a guard's control panel was provided in the driver's cab. The unpainted side panelling continued almost to the top of the roof arch; the roof top panelling was painted white. Internally the colour scheme was as the 1972 MkII stock, except for the cab end wall and saloon cab door which was bright yellow. Some, but not much, provision had been made for luggage as the door screens were repositioned to allow cases to be stood by the doors. As the testing of the new trains progressed, it was discovered that at a handful of locations there was insufficient clearance between the tunnel and the car roof, necessitating a lowering of the track at these places.

Once a passenger had actually entered a London tube train, he or she would expect to be treading on traditional maple wood flooring. But by 1974 maple was becoming expensive and difficult to obtain so LT experimented with some alternatives, including vinyl tiling and even carpet! A 1959 stock car (No.9153) was chosen for the latter experiment, bringing carpet back to the Underground for the first time since the withdrawal of the first class compartments on the Metropolitan back in 1940. The 1974 experiment was not regarded as a success, and the traditional wood flooring was to remain a feature of the London Underground train for the next twenty years.

In 1975 the Underground catered for 601 million passenger journeys. Although this was a reduction of 36 million over the total for 1974, it was still a creditable number, and the fact that in its 112-year history there had been so few mishaps only served to illustrate how generally safe the system was. Fatalities connected with train accidents were, and are, very rare on the Underground. In fact since the formation of London Transport there had been only two notable incidents. At the end of the morning rush hour on 17th May 1938 there was a collision between Charing Cross and Temple stations when a Circle Line train ran into the back of a District train held at a stop signal. Six people died and damage to the wooden carriages was considerable. The cause was a wrongly wired signal circuit, which had given the Circle train a green light to proceed. Just before 7pm on 8th April 1953 an Epping bound Central Line train ran into the back of the preceding train which was stationary in the tunnel between Stratford and Leyton. Trains in the area were being delayed because of a signal failure. Twelve passengers were killed and many others injured, including the driver of the Epping train, who was held largely to blame by the subsequent Public Inquiry for not carrying out strict observance of the 'stop and proceed' rule which had to be applied during signal failures.

The causes of these tragedies were quickly established, but the exact cause of the most serious accident hitherto on the Underground, which occurred at 8.46am on Friday 28th February 1975 at Moorgate on the Northern City Line, remains a mystery. A six-car train of 1938 stock, on entering the terminal dead-end platform simply failed to stop or even slow-down. It ploughed through the sand drag and smashed into the end wall at over 30mph. The first two carriages were completely crushed by the impact and damage to the following one was severe. The driver and 42 passengers were killed, and many more were injured. Rescue of the injured took until late evening of the 28th and the driver's body was not recovered until 4th March. Normal service into Moorgate did not resume until 10th March. The subsequent investigation failed to find any fault with the train, signalling or track. Much attention was focused on the driver, his state of health and mental condition, but no firm conclusions were ever reached and the Moorgate accident remains a mystery to this day. One immediate effect was the implementation of a 10mph speed limit on approaches to terminus platforms, and the alteration of signalling to ensure trains either stopped or proceeded slowly into the platform. The Northern City Line was scheduled for transfer to British Rail and after the last train on Saturday 4th October 1975 it was closed so it could be incorporated in the new Great Northern Electrics service from King's Cross and Moorgate to Hertford North and Welwyn Garden City.

The scene at Moorgate, Northern City Line, following the serious accident on 28th February 1975.

The tunnels are ready and the track is being laid. A scene at Hounslow West during the weekend of 12th/13th July 1975 just prior to the opening of the Piccadilly Line extension to Hatton Cross. The Hounslow West station building can be seen at the top left of this view. On 2nd December 1975, the last 1938 stock train ran on the Piccadilly Line. Its operation on the line had been spasmodic since July 1974, and for a time none were in service. Trips to Hatton Cross did however occur during the stock's last months on the line.

By July 1975 work on the Piccadilly Line Heathrow extension was well advanced. The time had come for the line to be diverted into the new orange and grey tiled sub-surface platforms at Hounslow West station. Over the weekend of 12th/13th July the change was made. Work began on the evening of 11th July, and the new track and signalling was in place by the morning of the 14th. For a few days trains terminating at Hounslow West reversed further on at the yet to be opened Hatton Cross station. This opened officially at 10am on Saturday 19th July, and a train of 1973 stock was used on the inaugural trip. The stock had not entered service by then, so its appearance on that day was strictly a one-off. The new Hatton Cross station was a modern affair with plenty of glass, and grey rough-faced concrete slabs adorning the roofline. Access to the platforms from the large ticket hall was by open staircases. The platform and trackside walls were tiled, beige for the trackside and orange and green for the platform walls, which included a 'Speedbird' motif. The effect was a refreshing change from the predominantly grey schemes of the Victoria Line. The first train of 1973 stock entered regular service on the Piccadilly Line on 18th August, initially in peak hours only. Further on towards Heathrow, all tunnel excavation was complete by the end of 1975, and track laying was well in hand. Similarly the bulk of the civil engineering work on the Fleet Line was complete and, as London Transport's Annual Report for the year was able to confirm, the installation of equipment and station finishes had begun. The flow of new 1973 tube stock to the Piccadilly was such that, by April 1977, over half the number ordered were in service. Sufficient displaced 1959 stock had been transferred to the Northern, a process begun in December 1975, to allow a start to be made on transferring the 1972 Mark II stock from the Northern to the Bakerloo.

Terrorist bomb attacks on the London Underground are unfortunately nothing new. The earliest were in the late Victorian era and involved the Fenians (Irish home rule extremists) who had already bombed several high profile London locations, including Scotland Yard in 1883. The first Underground attack was on 30th October 1883 on an inner circle train near Paddington (Praed Street) which caused extensive damage to that and a passing train and caused 62 injuries; part of the station and signal box was also damaged. Almost simultaneously another bomb went off in the tunnel between Charing Cross and Westminster, but no trains were damaged. The next was on 2nd January 1885 when three trains were damaged by a bomb near Chalton Street Signal Box (near Euston Square) but fortunately injuries were slight. The next bomb was hidden under a seat in a first class carriage and went off on 26th April 1887 near Aldersgate Street causing major damage to the carriage, some damage to the station and ten injuries, two subsequently dying.

Although Irish terrorism then calmed down it resumed with a vengeance as part of a campaign against key British Infrastructure at the start of 1939. In London alone there were over 70 separate attacks, though fortunately only two seriously affected the Underground. On 4th February 1939 two bombs exploded at stations, one at Tottenham Court Road and the other at Leicester Square, in each case being planted in suitcases deposited in the left luggage offices overnight. Both caused severe damage to the premises, and two people were injured, but the main consequence was to unsettle the travelling public.

Terrorist bomb attacks resumed in London in 1971 with an assault on the Post Office Tower and continued sporadically until 2003 with an attack upon Ealing. During 1976 there were two serious ones on the Underground. On 15th March an IRA bomb exploded in a Hammersmith & City Line train just west of West Ham en route to central London. It was still in possession of its owner who, realising what was about to occur, had thrown the bomb down the car and tried to escape through the driver's cab. The driver bravely gave chase, only to be shot dead by the terrorist. The following day a bomb exploded on a Piccadilly Line train reversing during the evening at Wood Green. Fortunately no-one was seriously hurt, but had the bomb exploded later as presumably intended, the train would have been packed with Arsenal supporters going home after an evening game at Highbury. As a security precaution, litter-bins were removed from Underground stations. In 1991 and 1992, in separate incidents, incendiary devices were found under seats in stabled trains at Hammersmith, Neasden (twice) London Road and Barking Depots, and a device went off on a train at Harrow-on-the-Hill. In at least one of these incidents all Underground services were briefly suspended towards the end of the morning peak so that all trains could be checked, and subsequently new inspection regimes were instituted. In 1992 there were also several explosions in Underground station car parks, and on the emergency stairs at Hampstead.

Returning to 1976 an order for 11 new 6-car trains of C stock was placed with Metro-Cammell for the Edgware Road to Wimbledon service, and an additional motor-car was included in the order to replace the one destroyed at West Ham. Also during 1976 the GLC approved the purchase of 75 new six-car trains for the District Line to replace the remaining CO/CP and R stocks. Design of the new stock was well advanced by the end of the year. Surface stock returned to the East London Line on 12th June 1977, when A stock from the Metropolitan took over from the 1938 stock. Service reductions on the Metropolitan had made sufficient units of A stock available for the conversion. On 29th July 1977 the first unit of C77 stock arrived from Metro-Cammell. It was virtually identical to the C69 stock apart from deeper anti-scuff rubber panels around interior bulkheads, and exterior white painted roof panels. This was the result of an experiment carried out on two C69 cars (Nos 5567 and 6567) in 1975 to see if in-train temperatures could be reduced. The trailer had also received tinted windows. An extra car was numbered 5585 and had been built to replace the C69 car destroyed in the West Ham bomb incident. This was to be the last C77 delivered, in November 1978. The C77 stock could run with C69 units, and the first entered service on the Hammersmith & City Line on 12th December 1977. Progress towards agreement with the Trade Unions for the operation of the C69/77 stock on the Wimbledon–Edgware Road branch was slow. As a result the first C stock train did not run on the branch until 17th April 1978.

A working site for the station that was to become Charing Cross on the new Jubilee Line, referred to on the site board by its original name of Fleet Line.

The devastating aftermath of the IRA terrorist explosion on a Hammersmith & City Line train at West Ham in March 1976 needs no description after a study of the photograph. The leading car of the train was damaged beyond repair and replaced by a new C stock motor car ordered as part of the C77 stock programme.

THE UNDERGROUND COMES TO HEATHROW AIRPORT

HEATHROW CENTRAL ✈

All the facts about
the Central London · Heathrow Airport
Underground service
scheduled to start December 1977

Tunnelling work for the Fleet Line was completed in 1976. All the new stations on the line provided interchange with the existing system and work progressed on escalator links at Bond Street and Green Park. A major task was under way at Charing Cross where, apart from the Fleet Line platforms and escalator links, the job of uniting the old Strand and Trafalgar Square stations went on in tandem with other work, to provide subway links to both sides of the Strand from the large new ticket hall. As Bakerloo Line trains would no longer be able to access Neasden depot once the Fleet Line became a reality, a new depot was constructed at Stonebridge Park on the site of an old British Railways power station.

The first evidence of the new Fleet Line was apparent in January 1977 with the opening of a new ticket hall and escalator shaft at Bond Street on Monday 23rd. It was the first stage of a plan to enlarge the original ticket hall which would eventually form part of a swish new shopping arcade called West One.

1977 was the Silver Jubilee year of Queen Elizabeth II. It was also GLC election year and the Conservative group on the Council proposed in its manifesto that the Fleet Line be renamed Jubilee Line as a commemoration of the event. The Tories won the election so the name change was introduced and was well into the parlance by the time the line eventually opened in 1979.

On 16th December 1977 Her Majesty the Queen formally opened the 1.6-mile, £30 million, extension of the Piccadilly Line from Hatton Cross to Heathrow Central, the name eventually agreed upon for this important terminus. From Hatton Cross the line continued in twin tunnels to the new station. The wide island platform had orange-tiled pillars; behind the seat recesses were Concorde tail fin motifs, designed by the artist Tom Eckersley. Other wall surfaces were tiled in grey and blue. Station names were illuminated. The ticket hall, which was reached by two banks of three escalators, had a Travel Information Office and a computerised machine telling passengers, in English, French or German, the best route to take to reach any other station on the system. It was little used and taken out within a few years. Wide subways equipped with moving walkways connected the ticket hall with the main departure termini, which again afforded under-cover access to and from aircraft. Now it was possible to travel from Toronto to Turnpike Lane without going out into the open air. The ticket hall entrance, adjacent to a large bus station, was a modest affair compared with Hatton Cross because of the limited space. A publicity campaign with the tag line 'Fly the tube' was launched, and by the end of 1978 eight million people, a figure way above LT's original estimate of 1.2 million, had done just that.

By early 1978 all the 1973 stock units had been built, the last two (one fitted with Westinghouse equipment, and the other fitted with GEC equipment) were designed as experimental three-car sets equipped with, among other things, thyristor motor control. These were to test features for incorporation into new trains for the Jubilee Line, the intention being that 1972 Mark II stock would be used on the Jubilee temporarily. The Westinghouse unit moved to the Central Line in February 1979 and began tests on the Hainault–Woodford section, although it did not enter passenger service until July 1983. It remained on the Central Line until June 1985. The GEC unit began tests on the Piccadilly Line in September 1980. The two units were eventually rebuilt with standard equipment and joined the other 1973 stock in passenger service on the Piccadilly Line.

On Friday 14th April 1978 the official 'last' train of 1938 stock ran on the Northern Line, completing almost 40 years continuous service. One of the driving cars on that last train, No.11182, can be seen today in London's Transport Museum at Covent Garden.

No.11182's work on the Northern Line had no doubt taken it almost daily along the 430-yard stretch of southbound tunnel between Golders Green and Hampstead which had been lined with blue asbestos in 1933 as part of an experiment to reduce noise levels. By the late seventies it had been recognised that blue asbestos contained deadly properties, making it essential that this very dangerous material be removed as soon as practicable under strictly controlled conditions. Emergency engineering work to remove the offending material was carried out in the four weeks between 25th June and 23rd July 1978. LT decided to operate trains in both directions through the northbound tunnel, an arrangement made possible only by the crossover north of Hampstead station. The Northern Line service was completely reformed for the duration of the work, and a fleet of special buses was used to augment the much-depleted Edgware branch service.

Mind the gap ma'am. Her Majesty the Queen steps from a 1973 stock train to inaugurate the new Heathrow extension of the Piccadilly Line. She is under the watchful eye of Mr J. Graeme Bruce, then the Chief Operating Manager (Railways) of London Transport.

A new train of 1973 tube stock emerges from the tunnel south of Southgate station.

The wide island platform at Hatton Cross station, opened in July 1975.

One of the last Underground lines to use destination headcode lamps was the District. The closure of signal boxes in the 1960s and 1970s had negated the use of the codes that had been a feature of the Underground since the early days. On 1st January 1978 the practice of displaying headcodes on the District ceased.

In July 1978 the GLC had approved LT's recommendation that tenders be sought for the design of a new ticket issuing and collection system for the Underground. Ticket fraud was estimated to be costing LT several million pounds each year in unpaid fares. During 1979 work continued on developing a new ticket and collection system. Years of experimentation had failed to produce a workable system which embraced both the automatic issue, and checking of the millions of tickets issued annually by LT. Authorisation by the GLC of the expenditure of £10 million towards developing the new system, enabled contracts to be placed with Westinghouse Cubic Ltd for the detailed development of the new £86 million system, which included designing new ticket gates, ticket issuing machines and automated ticket offices.

On 18th August test trains began running through the new Jubilee Line tunnels and in April 1979 the new Stonebridge Park depot came into use in readiness for the opening of the Jubilee Line, after which Bakerloo trains would have no ready access to Neasden depot. On 24th April the last 1972 Mark II train was transferred away from the Northern Line destined for Jubilee Line service. All was then ready for the official opening by the Prince of Wales, which took place on the morning of 30th April. The line was not opened to the public until the following morning. On the night of 30th April a mixture of 1938 and 1972 Mark II stocks which had been running on both Bakerloo Line branches was portioned out between the Bakerloo (1938 stock) and Jubilee (1972 Mark II stock). The new line took over the Bakerloo Stanmore branch and in the preceding weeks new track-plate maps, station and other signage bearing the silver-grey Jubilee Line legend had appeared along the route.

At Baker Street the Jubilee Line served a new northbound platform, but took over the southbound Stanmore branch platform. Previously all northbound Bakerloo trains had served the same platform (now served just by Bakerloo trains) regardless of their destination. The new platform walls were decorated with scenes from famous Sherlock Holmes adventures, designed by the artist Robert Jacques. Platform tiling was a poppy red, complemented by yellow panelling, with the station name on a silver-grey frieze. Platform station name roundels were illuminated. Broad bands of yellow roof vault panelling highlighted the location of the exit subways, a feature to be found on all new Jubilee Line platforms.

From Baker Street the line proceeded through new tunnels to Bond Street and interchange with the Central Line. The platforms here were decorated in dark blue tiling, incorporating a colourful hatbox motif by the artist Tom Eckersley. The new platforms at Bond Street were linked to the Central Line by new subways and escalators.

More colourful than the Victoria Line platforms of 10 years earlier, tile patterns behind the seats was an idea carried over at Bond Street and Green Park on the Jubilee Line. Green Park is shown at the time of opening.

TICKETS ↑

A view of the colourful ticket hall at Charing Cross built for the Northern and Jubilee lines. It was still easier to reach the Bakerloo Line via the Trafalgar Square entrance and ticket hall which was refurbished in 1983. The view, taken some years after the ticket hall opened, shows the automatic entry/exit ticket gates of the UTS Programme in operation.

The next station was Green Park, where the Jubilee Line interchanged with the Piccadilly and Victoria lines. Two banks of two escalators, separated by an intermediate landing, led down to the new platforms. The passageway and platforms were clad in orange tiles, bearing a motif of falling leaves, by the artist June Frazer. Interchange with the Victoria Line was by way of passageways and stairs, but to change onto the Piccadilly, a Jubilee Line passenger faced the prospect of going up to the ticket hall and down the escalators to the Piccadilly Line platforms. They would do so until a new interchange opened in April 2000.

The terminus for the new line was Charing Cross. The crossover was to the west of the new platforms, which were decorated in lime green tiles. Murals, by the artist David Gentleman, depicting different aspects of Nelson's Column adorned the platform walls. David Gentleman also designed the refurbished Strand Northern Line platforms, which reopened on 1st May 1979 as part of the Charing Cross complex. The stunning black and white murals, which ran the length of both Northern Line platforms and depicted medieval workers constructing the Eleanor Cross, were produced on special laminated panelling. The neighbouring Underground station that had been named Charing Cross until 1974 and then Charing Cross (Embankment) was renamed Embankment on the same day.

The spacious new ticket hall at Charing Cross was reached by subways from both sides of the Strand. It was finished and green, blue and black tiling and moulded plastic panelling. New banks of escalators led to the Northern and Bakerloo lines and another bank led down to the Jubilee. The old Bakerloo Trafalgar Square ticket hall was retained as part of the new complex and new subways linked the Northern and Bakerloo lines. This was only the first stage of the new Jubilee Line. The new tunnels had been driven some distance further east beneath the Strand in anticipation of the eastward extension. In its 1979 Annual Report, London Transport updated readers on progress for the eastward extension of the line. It reported that the GLC had agreed that lower cost alternatives to the full scheme for extending the Jubilee Line eastwards from Charing Cross to Docklands should be considered. One of these was a Light Rail system. LT was still anticipating that the Jubilee Line would head into south-east London, and continued to press for powers to extend the line via Fenchurch Street to Woolwich Arsenal and Thamesmead. As part of the original scheme, work began early in 1980 on the modernisation of the Bakerloo Line platforms and subways at Baker Street. These were to have new tiling, continuing the Sherlock Holmes theme already evident on the new northbound Jubilee Line platform. Work continued on modernising the Central Line ticket hall and escalators at Bond Street, the latter being completed during 1980.

Various attempts have been made to provide a satisfactory system that would allow passengers to open air-operated doors themselves. This was first attempted in 1936 when two new trains of Hammersmith & City M stock were delivered with air doors upon which were fitted push button switches; by pressing the switch the associated door or doors only would open, though under the overriding control of the guard. Being judged a success it was decided to equip all new and many existing trains and during 1938 this system came into use on the Northern and Central Lines. Unfortunately technical difficulties came to light and the system was withdrawn from January 1939.

After the war a modified system was introduced on the Central Line from October 1948 and most Underground trains were modified with it by 1956. There was never a time when all Underground trains were equipped and this must have caused some degree of confusion. PDC was abruptly abandoned in March 1959, reintroduced with the D stock and abandoned again – after first spreading to some other lines – in the late 1990s. Many trains still run with the button in place and passengers press them to no effect.

The first new District Line train for twenty years arrived from Metro-Cammell on 29th June 1979. The order for the new stock comprised 20 three-car double-ended units (M–T–M), and 130 three-car units comprising M–T–UNDM, the whole making up 75 six-car trains. The D stock, as the new trains were coded, differed from previous surface stock in many respects. The most obvious break with tradition was that access to the cars was by 3ft 6ins single-leaf push-button doors, each car having four doors per side. This, it was thought, would speed boarding and alighting. It certainly reduced the amount of door operating equipment required per car, thereby assisting overall reliability. The interior design was a departure too with flecked cream and orange melamine panelling predominating. Doors were painted orange. Seating was covered in yellow/black/orange moquette. The trailers and UNDMs seated 48, the motor-cars 44. The guard's position was in the rearmost driving cab. The cars were 60ft long, about 8ft longer than a car of R stock. The first D stock train entered passenger service on 28th January 1980. The preceding three weeks had been spent displaying the new train to District Line customers at various stations up and down the line. Local blind and disability organisations were particularly interested in the push-button doors. An extensive publicity campaign was launched to educate passengers on this important feature.

Sufficient new D stock units had been delivered by March 1981 to enable the last of the CO/CP stock to be withdrawn. On Tuesday 31st March, after almost 44 years service, the last train of the stock made its final trip. Two trains of CO/CP stock were running on the last day, and the last one arrived back at Ealing Common at 20.45. It was now the turn of the remaining R stock trains to be withdrawn as D stock delivery continued.

In October 1978 London Transport appointed its first woman train driver. Mrs Hannah Dadds receives the attention of the press by the cab of her District Line train.

The last 1959 tube stock train to operate on the main Piccadilly Line service was withdrawn on 5th October 1979, an event followed on 17th October by the replacement of the 1962 stock unit on the Aldwych branch, which went to the Northern.

In March 1980 Shadwell station became the first on the East London Line to have modernisation work completed. The old corrugated iron wall cladding was replaced by cream plastic panelling, and new fluorescent lighting was installed throughout the station. The ticket hall and staircases were also renovated. During the year work continued on other stations on the East London Line. The work was financed by the Government's Inner Cities Partnership, in association with the GLC. Shadwell was to feature in the second stage of the work announced during September 1980, which allowed for a new station building at Surrey Docks, a new ticket hall at Shadwell, the installation of escalators at Rotherhithe and modernised lifts at Wapping.

Another attempt to close the Epping–Ongar branch was made in May 1980. Buckinghamshire and Essex County Councils had refused LT's request to contribute financially to ease the growing deficit incurred in operating the Underground in their respective counties, whereas Hertfordshire had. Buckinghamshire did make provision in its 1981/82 budget, but nothing was forthcoming from Essex, hence LT's decision. Notices were posted announcing that the closure, subject to no objections being received, would take place on 6th October 1980. Not surprisingly objections were received, so the closure went to Public Inquiry. In March 1981 the Transport Secretary refused to grant LT permission to close the line, but did agree to the closure of the little-used Blake Hall station.

In line with the policy of the newly elected Labour GLC, fares on London's buses and the Underground were reduced by up to 25% from Sunday 4th October 1981 under the banner Fares Fair. For the first time a zonal fare structure was introduced on the Underground, initially in the central area, roughly the area bounded by the Circle Line plus some key stations like Waterloo and London Bridge. This area was divided into two over-lapping zones with 17 stations in both zones. Fares in this area ranged from 20p for travel in one zone to 30p for both, but there was also a 20p fare across the zone boundary. Outside the zones fares generally reduced by up to 40p. The £120 million per annum cost of all this was borne by London's ratepayers. For tube travellers outside the GLC area there was a 12% fares hike. But within a few weeks this bold scheme was scrapped following a Law Lords ruling that the GLC had acted illegally in reducing fare levels and forcing ratepayers to foot the bill. The matter had angered some south London borough councils, particularly those devoid of any Underground service within their boundaries, such as Bromley, whose residents relied largely on British Rail for commuting into central London. The GLC was given leave to appeal, which it did successfully, but the Law Lords upheld Bromley's objections, and on 17th December it was announced that the end had come for Fares Fair. The reality of the situation hit home on 21st March 1982 when fares rose by as much as 96% over 'Fares Fair' levels. A lot of bitterness surrounded this move. Soon the Underground was carrying 13% fewer passengers and road congestion, which had noticeably diminished during the Fares Fair period, increased once more. Apart from raising fares, LT announced that the Epping–Ongar, Aldwych–Holborn and Shoreditch–Whitechapel branches faced closure, along with some lesser-used stations like Edgware Road (Bakerloo), Fairlop and Regents Park.

Despite the threats of closure, the Epping–Ongar branch remained operational, as did the rest of the system, but a piece was technically lopped from it on 18th June when the Bakerloo peak hour service to Watford Junction was withdrawn. It was the first casualty of the service cuts resulting from the ending of cheap fares. In fact new schedules offering reduced services were due to be introduced on most lines from 21st June, but there was fierce Trade Union opposition to them, resulting in widespread industrial action across virtually the whole Underground system, lasting for several days. Eventually London Transport agreed to reintroduce the former schedules, including the Watford Junction Bakerloo journeys, and this settled matters, at least for the moment. However, the end for the Watford Bakerloo service finally came after the morning peak southbound journey on 24th September. Until 4th June 1984 the northern terminus of the Bakerloo in peak hours would be Stonebridge Park. On that date the service was reinstated as far as Harrow and Wealdstone.

On a more positive note, during 1982 London Transport placed an order with Metro-Cammell for 15 new trains for the Jubilee Line, with an option for 13 more. The trains were for delivery during 1983, and would enable the 1972 Mark II trains to be transferred to the Bakerloo, thus releasing for scrap the remaining trains of 1938 stock.

All the fuss over Fares Fare did not matter to the people who lived in the tiny Essex hamlet of Greensted, as their local station, Blake Hall, closed on the evening of 31st October 1981. Just 17 people had been using the station each day. A couple of days before, Epping Forest District Council had offered £20,000 to retain the seven-day service on the Epping–Ongar branch for a further year. LT reluctantly accepted this offer. It had been intended to reduce the service to peak hours only.

In May 1981 a dot-matrix destination indicator was tried out experimentally on the eastbound platform at St James's Park station. In August, a second machine was installed on the westbound platform. This one had a scrolling facility. It was the first of what was to become a common feature of the Underground over the next 20 years.

YES SIR, A BLACK UMBRELLA
HAS BEEN HANDED IN.

Property left on London's public transport goes to the Lost Property office at 200 Baker Street. The nature of the items left on the Underground and road services has changed over the years. At one time the office handled 25,000 umbrellas a year; today they get just 9,000, making them about level with mobile phones. Odder items that have been left include a box of assorted false teeth, a wedding dress, a postman's trolley, a 2½cwt bag of dried fruit, a lawnmower, a stuffed eagle, an outboard motor and a grandfather clock.

In September 1981, the GLC had announced approval of a £60 million ten-year rolling programme to modernise 140 stations, sixteen of them receiving major face-lifts accounting for two-thirds of the overall cost. By the end of that year work had begun on the first four projects, the Bakerloo ticket hall at Charing Cross, and the Central Line escalators and platforms at Tottenham Court Road, Oxford Circus and Bond Street. The modernised Bakerloo ticket hall at Charing Cross reopened on 13th December 1983. The platforms were unveiled at the same time. They had been modernised with murals comprising sections of paintings from the nearby National and National Portrait Galleries. One of the most striking was a scene from Henri Rousseau's 'Tropical Storm With Tiger'.

Expansion at Heathrow necessitated the building of a fourth terminal on the south side of the airport, and planning was well advanced by the end of 1979. LT sought powers to extend the Piccadilly Line to serve the new terminal and by the end of 1980 the GLC had agreed with LT's proposal that the best way to serve the new Terminal 4 was by a 'loop' extension of the Piccadilly Line. In July 1982 the Government finally approved a £25 million scheme to extend the Piccadilly Line by way of a single-track loop to the new Terminal 4 at Heathrow.

The first phase of the £10 million development of a new automated ticketing system came into being on 31st October 1982 when prototype equipment, consisting of ticket machines and gates, was introduced at Vauxhall station. The system's main aim was to reduce ticket fraud. It included two types of passenger-operated ticket machine; one called a Tenfare, selling the ten most popular single tickets, and an Allfare, which issued credit card sized single, return and cheap-day return tickets to all Underground stations. Both machines gave change. They were wall-mounted, and staff could service them from within the ticket office, thus removing the need to come out into the ticket hall to empty the machines of cash. The ticket gates were reversible, and could check season tickets as well. It was intended that evaluation of the new system would enable LT to decide on the adoption of a suitable system for the whole Underground. The Vauxhall experiment ran until July 1983, and the experience gained had proved valuable, enabling LT to decide how to take the project forward. A £100 million package was drawn up which included ticket gates for Zone 1 stations, the installation system-wide of automated wall-mounted ticket issuing machines selling a range of tickets, secure ticket offices for staff, and a Penalty Fare system with increased ticket checking on trains. The next stage of the project was to evaluate different ticket issuing equipment. In May 1985 the Transport Secretary approved a £135 million expenditure programme for the new ticketing system in line with the plans set out after the successful Vauxhall trials. At the time it was envisaged that the whole Underground Ticketing System (UTS) project would be complete by 1989. On 22nd May 1983 ticket zones were introduced across the whole Underground within Greater London, to simplify ticket issue. There were five zones 1, 2, 3A, 3B and 3C, the three 'Zone 3s' being regarded as one zone for bus travel, and tickets were priced depending on the number of zones passed through on each journey. The Travelcard, which included availability on LT bus services was introduced with this fare revision, and was an immediate success, far out-stripping the previous point-to-point season ticket sales. In fact the Travelcard became so popular that between April 1986 and April 1987 the Underground catered for 769 million passenger journeys. This was in stark contrast to the doldrum period post-Fares Fare in 1982 when the total was 482 million.

New timetables were introduced on all lines except the Victoria on 6th December 1982. They were designed to reduce off-peak services and match peak hour services more closely to demand. The Epping–Ongar branch was now peak hours only. The service reductions on the Northern Line threw up spare 1959 stock, which was transferred to the Bakerloo Line, enabling some 1938 stock to be withdrawn. Other rolling-stock allocation changes brought about by the service reductions included the allocation of spare 1962 stock to the Northern in seven-car formation. Four 1972 MkII trains also returned to the Northern from the Jubilee following the cuts.

The last link with the pre-war District Line era was severed on 4th March 1983 when the last train of R stock was withdrawn from service. The R stock had had a brief stay of execution while modifications were made to the D stock ventilation equipment, necessitating a return to Metro-Cammell. The last D stock entered service on the District Line on 15th July 1983, the final unit coming complete with the ventilation modifications. The District main line services were now operated with a fleet of trains all the same for the first time in 70 years. Also in 1983 there was extensive renumbering of 1962 tube stock trailers caused by the BR Derby built cars requiring a heavier, lengthier, overhaul than the Metro-Cammell built cars. As a result the trailers that returned to each unit after overhaul were not the original ones from that unit, but they were renumbered into the correct unit sequence.

The first unit of the £35.5 million order for 1983 tube stock for the Jubilee Line arrived at Neasden depot from Metro-Cammell on 27th August. The new stock was formed into three-car units (M–T–M) to make up six-car trains. The cars were 58ft 2ins long, and construction was of aluminium alloy. Apart from the usual end-door arrangement, the new cars had two single-leaf, push-button doors on each side; the driving cabs were the first on tube stock since 1967 not to have wrap-round windows. Inside, the new cars were the tube version of the D stock, with orange doors and panelling. Identical orange/black/yellow seat moquette was fitted. Seating was for 48 and was mainly longitudinal, but there were four transverse seats either side in the centre bay. One new feature was the concealed lighting. The fluorescent tubes were fixed behind frosted covers, which apart from providing the main in-car illumination also illuminated the advertising posters. The driver's cab was state-of-the-art, with a control panel which gave illuminated signals when faults occurred. Destination blinds were changed at the push of a button. There was also public address and train radio, then becoming the norm throughout the Underground fleet.

R stock last ran in passenger service in March 1983, but the flare-sided stock continued in use on the Underground for a time in the shape of Q38 pilot motor cars L126 and L127, seen at Acton Works in July 1983 in the company of engineers' vehicles converted from standard stock and 1903 Central London Railway stock.

1983 stock with 1972 stock far right in the Stanmore sidings of the Jubilee Line.

At Baker Street, the aim was to re-create the atmosphere of the original platforms from 1863. The original ventilation shafts, long since covered over, were fitted with lighting to give a sense of the daylight that would originally have shone down these.

The controversial change to one-person-operation (OPO) of trains on the Underground moved a step closer to resolution in early 1984 when the Trade Unions agreed to a twelve week trial on the Hammersmith & City Line. The experiment, which began on 26th March, was slow to settle down, with much late running. Passengers waiting for long periods on the Hammersmith & City platforms at Baker Street could at least marvel at the latest station modernisation project, unveiled on 10th April. 'Modernisation' is perhaps not the right word; 're-creation' would be better, because the platforms had been restored to their 1863 glory. All the old wall panelling had been removed to reveal the original brickwork which was carefully restored. When the station was built, natural light shone through shafts in the roof, and to recreate the daylight effect the shafts were lined inside with white tile and illuminated from above. The base of the shafts provided a fine location for platform seating and the station name frieze. The conversion of the Circle Line to OPO was implemented on 22nd October 1984 with the District following on 4th November 1985.

The first train of 1983 tube stock entered service on Tuesday 1st May 1984, but only to convey special guests to a celebration of the Jubilee Line's fifth birthday. The following day the train did the same for the media, although fare-paying passengers were allowed to ride on it later. Regular entry into service of the stock came on 8th May. In a way this event was historic because the 1983 stock was to end a 30-year tradition of unpainted trains on the Underground. Already design options were on the drawing board for a new fleet of trains for the Central Line, and orders had been placed for three prototypes, two from Metro-Cammell and the third from BR at Derby. The new trains were to be the first of the next generation of tube cars and they were being built to test some radical new construction and mechanical features, including the use of externally painted panelling, a feature not seen on a new tube train since the 1949 stock. The trains had been designed by David Carter Associates, and were due for delivery in 1986.

1986 was also the Government's target year for the dissolution of the Greater London Council. A right-wing Conservative government and a left-wing Labour-run GLC could hardly be a marriage made in Heaven, and since the Fares Fare debacle relations between the Palace of Westminster and County Hall had been far from harmonious. The Government planned to hand over most of the functions necessary to run London to the individual borough councils, but transport was a different matter, and the Government was anxious to wrest control of London Transport from the GLC before the 1986 dissolution. The Government believed that private enterprise should be given an opportunity to participate in providing services to public transport, particularly on the buses. To this end it introduced new legislation in the form of the London Regional Transport Act, which received Royal Assent on 26th June 1984. The LRT Act created a Corporation, London Regional Transport, which in turn was charged with setting-up wholly owned subsidiaries to run the various elements of London's public transport, including the Underground. Little time was wasted in

The 1980s' retiling of Piccadilly Circus has its admirers, though it is felt in official circles today to be rather too busy looking. Some other 1980s' schemes that were deemed less successful have already been updated with much simpler, and easier to repair, tiling.

bringing in the new order, for at midnight on 29th June 1984 London Regional Transport replaced the London Transport Executive in name only, but with a new reporting line to the Transport Minister. There then followed a period of several months when LRT was directly responsible for the operation of the Underground and the buses, while the new subsidiaries were being set up. On Monday 1st April 1985, LRT's new subsidiaries came into being. London Underground Limited started life with an issued share capital of £430 million. Out of all the new subsidiaries London Underground Limited (LUL) was probably the least affected by the change. The new bus subsidiary, London Buses Limited, soon found itself in the forefront of competition under the new rules for bus route tendering. LUL had its own management structure under Chairman and Managing Director, Dr Tony Ridley. LRT became an overall planning body which, among other things set fare levels.

The process of modernising and redecorating the principal stations on the network continued with work at Leicester Square, Holborn, Piccadilly Circus, Paddington and Finsbury Park beginning during 1984. Work was also under way on the Oxford Circus Bakerloo Line platforms where, in common with the situation at other sites, the contractor's materials were stored in a hoarded-off cross-passageway. On the evening of 23rd November a fire broke out in this area, gutting the northbound Victoria Line platform, and its associated cross-passageways with the Bakerloo Line. Many passengers were taken to hospital with smoke inhalation. The Victoria Line was suspended between Warren Street and Victoria until 17th December. The cause was thought to have been a discarded cigarette end or match, and a ban on smoking which had been introduced on trains on 9th July 1984 was extended, from 17th February 1985, to cover platforms, subways and booking halls of stations which were all or partly below ground.

The face of some of the busiest stations on the Underground was changing radically by the mid-1980s. By the summer of 1985 the Northern and Piccadilly Line platforms at Leicester Square were almost complete. The theme here was filmstrips with sprocket holes, black for the Northern, blue for the Piccadilly, all on a white tile background. Only the platforms at Leicester Square were redecorated, so as soon as the exit passageways were entered it was back to the traditional 1930s cream and blue tile. Thus Leicester Square was one of the most disappointing redecorations of the whole scheme, and a poor contrast to neighbouring Piccadilly Circus where swirls of green, red and blue tiling on an oatmeal tile background were used throughout the station below escalator level. At Shepherd's Bush the platform walls were clad in green square tiles; green and the countryside being the theme here. Ceilings and roof vaults were painted a speckled blue to represent a summer sky. At Finsbury Park, hot-air balloons in mosaic graced the Piccadilly Line platform walls. And so the programme went on. Work at Embankment, Gloucester Road, Bayswater, Green Park and Marble Arch was all well advanced at the end of the year, but in many cases it only served to paper over the cracks of a system whose base infrastructure in many areas was beginning to show serious signs of decay.

YOUR NEXT STATION WILL BE ARRIVING SHORTLY.

Dull. Dreary. Depressing.

These were just a few of the ways passengers described some of our stations in a survey not so long ago.

We weren't surprised.

After all many of the places they were talking about were the best part of a century old. And apart from routine upkeep, things had changed very little.

We felt a facelift was long overdue.

Which is why three years ago, we laid the foundation for our biggest ever

Finishing touches on the Bakerloo at Oxford Circus.

While mosaics of electrical colours highlight the musical and hi-fi connections of Tottenham Court Road.

Further afield at Shepherd's Bush, a new mural will soon ensure that West Londoners enjoy year-round blue skies.

Behind the scenes at night.

round of station modernization.

Today seventeen stations are under way.

But that's only the tip of a £70 million programme that will eventually spruce up nearly half of our stations.

Already most Tube users are getting a glimpse of the shape of things to come.

Key interchanges have been freshened up in a way that not only gives each station a character of its own, but also often reflects the character of the locality.

Charing Cross Bakerloo for instance, gives a preview of the nearby National and National Portrait Galleries.

And Baker Street rediscovers its historic roots.

Musical mosaics by Eduardo Paolozzi at Tottenham Court Road.

In short, the Underground is well on the way to becoming not only a nicer place to travel in.

But also an attraction in its own right.

At Tottenham Court Road, the centrepiece was a mass of mosaic murals by the artist Eduardo Paolozzi, stretching from the top of the escalators, down through the 'rotunda' to the Central Line platforms. The mosaic designs ranged from musical instruments and tape machines to butterflies, the whole effect being the colour and vibrancy of life at street level above this very busy and cosmopolitan station. At Oxford Circus the theme in tiles was 'snakes and ladders', by Nicholas Munro, reflecting the maze of stairs, subways and escalators making up the complex. At Bond Street the tile motif consisted of the words 'Bond Street' in maroon lettering on white. Common to each was the station name in white on a red conduit frieze running the length of each platform. Flooring was in small cream coloured tiles. While the station modernisation proceeded, a programme to renew the oldest of the 65 lifts on the system, some dating from the early 1900s, continued and was well advanced by 1985.

During 1986 more redecorated stations emerged from behind the hoardings. Bayswater and Paddington Circle Line platforms had been given the Baker Street treatment, at least as far as exposing and renovating original brickwork was concerned. The Bakerloo platforms at Paddington were decorated in tile depicting sections of tunnelling shields of 1818 by Sir Marc Brunel. As with all modernised stations, the new frieze ducting and seating were picked out in the respective line colour; that at Paddington being Bakerloo brown. At Marble Arch the platform walls were lined with enamel panels featuring various 'arch' designs by the artist Annabel Grey, who had also designed the mosaic balloons at Finsbury Park. New bucket-type seating was positioned by each Arch motif and formed part of the feature. More modest, but equally stylish work was carried out at Temple, Chancery Lane and St Paul's, which were retiled and equipped with new seating and lighting. Other schemes in progress during the year were at King's Cross, where the letters 'K' and 'X' in multi-coloured tiles adorned the Northern and Piccadilly Line platforms, and at Embankment where all the platforms were clad in white enamel panels bearing streaks of green, red, blue and yellow, depicting, rather obscurely, fireworks. The rebuilt northbound Victoria Line platform at Oxford Circus was complete before the end of the year. Platform walls were panelled in the red and grey snakes and ladders theme. The southbound platform was altered to match.

The highlight of 1986 was the opening of the extension to Terminal 4 at Heathrow. Work on the extension to Heathrow's new Terminal 4 was complete well in time in November 1985, but earlier in the year BAA had announced that disagreement among airlines as to which should serve the new terminal had delayed its opening, which was now scheduled for the spring of 1986. The delay gave LU engineers more time to complete the finishing touches so it would be ready when required.

The Prince and Princess of Wales performed the official opening ceremony for Heathrow Terminal 4 station on 1st April 1986. The new station was unusual in that it had only one platform. From Hatton Cross the westbound line separated with a new section running through a single tunnel to the new platform and station. The platform walls and floor were decorated in a beige coloured reconstructed marble topped with the station name frieze. Etched into the marble was a figure '4' motif. Apart from fluorescent strip lighting along the roof above the platform edge, concealed lighting above the frieze illuminated the walls to create a stylish effect. The platform was only a short walk from the ticket hall, one of the most spacious on the system, with surfaces clad in the same beige marble. The ticket hall was illuminated by uplighters set into columns around its perimeter. The new station was designed to make plane/train transfer easy for travellers; luggage trolleys could even be taken into the ticket hall. From Terminal 4 the single line continued in tunnel until it arrived at the original Heathrow Central station. This was renamed from Heathrow Central (Terminals 1, 2, 3), a renaming which had taken place in September 1984, to Heathrow Terminals 1, 2, 3. Heathrow Terminal 4 opened to the public on 12th April 1986, the day the new airline terminal officially opened for business.

At the start of 1986 the rolling stock in service on the London Underground could be summarised thus:

The most expensive of the mid-1980s station refurbishments was at Tottenham Court Road where mosaic murals covering large areas were designed by Eduardo Paolozzi. Following the King's Cross fire in 1987, much less expensive redecoration of stations became the norm with money diverted to elimination of fire hazards.

Bakerloo:	Circle/Hammersmith/	Jubilee:
1959 tube stock	Edgware Road:	1972 (MkII).
Central:	C stock	1983 tube stock
1960 tube stock	Met/East London:	Piccadilly:
1962 tube stock	A stock	1973 tube stock
District (main):	Northern: 1956/1959/1962	Victoria:
D stock	1972 (MkI and MkII)	1967 tube stock

Diana, Princess of Wales accepts a bouquet during the official opening of the Piccadilly Line extension to Heathrow Terminal 4.

The continuing programme of converting lines to OPO, and the need to release trains for conversion work to be done was soon to bring some changes. The Bakerloo Line was high on the list of lines to be converted and a series of stock relocations was drawn-up, which allowed for 14 trains of 1972 Mark II stock to be transferred from the Northern to the Bakerloo, in return for a similar number of 1959 trains. Four further 1972 Mark II stock trains from the Northern would then be sent away for conversion to OPO before returning to service on the Bakerloo. This would have left a shortfall of trains on the Northern, but help was in hand in the form of 1938 tube stock, which had lain unused since the previous November. On 15th September 1986 the stock made its return to the line on which it had first entered service 48 years before.

In the autumn LU ordered from Metro-Cammell a further 33 three-car units of 1983 stock for the Jubilee Line; with the existing stock these were enough to operate the whole timetable. The Metropolitan Line main service was converted to OPO on 29th September, and on 20th October the ATO equipment on the Hainault–Woodford section of the Central Line, which had provided the test bed for the Victoria Line, was taken out of service; the 1960 Cravens stock becoming conventional OPO trains from that date.

During the autumn two of the three prototype four-car trains for the Central Line were delivered from the manufacturers. The trains were given the codes A, B and C. First to arrive from Metro-Cammell on 25th October was train C, or the 'green' train, followed on 15th November by train B (the 'blue' train) built by BREL at Derby. The final one, Train A (the 'red' train) arrived from Metro-Cammell on 21st March 1987.

The new trains were a radical departure from tube stock built hitherto. They kept the basic dimensions of their forebears because of the confined space in which they had to work, but apart from this basic requirement they bore little resemblance to anything seen before. The bodies were constructed by welding together wide aluminium strips to create a single skin body. As a result the side doors 'hung' from the roof and did not open into a recess between the panelling skins as on previous trains. The side saloon windows extended into the roofline, (reminiscent of 1938 stock car 10306), as did the windows on the sliding doors. Double-doors made a re-appearance with the new trains as it was now acknowledged that single doors slowed down boarding times too much. The destination screen at the front worked on the dot-matrix principle. Inside the MCW trains all seating was longitudinal, but the BREL unit had some transverse seating. Train A cars seated 36, those in train B seated 32 and train C in third place at just 30, with additional perch seating for up to 12. The fact that the side windows occupied part of the roof space meant that car line maps and advertising panels were positioned at ceiling height. Seat colours matched the train identification colour, except in the red unit, which had grey seating but red grab poles. Gone were the 'straps', to be replaced by grab bars and poles. The emphasis was on energy saving and smoothness of ride. All axles were motored and thyristor control made for smooth acceleration and braking. The BREL train had steerable bogies to reduce wheel flange wear, an idea not pursued. There was enormous interest in these trains from the general media and the technical press, and they were put under a vigorous testing programme, including a spell in passenger service on the Jubilee Line between May 1988 and August 1989.

Looking quite unlike anything ever seen on the London Underground before, the 1986 stock laid the foundations for the next generation of tube train, with single-skin bodies, externally hung doors and painted exteriors. The front view is of the Metro-Cammell built train C, while the side view is of BREL's train. One of the motor cars from train C has been preserved by London's Transport Museum.

The fire at King's Cross in November 1987 was not the first on the Underground, but it was far more serious than any of the earlier ones and resulted in the deaths of 31 people. A consequence was an acceleration of the escalator renewal programme and the elimination of the remaining wooden escalators. The replacement for the escalators burnt out at King's Cross came into service on 27th February 1989. Meanwhile the opportunity was taken to replace the escalators leading from the middle concourse to the Northern Line. These came into service on 5th March. Northern Line trains did not stop at King's Cross until then in order to restrict the number of passengers using the station while the escalators and ticket hall were being replaced. Today, the only remaining station on the Underground with a wooden escalator is at Greenford, where the moving stairs take passengers up to the elevated platforms. The likely cause of the fire was a cigarette dropped by a passenger flouting the ban on smoking in subsurface areas of the Underground that had been introduced in February 1985. Within two weeks of the King's Cross fire, smoking was banned throughout the system.

The A stock returned to the East London Line on 9th May, replacing the D stock which returned to its rightful home on the District where increased services had been introduced. The prospect of increased services on the Victoria Line led to the allocation of five four-car units of 1972 MkI stock to the line between 1987 and 1989. The 1972 driving cars were formed into the middle of trains, where ATO equipment was not necessary. The Piccadilly Line was converted to OPO on 31st August 1987, the first tube line, apart from the Victoria, to go over to the system. The first of the second batch of 1983 tube stock arrived from Metro-Cammell on 11th October.

The last one was delivered in November 1988, by which time the Underground was going through a period of change unlike anything ever seen before. There was but one reason, the King's Cross fire. In a system that is below ground, the risk of fire is a particularly serious matter given the limited means of escape and the complications caused by fumes and smoke in a confined space. Only one other has been referred to in this chapter, but there had been others, including a very serious one at Finsbury Park in February 1976 caused by an electrical fault. Staff were trained to be alert to any 'smouldering', and had set-down procedures to follow. Thus there was no reason to believe that the small fire reported by a passenger just before 19.30 hours on 18th November 1987 on the up escalator from the Northern and Piccadilly lines at King's Cross was anything more than that. After a few minutes the Fire Brigade was called and dispatched four pumps and a turntable ladder from several local fire stations. The ticket hall at King's Cross gradually filled with smoke and in such a huge complex it naturally took time for an evacuation procedure to get under way. Deep below, trains continued to arrive and deposit their passengers, many no doubt anxious to make their main-line train connection quickly and get home. By 19.43 the first fire engine had arrived, and by 19.44 trains were non-stopping the station, although people were still coming up the Victoria Line escalator which fed into the same ticket hall as the Northern and Piccadilly escalator which was now well alight. The problem was that serious escalator fires (while not unknown) were unusual, and procedures at that time envisaged evacuation upwards to street level, necessarily through the ticket hall. At 19.45, as people were still being ushered out of the smoke-filled ticket hall from the Victoria Line escalator, a huge fireball swept up from the Northern and Piccadilly lines escalator shaft and engulfed the ticket hall. Thirty-one people perished, including a fire officer. The fire raged for several hours and was not completely contained until 01.46 on 19th November. The subsequent high-profile Public Inquiry into its cause made recommendations that affected every station, every train and every member of staff on the Underground. The issue was not only one of removing all flammables (few though they were), it was about removing every possible fixture or finish that performed badly in the event of a fire starting elsewhere, perhaps by creating dense smoke or poisonous fumes or which could further fuel a serious fire. It also focused on introducing advanced detection systems that could detect fires while still containable. Evacuation procedures were also drastically revised. Wednesday November 18th 1987 was without doubt one of the saddest days in the long history of the system and badly knocked confidence, but its aftermath served to make the Underground as safe as humanly possible.

A new dawn for the heart of London.

Promise of a New Dawn

The last 1938 stock train ran in passenger service on the Underground on 19th May 1988. This was also the last red painted train on the system. For six months no fully painted trains operated in passenger service on the Underground, but the exclusive reign of unpainted aluminium trains was ended with the first attempts to find a new corporate livery.

The Public Inquiry into the King's Cross fire began at Church House, Westminster on 1st February 1988. It lasted 91 days, ending on 24th June 1988. It was presided over by Desmond Fennell OBE QC and its weighty 248 page report, plus diagrams, charts and maps, was published on 10th November 1988. The Report made 157 key recommendations on safety, ranging from safety procedure and operation of escalators, through safety management communication and staff training. There was a clearly defined role for the Railway Inspectorate, and some of the recommendations were down to the Fire Brigade, Police, Ambulance service and British Rail to implement in conjunction with London Underground. All trains were to be fitted with public address. All wooden escalator components, including side panelling and treads, were to be replaced by stainless steel. London Underground acted swiftly to implement the Report's recommendations. It also undertook a top to bottom review of its entire management structure, embarking on a period of radical change of a magnitude never before seen in the organisation. The Chairman of LRT and the Chairman of London Underground both resigned as a result of the Fennell Report. Those who succeeded them took up the reins of the new challenge with a vigour and enthusiasm that resulted in 125 of the 127 recommendations specifically for LU to implement being in place by July 1990.

The King's Cross aftermath dominated events on the Underground at the end of the decade, but other important things were happening. On 4th May 1988 the three 6-car prototype trains of 1986 stock entered service on the Jubilee Line, newly converted to one-person operation from 20th March, to undergo service trials. The trials lasted until August 1989, being ended abruptly by a derailment of one of the units, by which time London Underground engineers felt they had gained enough information to decide on the design and build of the train fleet to replace the 1962 stock on the Central Line. One line on which there were no immediate plans for OPO was the Northern, and it was there, on 19th May 1988, that the very last 1938 stock train ran in normal public service on the Underground, just one month short of its 50th anniversary. It was only to be a brief absence from service however, for BR had already decided to replace the standard stock on the Isle of Wight Railway with 1938 stock. Eventually twenty cars were moved to the island, the first full train entering service on 13th July 1989.

A number of features, which today are commonplace on the Underground, were first seen in 1988, some admittedly in embryo form. In June a £15 million passenger security scheme was launched. It was trialled at twelve stations, six on the eastern end of the Central and six on the southern end of the Northern. Included were staffed 'Help Point' booths and 91 pill-shaped wall mounted alarm panels, which put passengers in direct contact with staff in station operations rooms or the British Transport Police. More police were promised too, along with 'safe' waiting areas, see-round-the-corner mirrors for subways, and CCTV. These much needed measures arose from the 1986 *Crime on the Underground* report, and it was just one of the measures aimed at making the Underground a safer and more pleasant system.

Other major projects either proposed or sanctioned during 1988 included a £20 million scheme to completely rebuild Angel station with a new ticket hall, and escalators leading down to a completely new northbound platform and a much-enlarged southbound platform. The icing on the cake came on 11th October when the Government gave the go ahead for what in the event was to prove a problem-ridden £720 million modernisation of the Central Line with 85 new trains, new signalling and track and centralised service control.

An event of some significance took place on 16th November 1988 when a newly painted train ran on the East London Line. Seventy-five per cent of the cost of painting the train had been met by the London Docklands Development Corporation (LDDC), and it owed its existence to the unhappily prevalent fad of graffiti vandalism. The Underground had been a target of graffiti vandals for some years. Stations, trains, bridges, all had been targeted by youngsters, and some not so young, looking for danger and notoriety. The danger came in gaining access to station premises, depots and the trackside. There were some fatalities, but even this did not deter those seeking the dubious pleasure of knowing their 'tag' was being viewed from one side of London to the other. Spray paint applied to a bare aluminium surface was difficult to remove effectively, usually leaving tell-tale stains where it had soaked into the porous surface. Now London Underground began fighting back and the painted A-stock on the East London Line was the first assault on the problem. The paint used combined primer, finish and lacquer and was easy to clean of ugly daubings. The A stock and the 1962 tube stock had been particularly badly hit by vandalism.

The painted train returns to the Underground, firing the first salvo in the war against the graffiti vandal. From this modest beginning on the East London Line in 1988 has come a train fleet which is almost universally externally painted. In 2001 the exception was the District Line D stock, and plans were well advanced for a refurbishment programme, including external painting, for this stock as well.

Anti-social behaviour on the Underground – a passenger sits with his feet up inside a graffiti scrawled car of A stock.

The eventual success of the painted trains sounded the death knell for the unpainted Underground train, but before then more trials were carried out to determine possible styles for a fleetwide refurbishment. These included three trains of 1972 MkI stock on the Northern. A trial train refurbishment programme was unveiled at Acton Works on 13th September 1989. The invited guests and the media were able to inspect units of A stock, C stock and 1967 tube stock which had been completely refurbished, with light coloured fire resistant interior panelling, new lighting, flooring and seating. Draught screens were redesigned, and the C stock now had all longitudinal seating. Anti-vandal seat cushions were fitted, containing a mesh sheet and covered in a new design of seat moquette. Grab rails were in the respective line colour. Better ventilation and public address were also included.

Three firms had undertaken the design work for the trains. The A stock had been developed by David Carter Associates, with the modification work being undertaken by Metro-Cammell. The C stock had been redesigned and rebuilt by British Rail Engineering Ltd (BREL), while the 1967 units had been designed by Transport Design Consortium and rebuilt by both Aston Martin Tickford and the Vic Berry Company. The refurbished units underwent exhaustive service testing and market research in advance of contracts being let for the full-scale refurbishment of the A, C and 1967/72 Mark II stocks in March 1990.

A large new ticket hall was opened at Tower Hill on 23rd November 1988. This busy but congested station benefited considerably from the extra space provided. The new ticket hall was used for way-in passengers for most of the day, the original ticket hall being exit only. At night the new ticket hall became bi-directional. A novel feature was a display case containing artefacts from the nearby Tower of London.

In June Piccadilly Circus station was officially reopened by the Lord Mayor of Westminster, following its refurbishment begun in 1987. Much was done to restore the ticket hall at the showpiece station to its 1920s magnificence. Bronze, which had featured strongly in Underground stations in the 1920s and 1930s, was evident once again in the wall fitments as well as in the red supporting columns for lighting. All the subways to street level were restored too. One feature evident now at Piccadilly Circus, not there when the ticket hall was originally built in 1928, was that of the automatic entry and exit gates and wall-mounted ticket machines of the UTS system. But they were there in 1989 as they were at the bulk of stations in the central ticket zone (Zone 1). Also in June the restoration of the Piccadilly Line platforms at South Kensington was completed. The theme was based around the nearby Natural History Museum and the images reflected a range of wildlife, both contemporary and prehistoric, by the artist Alfred Waterhouse.

September 1989 was a busy month on the rolling stock front. Apart from the launch of the refurbished train programme mentioned earlier, a new equipment overhaul shop opened at Acton and a £300 million order for new Central Line trains was placed with BREL. The order was a large one comprising 85 eight-car trains, plus twenty similar cars for British Rail's Waterloo & City Line. By this time work was well under way on carrying out modifications to rolling stock which had been recommended in the Fennell Report. The most noticeable changes were to the 1959/62 tube stock, which were fitted with new push-button passenger alarms and public address. TB Precision carried out the safety modification work to the 1959 stock at Highgate depot. BREL undertook the modifications to the 1962 stock at its Derby and Crewe works. The modifications were completed in 1990.

In 1989 some cars of 1959 stock on the Northern were given brighter interior colour schemes. While this succeeded in improving the interior specification, exteriors were still being ravaged by graffiti vandals, making much of the stock scruffy and drab.

In July 1989 the Chesham branch of the Metropolitan celebrated its centenary by holding two weekends of steam specials. The event was so successful that similar steam weekends under the banner 'Steam on the Met' were held in many of the years since. Steam locomotives were loaned from the many preserved railways up and down the country and ran with former Southern Region 4-TC units, usually accompanied at one end by ex-Metropolitan electric loco 'Sarah Siddons'.

One train of 1959 stock did receive a 'new' colour scheme. Units 1031 and 1044 were repainted externally and internally in the 1923 livery worn by standard stock when new, to celebrate the centenary of the tube in 1990. The retro-look was authentic, right down to the seat moquette. The last 1959 stock train was transferred away from the Bakerloo Line on 7th July 1989 in readiness for the line's conversion to OPO, which took place on 20th November 1989.

The station modernisation programme continued into the new decade. In April 1990 work began at St John's Wood which, although not part of the main programme which by this time was very evident in the central area, is significant because its aim was to restore the station to its 1930s glory. The scheme included the restoration of the bronze uplighters on the escalators. Similar restoration was the theme at Edgware Road Bakerloo Line station, which blended the old and the new. In the ticket hall the Edwardian tiled ticket office window surrounds were restored and the tiling in the rest of the station renewed. Help Points, the name now being applied to the wall-mounted pill shaped modules, were installed. The station was closed from 25th June 1990 until 28th January 1992 as part of the refurbishment scheme included lift renewal. Work on restoring Gloucester Road station was under way too during the year. The original entrance, ticket hall and District and Circle Line platforms were brought back to Victorian splendour. Straddling the tracks, just below the ticket hall, was a continental style saloon which was to have been a wine bar. Unfortunately those who wished to view the hustle and bustle of the platforms below with a glass of something pleasant to hand were to be disappointed. LU decided not to proceed with the idea and the saloon remains just a shell. The Piccadilly Line platforms at Gloucester Road were left largely unaltered by the scheme. Further out, work began on a new £10 million station for Hillingdon at the start of 1991. It was needed because the main A40 trunk road, which crossed the Metropolitan Line close to the station, was being realigned and the old wooden station stood right in its path. The new station was positioned to the west of the old one. Its design was a complete breakaway from anything done on the Underground before.

If train liveries had remained unchanged in the 35 years which separated the first standard stock from the 1959 tube stock then this is how the latter might well have looked. Unit 1044 wears its 'retro' look well.

Recognition of the Underground's heritage went hand in hand with refurbishment of the system. Accurate modern copies of the classic Underground bullseye were used where appropriate.

In 1993 a trial refurbishment was given to 1959-stock units 1028 and 1043. It much enhanced the appearance of the graffiti ravaged cars but unfortunately it was, in the event, strictly a one-off. The bulk of the 1959 and 1962 stocks went to the scrapyard still bearing the scars of the graffiti craze of the 1980s and '90s.

The little-used Epping–Ongar service reverted to peak hour operation only from 8th April 1991. A limited through service in both directions around the Hainault loop was also introduced. The Central Line was due for a dramatic change, as work began on the £750 million scheme designed to completely modernise the line's basic operational infrastructure, track, power supply, communications and equip it with a fleet of new trains based on the evaluation carried out on the 1986 prototypes. Station refurbishment was also an element of the scheme. All this high profile activity resulted in disruption to the service while it was being carried out, chiefly at weekends. Passengers affected by the disruption were promised that, when everything was in place, the Central Line would offer higher standards of comfort, safety and, because the new signalling would allow for up to 33 trains per hour in the central area, an improved peak hour frequency. In fact only 30 trains per hour were achieved.

On 1st July 1991 the Docklands Light Railway was extended to Bank. The huge complex at Bank/Monument was the City's busiest station and here one of the biggest station modernisation projects was under way. It had begun in 1991 and was of such magnitude that it took seven years to complete. Every square inch of the station complex, three ticket halls, six platforms, 15 escalators, four lifts, and a labyrinth of subways, was to be refurbished. The DLR was linked to all parts of the complex, adding more subways and escalators to those already there. Being deep in the bowels of the station, its most convenient interchange was with the Northern Line. The District, Circle and Central Line platforms were reached by long walks through subways and escalator connections.

A full-scale launch of the refurbished trains project was held at Rickmansworth sidings on 16th July 1991. On display were fully modernised units of 1967, 1973, A and C77 stocks, together with unrefurbished units of the same type so a 'before and after' comparison could be made. The Secretary of State for Transport, Malcolm Rifkind, inspected the trains, which were the culmination of many months of testing and research into design and materials, with fire safety a particular consideration. All the trains were in the new corporate livery of red cab fronts and passenger doors, white side panelling with a blue skirt, and grey roofs. Under the first phase of the project the C stock and the 1967/1972 (MkII) stocks were to be refurbished. No Government money was yet available to make the same transformation to the 1973 tube stock or the A stock, although trial refurbishments were on display to show what could be achieved. All the trains had improved communications in the form of better public address.

The C stock was refurbished by RFS at Doncaster under a contract awarded in 1990, while the 1967/72 tube stock was refurbished by Tickford Rail at the Royal Rosyth Dockyard. In April 1992 a contract for the refurbishment of the A stock was awarded to BREL in Derby. The first refurbished trains entered service on the Metropolitan Line in September 1994.

Passenger safety and security remained high on the Underground's agenda during the early 1990s. The Ladbroke Grove Security Control Room, on the Hammersmith & City Line, opened in October 1991. The eight stations from Hammersmith to Paddington were under the watchful eye of control room staff who could monitor most areas of the eight stations, all of which had been equipped with CCTV for the purpose. Help Points, many with CCTV cameras positioned above, enabled a verbal and visual link to be made by control room staff and the people seeking help. All blind corners were fitted with convex see-round-the-corner mirrors.

On 26th November 1991 LU launched a radical and far-reaching Company Plan. The Monopolies and Mergers Commission had acknowledged in a June 1991 report that the Underground had suffered from chronic under-investment over many years, making it impossible for the Company to keep essential infrastructure up to date. More funding was promised from central Government, both in the immediate and long term. London Underground was expected to play its part by running an efficient and more cost-effective operation, and more than £700 million in cost savings were identified. To implement these savings some major changes to staffing levels and organisation were proposed. For the first time some of the Underground support services, like cleaning and train maintenance, were to be offered out to the private sector under tender. A large-scale reorganisation of station and train management structures resulted in a staff reduction of around 5,000 during the following four years. The plan touched all areas of LU's operation, including safety, train services, maintenance and signalling; but the emphasis was on customer focused accountability and performance measures, which were regularly published through a Customer Charter launched in August 1992.

On 17th September 1992 Angel station reopened after its £70 million rebuilding scheme. A large new entrance and ticket hall had been built in Islington High Street to replace the original one in City Road. The old station with its worn-out lifts gave way to a bright, modern and spacious station, everything an efficient tube station should be. From the ticket hall three escalators, the longest on the Underground with a vertical rise of 27.425 metres, led down to an intermediate level. From there three shorter (8.32 metre) escalators led down to the platforms. The southbound platform is the original island platform with the northbound track filled in to create a wider waiting area. A completely new northbound platform was built, clad in vitreous enamel and marble, the marble extending to subways and the ticket hall. On 23rd October 1992 Mornington Crescent station closed for refurbishment and the replacement of its original 1907 lifts. It was to remain closed for almost six years.

The impressive line-up of refurbished trains await inspection by those who can sanction the expenditure for a large-scale refurbishment programme. The scene at Rickmansworth sidings on 16th July 1991.

Transformation at Angel. The old island platform (left) was rebuilt to create a wide southbound platform and a new northbound platform was added in the new tunnel.

Large windows at the ends of each car of 1992 tube stock gave added security for passengers. All new trains have these as standard and some refurbished older stock has also been equipped.

Delivery of the new Central Line trains continued until February 1995. At the time the 1992 stock was being ordered, British Rail was considering replacement of the 1940 vintage class 487 stock on the Waterloo & City Line. It was decided that a good option would be to buy some 1992 stock as a replacement as this would obviate the need to design and build anything bespoke for the short line. An order for twenty cars (five 4-car trains) was added to the Central Line order. One of the new trains is seen here at Bank.

The first of the 85 trains of 1992 tube stock entered passenger service on the Central Line on 7th April 1993, running initially only during off-peaks between West Ruislip and Liverpool Street. Peak hour appearances had to wait until June. Deliveries had begun on 17th May 1992. The build of the stock was based on the 1986 prototype. The bodies are constructed of welded aluminium panels, thus saving weight and cost. Passenger and driver side cab doors are pneumatically operated and externally hung, to save giving the car bodies a double-skin. Each motor car has two sets of double-doors and one single-leaf door, while the trailer cars have a single-leaf door at each end. The double-doors open to give 1.66 metres entry space, the widest so far on a London Underground train. The cars have end windows to increase vision and security. These had been introduced on refurbished cars of the Victoria Line 1967 stock, but the 1992 stock was the first new fleet of trains to have them and the feature is now standard on new Underground rolling stock. Also now standard are the warning beeps which sound just before the doors close – though previously most passengers had the intelligence to detect this was going to happen when they heard the click of the pneumatic door motors. The Central Line had been involved in an experiment 45 years earlier in which sirens, hand-operated by platform staff, were sounded at Liverpool Street station 25 seconds after a train had arrived to hurry any passengers still about to board. It did not extend to any other stations.

Driver's cabs are fitted with CCTV to enable drivers to see when to close the doors at stations. Train radio, incorporating the latest digital technology, and an information diagnostic system to aid fault finding without needing to delay train services, are also part of the package. Mechanically all axles are motored and fed by DC chopper-controlled traction equipment for higher maximum speed, smooth acceleration and regenerative braking.

Work on the Central Line modernisation, which was to be plagued with serious technical problems, was well under way by the start of 1993. New coded track circuit based signalling was being installed and commissioned at various locations. Trials with the new trains continued, one actually being sent to Ongar in July. But the locals at North Weald were mistaken if they thought their bit of the Central Line was in line for the new trains. In May new proposals were announced for the closure of the Epping-Ongar branch; they came a few months after a similar announcement of the intention to close the Aldwych branch. Objections were received to both proposals so they went to Public Inquiry.

On 28th May 1993 British Rail's Waterloo & City Line closed for six weeks to get the line ready for its new 1992 stock trains. The last of the old 1940-vintage class 487 ex-Southern Railway cars were withdrawn. When the line reopened on 19th July it had five smart new four-car blue and white class 482 trains of the same design as the new Central Line stock. Also in May a contract was placed with RFS in Doncaster for refurbishment of the 1973 tube stock on the Piccadilly Line.

The contract for a new fleet of trains for the Jubilee Line was placed in late 1992. It went to GEC Alsthom, the parent company of Metro-Cammell in Birmingham, where the new trains would be assembled. The original intention had been to refurbish the 1983 tube stock and build some new cars to make up the extra trains required for the extended Jubilee Line. The idea was eventually dropped because the cost was calculated as being about the same as building a fleet of completely new trains for the Jubilee.

Station modernisation projects were still progressing during 1993, although a cutback in Government funding was putting other projects which were not 'ring-fenced' on ice. The first stage of the new Hammersmith (District and Piccadilly) station Centre West complex opened on 5th July. A wide shopping mall led from Hammersmith Broadway and a new ticket hall was incorporated into it. The old ticket hall was gone. Passengers entering and leaving were segregated, to reduce congestion.

As part of a major commercial development of London Transport property, Hammersmith became the first post-modern Underground station when impressively rebuilt platforms came into use in 1993. It was followed soon after by a stunning new station at Hillingdon, where rebuilding was required because of improvements to the neighbouring A40 trunk road.

For many years discussions had been under way on how best to provide rail links to serve the growing population of south-east London, not only in established areas like Greenwich and Woolwich, but also on the large new residential Thamesmead estate at Plumstead. The problem gained impetus during the 1970s and 1980s, with proposals for the rejuvenation of the area around the old London docks and the need for an effective transport link to the surrounding area which would be required. A number of options were looked at across the two decades, one of which ended up as the Docklands Light Railway. As the years passed and the traditional industries and dockyards closed, a proposal emerged for a giant £4 billion business and office complex on the Isle of Dogs, an area largely devoid of surviving rail links. It was to be an 'annex' of the City of London. The London Docklands Development Corporation was set up, and was instrumental in creating the DLR with London Transport. It was recognised quite early in the development of Docklands that the DLR would not have sufficient capacity for the numbers who would eventually be travelling to work each day in the redeveloped area as well as those who would live in the many housing projects planned.

At the centre of Docklands was Canary Wharf, and the huge development there, including its transport links, was being promoted by a consortium led by a wealthy American, G. Ware Travelstead. Various extensions to the Docklands Light Railway were proposed, including one to Bank, one to Lewisham and another to Beckton. But these were not expected to be sufficient, even operating at full strength. Office accommodation was likely to increase at a phenomenal rate and everyone became nervous at the prospect of the area failing through lack of sufficient transport. A new tube railway, linking Waterloo and London Bridge with Canary Wharf and south-east London was proposed and was the subject of detailed planning by London Transport and Olympia and York, the successor to the Travelstead consortium. LT favoured an extension to the Jubilee Line, which would connect the West End with Waterloo, London Bridge, and Canary Wharf and then continue to Stratford. An extension to the Bakerloo Line had been considered as an alternative, but rejected.

Eventually the proposal made in the East London Rail Study, which had looked at various options for rail links between central London and the east London corridor, was agreed upon. It was in line with LT's thinking on the Stratford option. In November 1989 a private bill was submitted to Parliament. Following a further bill in November 1990, which slightly amended the route, the Bill to extend the Jubilee Line through south-east London and Docklands to Stratford received Royal Assent on 16th March 1992.

The Government of the day quite reasonably looked to private enterprise, which would reap much of the benefit of the new line, to play its part in contributing to the cost of building the extension. The sum needed was estimated to be £1.3 billion. Olympia and York offered to pay £400 million towards the cost if the Government met the remainder. But a recession in the early 1990s threw Olympia and York into receivership, and the project froze as the Government were unwilling to finance the whole thing. After more than a year when nothing moved, a consortium under the name Canary Wharf Ltd, and led by several banks, agreed in their own interests to contribute the £400 million funding previously promised by Olympia and York, but spread over 25 years and thereby greatly reducing its value. On 29th October 1993 the Government gave London Transport the go-ahead to begin building the extension, raising the curtain on seven hectic and fraught years for London Underground. No time was lost in starting work on the massive project. By December construction work was under way. The total bill was to exceed £3.5 billion.

No doubt with more people present than at any time in the quiet branch's history, locals and enthusiasts from farther afield congregate on Ongar platform on the last evening of passenger service, 30th September 1994.

The last train from Epping to Ongar, pausing a little longer than usual at North Weald for people to get off the train to take photographs. This one was taken from the foot crossing at the station's eastern end.

At different times in its life threatened with closure and promised a link with Waterloo, Aldwych station finally closed to passengers on the same evening as the Ongar service.

On a smaller scale, another extension was being actively considered during the early 1990s. This was the Croxley Rail Link, a scheme by which the Metropolitan Line would be diverted from its route between Croxley and Watford, and run instead via Croxley Green to Watford Junction. The scheme was still on the back burner in 2005.

On 13th March 1994 a partial OPO service was introduced on the Central Line, where 30 trains out of the 71 required for the Monday to Friday peak service were of 1992 tube stock. One-person operation continued to be phased in on the Central Line until completion in 1995. By this time the promise of a first class service for Central Line customers was being regularly tainted by delays due to the on-going modernisation work, especially to problems relating to the new signalling and its interface with the old signalling it was replacing. A serious power failure on 24th November 1993 affected a wide area of the Underground in east London and stopped trains not only on the Central Line but the District and Hammersmith & City as well. It was traced to a fault in worn cabling at Newbury Park which in turn damaged cabling at Lots Road. Power was not restored until the following evening. On 26th November the power failed again and the Central Line service on the east side of London had to be covered by an emergency bus service. The Central Line did not run normally again until 30th November, over a week after first failing. This was the last straw for many of the line's passengers who had suffered numerous delays due to problems with new signalling and train equipment.

On 1st April 1994 five stations were added to the list of those managed by London Underground, when LU took over from British Rail the management of East Putney, Southfields and Wimbledon Park stations and the Waterloo and City Line with its platforms at Bank and Waterloo. With the latter LU also took over the 20 cars of 1992 tube stock in their blue and white livery. The take-overs were due to the impending privatisation of Britain's railway network. On 3rd April the Underground introduced a £10 Penalty Fare for anyone found travelling without a valid ticket.

On 1st September 1994 the Secretary of State for Transport gave London Underground permission to close the Aldwych branch of the Piccadilly Line and the Epping-Ongar branch of the Central Line. Both branches were losing money heavily; the Epping-Ongar service, with its 100 or so passengers a day, was losing in the region of £185,000 a year, while annual losses on the Aldwych branch totalled £150,000. The closures took place on the evening of Friday 30th September. The last train from Ongar was bursting at the seams with enthusiasts determined to take part in the last rites. LU was instructed by the Minister to keep the tracks of the Epping-Ongar line in place for three years while a buyer for the line was sought. Aldwych station was closed and mothballed, although the front fascia was subsequently restored, revealing the name Strand station. In July 1995 the Epping-Ongar line was put up for sale and interested parties were invited to register their interest with London Underground. A Sunday only service operated by the Epping Ongar Railway began in November 2004 using 40-year old diesel stock. This terminates about a mile short of Epping at Coopersale.

1994 had been the first full year of the Jubilee Line extension construction. It was the biggest construction programme then under way in Britain and a huge project team had been assembled to oversee each element of construction. As with the excavation of previous new lines, the extension work was carried out concurrently at several different locations. Seventeen major engineering contracts, totalling between them £649 million, had been placed with some of the country's biggest engineering firms, including Balfour-Beatty, Costain, Taylor-Woodrow, McAlpines, Wimpey and Mowlem. Fourteen electrical and design contracts, totalling £583 million, and covering rolling stock, signalling, escalators, lifts, power cabling, ticketing systems, track and communications had also been placed. The biggest of these, £249 million, went to GEC Alsthom Metro-Cammell for the new Jubilee Line train fleet. The Westinghouse group of companies received contracts to supply signalling and ticketing systems, and platform edge doors. Everything connected with the project was on a huge scale. Eleven 200 tonne tunnel boring machines were loaded into their respective shafts for tunnel excavation. Each was capable of boring through 13 metres of ground each day. Much of the spoil from the excavation was taken down the Thames by barges from specially constructed jetties close to excavation sites.

 All was progressing well when on 21st October 1994 a tunnel being built for the Heathrow Express rail link using the New Austrian Tunnelling Method (NATM), collapsed. The NATM method allowed for quick setting concrete to be sprayed directly onto a newly excavated tunnel section with steel mesh and lattice arches then being embedded into the concrete which was then anchored into the surrounding ground. The system had been used effectively for short and temporary tunnels; its success depending on the type of ground being excavated. The NATM method was being used in the preparation work for the Jubilee Line extension tunnels between Waterloo and London Bridge. Following the Heathrow collapse, work on this section was suspended. This was to cause a serious delay to the programme as work on the section did not restart until August 1995. However in November 1994 the first of the three Thames crossings of the extension, between North Greenwich and Canning Town was completed. The tunnelling for the whole 20km extension was completed in August 1996.

On the operational railway the Central Line modernisation continued, albeit more slowly than planned, a landmark being passed on 17th February 1995 with the withdrawal of the last 1962 tube stock train, almost 33 years since the first of the type had entered service on the line. It was not the end of the 1962 stock because a handful of units had passed to the Northern Line and a few more were being employed on various works duties, including piloting new trains to their home depots.

For some while, concern had been expressed about water ingress into tunnels on the existing Underground system where they passed beneath riverbeds. London Underground engineers had identified several sites where tunnels would need to be sealed and strengthened to safeguard them for the future. Some of the work was relatively minor and much of it could be carried out with little or no disruption to services. However two schemes necessitated the closure of sections of line, and a third was to result in a planned seven-month closure of the whole East London Line, where Brunel's historic Thames Tunnel was one of the tunnel sections requiring strengthening. Complete closure gave LU engineers the opportunity to construct the base infrastructure of the new Canada Water East London/Jubilee Line interchange and other upgrading work such as new signalling, track replacement and station refurbishment. The line closed on 25th March 1995, but immediately the project was thrown off course when the Secretary of State for National Heritage gave Brunel's tunnel a Grade II* listing just hours before the work was due to start. LU had intended to shotcrete the tunnel with new concrete, thus erasing much of the historic structure from view. A panel of engineers was hastily convened to work out a compromise solution, and eventually one acceptable to all sides was found. It involved restoring four of the historic arches which did not lie beneath the river, and relining the remainder. Work finally began in January 1996, nine months later than originally planned. Since the closure, replacement buses had been running covering all affected stations. The buses were painted in East London Line orange.

In April 1995 the refurbishment of the 1972 MkII stock for the Bakerloo Line was completed. The following month the last 1967 stock train arrived back from the refurbishers. Some design modifications had been made to the last unit (No.3186). There was additional standing space for passengers around the door area, resulting in some different profile seating in the trailers. This was to test the concept of perch seating in the 1995/1996 tube stock then being developed.

Tunnelling on the Jubilee Line extension was completed in August 1996. The tunnel boring machines used on the Jubilee Line extension were larger, more powerful, more accurately steered and much faster than the Price rotary excavators used in part on the Yerkes tubes of the Edwardian era, but used the same principles. A rotating frame with cutting teeth carved out the ground at the leading edge with the frame and protecting shield forced forward hydraulically. Depending on ground conditions (some of which were treacherous) additional technologies were available to maintain pressure on the tunnel face to prevent collapse. Most running tunnels were built in concrete expanded against the clay, the pressure of which keeps the segments locked home without bolts.

The first all-over advertisement tube train entered service on the Piccadilly Line on 19th June 1995. A complete 1973 stock train had been painted in blue United Airlines livery. It was joined in February 1998 by a C stock train clad in an all-over display for Yellow Pages. This one (above) survived until May 1999 when the transfers were removed. It was subsequently repainted back into the more traditional colours. Apart from these two, no further examples of mobile purchase inducements had appeared on the Underground by the end of 2000.

One of the first steps taken by LU into the realm of the Private Finance Initiative (PFI) had been the awarding of a £400 million contract to GEC Alsthom in 1994. Under the terms of the subsequent contract the Northern Line trains, including initially the 1959 and 1972 tube stocks, would be owned and maintained by GEC at Northern Line depots, LU paying GEC to provide sufficient trains to operate the Northern Line service. Performance related payments were part of the package, GEC incurring penalty payments if the number of trains supplied for service was below the number required. On 26th November 1995 GEC Alsthom took over the maintenance of trains on the Northern Line under the PFI deal, which involved the transfer of 170 staff from LU to GEC. The contract with GEC Alsthom was to run for 20 years with an option for a further sixteen years on top of that. It was a major change in the way the purchasing of new trains is financed. The 106 new hi-tech trains GEC would provide for the line would be the star turn of a £1 billion package of improvements for the Northern Line to include a new signalling and communication system, a new control centre, upgraded track, station refurbishment and bridge and embankment works. At the end of 1995 this must have seemed light years away to the ordinary Northern Line users told by the media for so long that they travelled on the 'misery line'.

Operation Hard Hat gathered momentum in 1996. The term was LU's way of describing the multitude of engineering works then under way or in the pipeline, many of them connected with tunnel strengthening. A high-profile advertising and publicity campaign was rolled out to tell LU's customers why the work was necessary and what was involved. Apart from the East London Line two other large tranches of disruptive tunnel strengthening work took place during the year. The first was a closure of the Northern Line Bank branch between Moorgate and Kennington from 1st July until 20th October. It was followed by a closure of the Bakerloo Line between Piccadilly Circus and Elephant and Castle between 10th November 1996 and 14th July 1997. The latter scheme was particularly high profile because it necessitated the erection of a huge cofferdam in the Thames. The Bakerloo tunnels were literally boxed-in with concrete to seal them. In both instances a high intensity alternative bus service was provided between the affected parts of the lines. The Bank branch closure allowed work to continue on the construction of a new southbound platform at London Bridge to create a bigger circulating area for passengers interchanging to the new Jubilee Line.

Between 29th and 31st May a driving motor-car of 1996 tube stock was put on display at Canary Wharf. It would be many months before the first train entered service, but the display gave interested onlookers a glimpse of what was in store for them when the extension eventually opened. The 1996 stock is an odd mixture in more ways that one. It is formed into six-car trains made up of two three-car units. The basic construction is similar to that of the 1992 stock with welded aluminium panels. However, apart from the exterior livery and the exterior hung doors, there is little similarity to the 1992 stock. The window depth matches that of the 1983 tube stock which, had the original plan being carried out, would have been refurbished to run with new trailer cars of 1996 stock. The new trains were assembled by GEC Alsthom at the Metro-Cammell factory in Birmingham, but they are a real cocktail of ancestry. For instance, the body shells were manufactured in Spain, the bogies in France and the doors in Canada. The first completed 1996 stock train arrived at Ruislip Depot on 18th July 1996.

While all attention focused on the Jubilee Line during the mid 1990s, one former showpiece line was receiving investment from an unusual source. A £4.5 million scheme to modernise the ticket hall and provide lift access to the Victoria Line platforms at Tottenham Hale was funded jointly by the European Union and Haringey Council. The scheme also included refurbished platforms, with new lighting, CCTV and Help Points linked to a security room. It was one of the first step-free access projects to be undertaken by London Underground, part of an initiative to help the mobility-impaired which saw similar installations at other stations where the necessary lift equipment could be accommodated. On the Wimbledon branch of the District Line, a one million pound refurbishment of Wimbledon Park station was unveiled by the local MP on 18th October 1996. It was part of a £4 million programme in which the three stations taken over by LU in 1994 had been completely refurbished.

The Private Finance Initiative embraced another vital part of the Underground's infrastructure in March 1997 when the consortium Seeboard Powerlink was selected to run a 30-year contract to provide high voltage electricity supply for the Underground. Seeboard Powerlink would lease the giant Lots Road Power Station from London Underground until it could be decommissioned. Around 780 staff would transfer to the new organisation. The changeover was made at a special switchover ceremony on 16th August 1998.

There being no windows in the roofline of 1995 and 1996 stocks, there is more space to display map publicity and commercial advertising in their traditional positions. All seating is longitudinal, the motor cars seat 32 with the trailers/UNDMs seating 34. Perch seating is provided on either side of the double-doors in the middle saloon section. The basic internal livery is ivory, complemented by light blue panelling around the doors and the roof lighting. Grab poles are pale yellow. The seat moquette is a mixture of mauve, grey, white and blue. One new feature is an internal dot-matrix 'next station' indicator augmented by digitised speech announcements. The trains have dynamic regenerative braking. As the first of a new breed of tube train arrived, so the first of an old breed departed. On 21st May 1996 the last of the 1956 tube stock prototypes was withdrawn from service on the Northern Line following a curious incident when it ran over a metal storage bin that had come adrift and got stuck beneath the train.

The first refurbished train for the Piccadilly Line entered service on 17th June 1996. Once again the result was a transformation. The cars had all-new panelling, flooring and lighting, along with longitudinal seating throughout. Bright red, white and blue seat covering and blue grab poles completed what was a very stylish interior. A 1996 tube-stock style information system with dot-matrix information panel scrolling the name of the next station, and complemented by digital speech verbal announcements, was included. The work had been carried out by Bombardier Prorail, which had assumed control of the £76 million project after the original contractor, RFS Engineering, had gone into receivership. The refurbishment of the 85 trains of 1973 stock continued until the end of 2000.

If the Conservative Government, which had been in office since 1979, hoped to get re-elected on a platform of massive investment in the Underground, there was no sign of it as the General Election of 1997 approached. Spending for the financial year 1997/1998 had been reduced in the Government's 1996 Autumn Statement. The £2 billion of work identified by the Monopolies and Mergers Commission in 1991 had been reduced to £1.2 billion, making it impossible to catch up on much-needed infrastructure work on the existing railway. Many important projects were put on hold including numerous escalator renewals, station refurbishments and track upgrading projects. Among the projects which did continue were the tunnel strengthening works under the *Operation Hard Hat* banner including the modernisation of the East London Line, Metropolitan and Piccadilly train modernisation and new rolling stock for the Jubilee and Northern lines. Work on the Central Line project continued. In amongst all the cut-backs there were some successes. A fall in crime on the system, a continuance of the trend over the previous ten years, made the system now one of the safest in the world.

On Thursday 1st May 1997, the nation elected a Labour Government for the first time in 18 years. The new Government announced its plans for the future of London Transport in a White Paper published on 20th March 1998. A new Greater London Authority was to be set up, and with it a new organisation Transport for London (TfL) to implement an integrated transport strategy for the Capital. TfL would take over the roles of LRT and its subsidiaries, together with responsibility for the Docklands Light Railway, taxis and Victoria Coach Station, as well as London's roads and cycleways. The new authority took up the reins in July 2000 following the mayoral election, as a figurehead Mayor (New York style) was a key element of Labour's strategy for London government. Also in 1998 the Government announced its preferred option for funding the Underground. This was a Public-Private Partnership (PPP), the public element being the operation of the train service, including running trains, stations, setting fares, controlling safety and signalling etc, while the private sector would provide and maintain the infrastructure used by the public operating body. The main advantage of this system, the Government believed, was that private sector skills and finance could be used to improve and maintain the network.

Early in 1998 it was announced that traditional fixed block signalling, rather than insufficiently developed moving block signalling which had promised to give additional line capacity, would be used on the Jubilee Line extension. The new signalling did make full use of the latest radio-based technology, but the increased service that the moving block system had promised would not be possible. In July 2001 it was announced that the signalling on the extension would have to be completely renewed because of its inability to cope with extra trains.

On 12th June 1998 the first train of 1995 tube stock entered service on the Northern Line. Its arrival was several months late because of the need to thoroughly test the stock before putting it into service. A backlog of new trains had built up, resulting in many being stored at various locations including a Ministry of Defence site in Warwickshire. On 9th July the last train of 1983 tube stock was withdrawn from service on the Jubilee Line. The bulk of the first batch of the stock went for scrap while the second batch was earmarked for refurbishment and possible use on the Piccadilly Line. Spare tracks in various depots and sidings were soon filled up with 1983 stock awaiting the day when some railway engineers would do to them what had been done to such good effect on the older stock on the system. But this did not happen and the second batch followed the same fate as the first.

The arrival of the 1995 stock on the Northern Line quickly resulted in the withdrawal of the 1972 (MkI) stock. At the start of 1998, twenty trains of this stock were still running on the Northern, but at the start of 1999 there were just two. The last one was taken out of service on 3rd February. A start was then made on withdrawing the 1959 tube stock and also the last guards on the London Underground. The last passenger train journey under the control of a guard arrived at Edgware at 9pm on Thursday 27th January 2000.

One of the projects that had carried on despite the 1997 cutbacks was the £45 million redevelopment of the Bank-Monument station complex. The Corporation of London had contributed £2.5 million. All surfaces were lined in marble tiling and the Central and Northern Line platform walls were adorned with griffin images. Five new escalators were installed and there was new lighting and signing. The project was completed in 1998. The photograph shows one of the grubby Northern Line platforms prior to refurbishment.

A car of 1995 stock at Edgware. Rubber inter-car barriers to prevent people falling between cars were introduced as standard fitments on the 1995 and 1996 stocks.

The East London Line reopened on 25th March 1998, three years to the day after it had been closed. During the extended closure it had been transformed from a damp and down-at-heel backwater railway, into a bright and modern inner urban railway. The £100 million modernisation had brought about refurbished stations, new track and signalling, a new station at Canada Water with the Jubilee Line, and a strengthened Thames Tunnel. The line also benefited from refurbished A-stock, the last unit of which returned from Adtranz on 11th February 1998. Shoreditch station reopened on 27th September following completion of its refurbishment.

Since the completion of the tunnelling works on the Jubilee Line the mammoth task of equipping the station tunnels, and the multitude of other elements needed to make the line into a working tube railway, had been progressing. The JLE stations were to be quite unlike anything seen on the Underground so far. Whereas the Victoria Line platforms were all practically identical in design and colour scheme, each of the eleven stations on the Jubilee Line extension were different from each other and a number of celebrated architects had been invited to submit designs for them. Many of the stations would have new surface level entrances, unlike the Victoria Line, which interchanged with other lines at existing stations for almost all its route. By late summer 1998 the Jubilee Line extension had reached a crucial phase. Already nearly six months late in completion there was still no certainty when the line would open. LT had appointed Bechtel, a leading engineering and construction firm, to appraise the way work on the project was being planned and implemented. The result was a complete takeover of the project management role by Bechtel. The company recommended that the line be opened in phases, rather than in one go as had been planned, and it began its important task with that aim as a key target.

In 1996, with an eye to the future, LT had invited tenders under its PFI initiative for the development of a scheme to revolutionise ticket purchase and use, with the emphasis on Stored Value Ticketing (SVT) using Smartcards. The contract for the scheme, which went under the name Prestige project, was awarded to a consortium led by Electronic Data Systems (EDS), with SVT and Smartcards being expected to make their debut early in 2002. On 14th August 1998 the consortium began work on the project, an important element of which was the installation of UTS gates across the whole Underground system.

One welcome measure from the Government had been a £1 billion investment package launched under the banner 'Tube 2000'. Every line was to benefit from the funding through projects covering many vital aspects of operations, including track and escalator upgrading, better communications, safety and station refurbishment. In July 1999, the Government awarded an additional £517 million to enable more vital improvements to be made on the Underground. LU quickly drew up a spending list, which was announced at a special meeting at London Transport's 55 Broadway Headquarters on 22nd July attended by Prime Minister Tony Blair and Deputy Prime Minister John Prescott. Improvements to train services on the Northern Line, track upgrades on the Bakerloo, Victoria and Metropolitan lines, infrastructure works, escalator refurbishment, step-free access for mobility impaired passengers at many stations, more CCTV and Help Points, and schemes to end overcrowding at Vauxhall, Brixton, Russell Square and Knightsbridge. The Government also endorsed LU's plans to reorganise its operations in preparation for PPP. The reorganisation was implemented on 18th September 1999 with the company being divided into the parts which would remain in public ownership (Opscos) being separated from those which would be controlled by the private sector (Infracos). The whole reorganisation was based around three line groupings, the Bakerloo, Central and Victoria lines, Jubilee, Northern and Piccadilly, and finally the sub-surface lines. The private sector consortiums would bid for ownership of one of the three Infracos based around the line groupings.

On 12th June 1999 work began on the first major piece of engineering work under the Tube 2000 investment banner. The tunnel roof on the section of the Circle Line between High Street Kensington and Gloucester Road needed strengthening, and the only way it could be achieved was to close the section of line for nine weeks. The Circle Line resumed on 23rd August, by which time a further large slice of engineering was under way on the Northern Line's Bank branch, which had been closed for tunnel strengthening in 1996. This time the target was the track, which was to be upgraded so that a number of permanent speed restrictions could be removed. Some tunnel enlargement work was also carried out. The section from Kennington to Moorgate was closed from 5th July until 6th September.

In May 1999 the Central Line's new communication system took a giant leap forward and the platform dot-matrix destination indicators, which had been misleading passengers with incorrect information for the past five years, were activated to show the correct destinations and arrival time of the next three trains. In September the new Wood Lane Control Centre began controlling the signalling on the western side of the line from Bank, and by the end of 1999 the Centre was controlling signalling as far east as Newbury Park. In December the training of Central Line train drivers for Automatic Train Operation began.

A night-time view of Stratford station showing the automatic ticket gates to and from the new Jubilee Line platforms.

The Government and other interested parties exerted considerable pressure on London Transport to get the Jubilee Line extension open in time for the Millennium celebrations on 1st January 2000 and the opening of the Millennium Dome, a huge edifice built to house a mammoth exhibition to celebrate the dawn of the third Millennium. The Jubilee Line was to provide the main transport for the guests who had been invited to a huge gala night at the Dome, which was deliberately devoid of any car parking facilities.

On Tuesday 14th May 1999 the Deputy Prime Minister opened the first section of new line from Stratford to North Greenwich. Initially trains ran only between 06.10 and 20.30 on Mondays to Fridays. On 19th August local MP Simon Hughes opened the new ticket hall and new East London Line platforms at Canada Water. It would be almost a month before East London Line passengers could interchange to the Jubilee Line at Canada Water, but their chance came on 17th September when the line was extended from North Greenwich to Bermondsey. As there was no reversing facility at Bermondsey, trains ran on to Waterloo to turn. Waterloo opened on 24th September, but trains did not stop at London Bridge until 7th October, or at Southwark until 20th November. This was the day the two halves of the Jubilee Line joined at Green Park and the section to Charing Cross closed to regular passenger services, though the very first scheduled train over the extension had to be cancelled because of signal failure. Westminster station eventually opened on 22nd December, nine days before the New Year's Eve deadline.

The Jubilee Line extension was quite unlike anything that had gone before. For a start there had been little or no constraints on space. The architects and designers who worked on it, overseen by leading architect Roland Paoletti, had virtually a free hand and could design stations where the service infrastructure, ventilator shafts and cable tunnels could be kept away from passenger areas, but have easy access and maintenance. Natural daylight is included in the designs wherever possible. Escalators, and lifts for the mobility impaired, are in abundance everywhere. There are 118 new heavy-duty escalators and 34 lifts on the extension. A new design of passenger operated touch-screen ticket issuing machine was developed for the extension, and by January 2001 a modified version had been installed throughout the Underground to replace the original Multifare model.

Some bold and assertive designs emerged for the Jubilee Line extension, each one different from the next, but all linked by the common purpose of making travel on this new part of the Underground safe, convenient, easy and enjoyable. The basic station scheme colours are grey and blue, and there is plenty of raw concrete and stainless steel. Indeed many areas of platform walls, ceilings and escalator shafts retain their raw lining segments without the finished over-panelling.

Nonetheless the variety of materials used, combined with the sheer scale of everything, make a ride on the 16 kilometre Jubilee Line extension an exciting experience. The experience starts as soon as you step onto the line at Stratford.

Stratford, designed by the architects Wilkinson Eyre, was already a busy interchange when the route for the Jubilee Line extension was agreed. A huge glass-fronted entrance building with a curved roof sloping down towards the rear sits parallel to the westbound Central Line track. It leads to two large concourses separated by the former North London Line (now Silverlink Metro) platforms and tracks which pass beneath the Central Line and Great Eastern platforms. Each concourse has a ticket office. A footbridge links the main entrance concourse to the Jubilee Line concourse and platforms. New and refurbished subways link the new entrance and concourses to the Central, DLR and GER platforms, which themselves required some rebuilding and refurbishment. Jubilee Line trains terminate in one of three open-air platforms.

At West Ham the Jubilee Line interchanges with the District and Hammersmith & City lines, c2c (formerly LTS Rail) and Silverlink Metro services. The old station has been transformed through a design by the architects Van Heyningen & Haward. The main entrance to the station and a new ticket hall are now around the corner in Durban Road. The original station entrance in Manor Road was closed and the old ticket hall merged into a refurbished subway beneath the District Line platforms. The new complex was built in red brick to blend in with the local area. In 1999 LTS Rail opened a new interchange platform, the first time trains on the line from Fenchurch Street had called there since the LMS closed the original platforms in 1940. From the new ticket hall the route to the Jubilee Line platforms is via an overbridge, clad in frosted glass blocks, across the Silverlink platforms.

From West Ham the line remains in the open, running parallel with the Silverlink service, to Canning Town where it meets up again with the Docklands Light Railway.

The Jubilee Line platforms at Canning Town are constructed mainly of concrete with two rows of 'Y' shaped pre-cast supports holding up the DLR platforms above. The spacious lower ticket-hall concourse, which is lined with grey aluminium panels, is lit by daylight from two glass-sheeted roof lights. There are ten escalators, four linking the concourse to the Jubilee platforms, two linking the concourse to the Bus Station, and four linking the Jubilee and DLR platforms. Three lifts link the lower concourse with a subsidiary entrance at Bow Creek, a large new Bus Station and the Jubilee Line. The main station structure was completed in 1998 with DLR trains using the new 'upstairs' platform from 5th March 1998, with a temporary staircase and a 'portakabin' serving as station buildings and Silverlink ticket office. The new Bus Station opened in May 1999.

From Stratford the line passes the huge Stratford Market depot, designed by Hyder Consultants. Stratford Market depot is one of two new buildings built especially to service the extended Jubilee Line (the other is the Neasden Control Centre, which apart from controlling train service from Stratford to Stanmore also acted as a training centre for staff working on the new line). The new depot, whose massive 89metre wide expanse must contain several miles of steel tubing, has the capacity to stable 33 trains. There are 11 roads undercover for train maintenance, repair and inspection. The roads were especially designed to obviate the need for engineers to work in pits as five of the roads stand on stilts to allow easy access. The depot also has train-washing facilities with the option of a simple side and roof clean or an all-over wash.

The first deep-level station on the extension is North Greenwich, the platforms being 25 metres below the surface. Designed by Alsop, Lyall & Stormer, the original plans involved leaving North Greenwich open to the sky with an oval shaped concourse suspended from support beams across the open 'roof'. A garden was to have featured in the design, but British Gas, which owned the site, objected to the plan and North Greenwich got a roof. However the basic design elements, with the concourse suspended over the platforms, remained. Six, free-standing escalators lead from the three platforms to the main concourse which is composed of stainless steel cladding. Massive dark blue 'V' shaped columns rise up from the platforms to act as a roof support.

The North Greenwich peninsular was selected for the site of the Millennium Exhibition housed in a huge dome structure. The Exhibition was open only during 2000 and there were high hopes for large attendances. It was surprising then that only three escalators to street level were provided at North Greenwich; two going right to the entrance level, the other stopping mid-way with the journey being finished up fixed stairs. In the event the Dome attracted only about half of the 20 million visitors expected. Originally there was to have been a subway through to a large car park close to the station, but that was before the Dome was conceived, and in the environmentally conscious 1990s the Dome was not to be accessible by private car, only public transport. The station building consists of a crescent-shaped glass structure outside which is a large Bus Station.

Canary Wharf, and the acres of prestige office development it has spawned, naturally merited a showpiece station and the result lives up to the high expectations originally envisaged for it. Designed by Sir Norman Foster, Canary Wharf boasts the biggest capacity area of any of the new Jubilee Line stations. It is 24 metres deep by 280 metres long. To build it, the old West India Dock was drained and the station excavated, like North Greenwich, using the cut-and-cover method. Interchange with the DLR is circuitous, although in April 2000 a new subway was opened linking the two via a new underground shopping arcade. Concrete dominates this mammoth structure and the station direction signage, suspended on long poles from the distant lofty roof, is perhaps its only incongruous feature.

Canada Water, designed by the JLE Project Team with Herron Associates, was built as part of the original Surrey Quays Development programme. The Jubilee Line platforms here are 23 metres below ground, and like North Greenwich and Canary Wharf, are separated by a wide island platform. A bank of escalators lead up to a concourse where access to the two East London Line platforms is gained. Canada Water was slotted in on the East London Line between Rotherhithe and Surrey Quays and the distance between it and the two adjacent stations is extremely short, 0.32 km in the case of Rotherhithe. From this concourse another flight of escalators leads up to the spacious L-shaped ticket hall and control room. Stairs and lifts then lead up to the three main entrances, one beneath a huge glass drum structure. Daylight through the drum penetrates much of the lower levels. Here one gets the feeling that the great days of 1930s station building were not far from the designers' minds. The 'drum' is flanked by a new roofed bus station.

A bird's-eye view of the new platform-edge doors at North Greenwich, an added safety feature evident at all new sub-surface stations on the Jubilee Line extension.

At Canary Wharf, huge load-bearing columns run the length of the station platform, itself a wide-open space, and support the station roof and the park cultivated above. Nine free-standing escalators take passengers to and from the ticket hall concourse, which is as wide as a football pitch. A second entrance, built at the same time but not opened initially, came into use on 19th March 2004.

The foot of the escalators at Bermondsey station.

On arrival at the concourse at Southwark, passengers find themselves opposite a giant 40 metre long by 16 metre high cone wall designed by Alexander Belechenko. It is made up of 630 triangular panes of blue enamel glass fixed to a steel framework. The street level building is seen on opening day, hence the balloons.

The construction of the next station, Bermondsey, which serves the large residential area around Jamaica Road, utilised both cut-and-cover and bored sections. It was designed by Ian Ritchie Architects, and is the smallest station on the extension having only three escalators and one lift. The stainless steel panelled platforms are separate, the main concourse being at the western end. The concourse, which leads to the tall escalator shaft lit by natural daylight from above, is dominated by concrete support and cross-members. The use of secondary finishes, over the basic concrete, is minimal. The surface building is largely glazed and contains shop units.

The new Jubilee Line element at London Bridge lies at the front of the main line station beneath the Bus Station. The building package here also included a new southbound Northern Line platform, together with new ticket halls at Joiner Street and Borough High Street. The Jubilee Line platforms are lined with dark blue panelling bearing the station name below the glass station name frieze and grey slatted panelling above. The station layout is fairly traditional in as much as the platforms are linked by cross passageways. The new station accounts for 22 new escalators and four lifts.

Southwark, which offers an interchange with National Railway's Waterloo East Station, is perhaps the most agreeable station on the whole extension. Its overall design was by the architects MacCormac, Jamieson and Pritchard. The platform walls are lined with concrete, relieved only by the glass frieze bearing the station name. Escalators in separate shafts lead to an intermediate concourse where passengers making for Waterloo East station separate from those going out to Blackfriars Road. The circular ticket hall is reached by eight escalators and is at an intermediate level from the concourse and the street above which is up a short staircase.

At Waterloo, which at only 0.44 km from Southwark is the shortest distance between any of the new stations, the Jubilee Line interchanges with the Bakerloo, Northern and the Waterloo & City lines as well as with numerous National Rail services. But the tube lines are a long way from the Jubilee. So much so that two 140-metre level moving walkways take passengers between them. Because of the NATM problem the original plan devised by the in-house JLE architect team, which was to excavate a large tunnel containing both the eastbound Jubilee Line platform and interchange subway, was dropped in favour of a more traditional layout with separate platforms. These are lined in a grey mosaic pattern and are linked by cross passageways. Six escalators lead up from each end of the platform to the main subway and moving walkways, which take passengers to the Bakerloo and Northern lines and the South Bank. Four more escalators lead to a new ticket hall in Waterloo Road built within the Edwardian Colonnades, previously the site of a bus stand.

At Westminster the sheer size of the interchange area between the new Jubilee Line platforms, which are lined with steel-grey panels, and the District and Circle lines takes the breath away. It was here that great concern was expressed at the possible dangers of deep level excavation to the delicate foundations of the Big Ben tower. This affected the final layout of the new station designed by Michael Hopkins & Partners in as much as the Jubilee Line platforms were built one above the other rather than on the same level. This was to avoid the danger of ground movement, which was closely monitored throughout construction. The station was excavated out from beneath the land now occupied by another Michael Hopkins creation, Portcullis House, and for a few weeks one could stand on Westminster station District platforms and gaze up at the face of Big Ben above.

From the westbound platform passengers enter the lowest part of a huge auditorium 39 metres below ground. Between here and the station exit are no fewer than seventeen escalators and four lifts connecting two more levels with the surface and with the District Line platforms. The next level up from the westbound Jubilee platform serves the similarly finished eastbound platform. As soon as they leave Jubilee Line trains, passengers must decide whether to change to the District and Circle platforms, which were modernised as part of the overall scheme, or to exit from the new ticket hall which opened in 1998, because all upward travel is skilfully segregated. The large ticket hall, with its high-profile control-room, has subway exits to Whitehall, the Embankment, Big Ben and Westminster Bridge. The overall effect of Westminster station is as far removed from the traditional tube station interchange as could be imagined. Anyone could be forgiven for wondering if they were in some huge top secret underground weapons establishment.

Thus the Jubilee Line extension was fully open in time for it to assume its important role in all the celebration and pageant in the biggest night for 1000 years, 31st December 1999. A mammoth firework display, including an ambitious plan to set light in a split second to the River Thames – a river of fire – had been planned and drew several million people. To get them there, and home afterwards, London Underground ran trains over most of the system throughout the night, for the first time since the Coronation of King George VI in 1937. Stations adjacent to or close to the river were closed, as were the roads in central London. Over two million people used the tube that night, and 6000 staff volunteered to work, being paid generous overtime payments to forgo their own celebrating and help get people to and from London's gigantic party. The last big challenge for the Underground in the 1900s had gone fairly smoothly and very safely and was a credit to the staff involved in planning and running it.

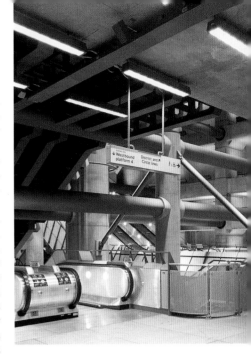

For engineering reasons the westbound Jubilee Line platform at Westminster is below the eastbound rather than alongside and is reached by two flights of escalators.

On the journey from the lowest level to the surface at Westminster, escalators criss-cross one another and huge steel supports driving into huge walls of concrete which form the foundations of Portcullis House.

The Infracos are responsible for enhancing the passenger environment and their contracts allow for a number of comprehensive refurbishment schemes. Where major schemes are required beyond those for which the contracts provide, the Infracos will undertake the work at London Underground's expense. At Wembley Park it has become necessary to make major changes to the station to update facilities and to cope adequately with the traffic to the new stadium. The work is undertaken by Tubelines on behalf of London Underground and receives funding contributions from the stadium developer and the Mayor's single regeneration budget. This particular modernisation has proved to be one of the least successful visually, old and new elements having been forced together very uncomfortably.

Private Finance Again

The concept of Private Finance Initiatives had first emerged in the mid-1990s, and was originally for projects such as hospitals, prisons and schools. The immediate reward to the contractors lay in the rental payments from the public sector. London Underground had used this Private Finance Initiative framework for projects such as a new ticket issuing and checking system and for devolving power generation to allow the closure of Lots Road power station and rely on the national grid instead.

As described earlier, a significant step forward was taken in 1994 when a suggestion originally made by the rolling stock manufacturer Adtranz was taken up by London Underground. The deal was tendered and the winner was GEC Alstom with a proposal to build 106 6-car trains known as the 1995 stock. The deal saw the private company funding, building and maintaining the trains themselves with London Underground paying a daily service charge for their use; GEC were subject to significant penalties for trains it could not provide to meet the scheduled service, or for failures of trains in service that were found to be its fault. The contractor also assumed responsibility for the depots at Golders Green and Morden. The effect, together with signalling, communications, stations and track in due course moving to the private sector was to remove from London Underground all the short- and long-term engineering decisions. The archaic Treasury practice of allocating capital funds in annual budgets had ensured that London Underground had no assurance that funds would be available to complete a project.

Apart from these structural financial difficulties, the government had, over the course of several years, acquired grave doubts about the ability of London Underground management to handle major projects, with particular reference to the farcical Central Line modernisation scheme, and problems with the Jubilee Line extension to Stratford.

Soon after the Labour government was elected in May 1997 it created an interdepartmental committee to devise a more effective way to invest money in the London Underground. The firm of Price Waterhouse won a consultancy competition and was charged with the task of devising a new, better system. Its report of October 1997 recommended splitting LUL into three groups to look after its infrastructure, and one or more groups to operate the services. A press conference was held on 20th March 1998 at which the Deputy Prime Minister announced the intention to establish a Public-Private Partnership to bring stable, increased investment into London Underground, and to tackle an investment backlog of £2 billion. London Underground

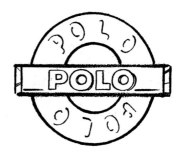

Tube for sale 16p.

Polo. The mint with the hole.

The operation of underground railways in London has rarely been profitable and even in Victorian times railways looked for property and other commercial income to supplement fares revenue, the development of air space over stations being an obvious opportunity. In recent years London Underground has sought to use development opportunities to gain major station improvements at the same time. An example is Fulham Broadway, where there has been an air space development over the platforms, resulting in a new entrance being built, the old entrance being incorporated into the property scheme.

would be a publicly-owned holding company responsible for delivering services, The three privately-owned infrastructure companies (the 'Infracos') would jointly aim to deliver £8 billion of investment in LU over the next 15 years. The contracts would be for a limited period, after which the upgraded assets would revert to the public sector. The successful bidders would be subject to a strict code of service delivery, with fines for failing to deliver all the constituents of the timetabled service and bonus payments for providing an exceptionally good service. The successful bidders (chosen on the basis of value for money in their promises to deliver investment and improvement) had to purchase their franchises from London Underground (£60 million from each member of the Tube Lines consortium, and £75 million from each member of Metronet) but, provided that they fulfilled their side of the bargain, would be able to rely on receiving a regular service charge for up to 30 years.

In July 1998 the Chief Executive of London Transport chaired a conference of industrialists and financiers with the aim of involving prospective investors in the design of the contracts for the PPPs.

By spring 1999 the allocation of lines between the Infracos had become clearer. One obvious grouping was to embrace the sub-surface lines, i.e. the Metropolitan, District, Circle, Hammersmith & City and East London, known collectively as 'SSL'. For the deep-level tube lines two groups were formed, 'BCV' comprising the Bakerloo, Central, Victoria and Waterloo & City, and 'JNP' (known as 'Tube Lines') comprising the Jubilee, Northern and Piccadilly. There was a degree of logic in the tube groupings, including similarities in rolling stock and signalling and in the type of work that needed to be done.

On 18th September 1999 London Underground was divided into the parts which would remain in public ownership (mainly the operational side) and those which would later be taken over by private enterprise but for the time being would remain in the public domain and be tested by 'shadow running'.

The framework with which the bids had to comply was that the franchises should be for a period of 30 years, but that a review of progress, costs and charges would be held after 7½ years, which would give the bidders an opportunity to seek a review of their fees.

Some light relief in the serious business of bidding was introduced by the bizarre intervention of Railtrack, who had expressed interest in the SSL franchise in spring 1999. In the light of the subsequent history of Railtrack it is noteworthy (and a little alarming) that in these early days the government expressed disappointment that Railtrack was not bidding for the deep level tubes as well.

Overnight repairs halt Tube again

By Dick Murray
Transport Editor

TUBE commuters faced delays today when overnight engineering work again failed to finish on time.

Most of the Victoria line was suspended, with only a shuttle service running between King's Cross and Victoria.

Even when the line was reopened there was disruption throughout the morning peak period.

Engineering work on the Victoria line is being carried out by Metronet, the consortium responsible for maintenance over two thirds of the Tube.

The National Audit Office last week raised the problem of night engineering work finishing late — causing 226 morning delays last year.

The first noticeable signs of the takeover of maintenance of the Underground by private companies were a deterioration in morning peak reliability, often caused by engineering work overrunning, and – on a more positive note – improved reliability of signalling and trains. A new programme of station refurbishments got under way, but was well behind schedule according to a March 2005 report to the London Assembly. Track replacement was also below target.

At that time the City of London was being particularly vociferous in demanding a direct rail route between the City and Heathrow Airport. For those using maps as their sole source of information, there appeared to be a quick solution by making a connection from the Heathrow Express line near Paddington to the Hammersmith & City line, and then continuing with trains of main line loading gauge via the Hammersmith & City and Circle lines. The government was so pleased at the possibility of avoiding paying millions of pounds for CrossRail that it gave Railtrack 'preferred bidder' status in the race for the SSL franchise. When the proposal was examined more carefully, however, it was discovered that (i) the Circle platforms were too short for the Heathrow Express type of train, (ii) the Circle Line infrastructure was in other ways unsuitable and (iii) there was no spare line capacity on the northern half of the Circle Line. So, the idea was a non-runner, and Railtrack lost its preferred bidder status in November 1999. In June 2001 it was announced that the PPP contracts were being modified to give greater co-ordination and unification of control. Further modifications were made in October 2001 to strengthen the safety provisions.

The National Audit Office stepped in on 22nd August 2000, saying that it would publish a report in November of that year, which originally would be one month before the preferred bidders were selected. However, this time scale proved to be far too tight for an investigation of such a complex subject, and the NAO returned later.

On 2nd May 2002 the preferred bidders for the two tube PPPs were announced. For the JNP (or Tube Lines) Infraco the winning consortium comprised the firms of Amey, Bechtel-Halcrow and Jarvis. For BCV the winning consortium was Metronet which comprised Balfour Beatty, W. C. Atkins, Thames Water, Seeboard and Bombardier Transportation. Seeboard had been a member of the consortium which had agreed to take over the London Underground power supply by supplying current from the national grid.

Ten days after the announcement of the preferred tube bidders, the National Audit Office began a detailed enquiry into the PPPs, and published its report on 17th June 2004. The enquiry was entitled 'London Underground PPPs – were they good value for money?' The report did not live up to its sweeping title – it was much too early to answer the question, and several years would have to elapse before the value – or otherwise – of the laboriously-constructed and immensely complicated new regime became apparent.

Transport for London, created by the Greater London Authority Act of 1999, was viscerally opposed to the PPP concept, and used every legal procedure to try to halt the whole process. Its political complexion determined that it should oppose any transfer of the publicly-owned London Underground to the private sector. London Underground would not be transferred to TfL until all the PPP deals had been completed. TfL tried to obtain a judicial review but eventually the two sides realised that further argument was useless.

When PPPs were first suggested the fond hope was entertained that the government would no longer have to make up the deficit in London Underground's revenue. However, as the PPPs settled down and the true magnitude of the arrears of maintenance became apparent, this hope was soundly dashed.

The contracts included some relatively severe penalty clauses (called 'abatements', i.e. deductions from the regular Infraco service charge) for failures to provide the foundations of a satisfactory service. These included failure to complete escalator overhaul projects on time, over-runs of overnight engineering works, causing late starts to the service, prolonged station closures; in fact all major delays which were judged to be the fault of the franchisee's team. Any attributable accidents which caused any suspension of services for days on end naturally incurred heavy penalties. On the other side of the coin there were bonuses for good service, but the rate per hour in money is only half the rate for the abatements. The basis of the calculation is a nominal assessment of the value of a passenger's time. The monetary amounts of these payments, although huge in themselves, and especially for reduced availability at busy stations at peak times, are relatively minor in relation to the regular payments made to the franchisees, averaging 1–2% of the payments made by London Underground. Calculating the abatements and bonuses was not merely a simple matter of reading the correct amounts from a table as there was much horse trading involved.

Metronet has had quite a few troubles. On 25th January 2003 a Central Line train derailed at Chancery Lane as a consequence of a traction motor becoming detached. This generated some debate between London Underground and the Infraco (at that point still owned by LUL) about maintenance procedures and culminated in the withdrawal of the entire fleet for inspection and subsequent modification. Central Line services were entirely withdrawn and were progressively reintroduced between 14th March and 2nd June. Tube Lines had an analogous problem following a derailment at Camden Town on 19th October 2003 when the rear car of a Barnet-bound train from the City derailed and struck the headwall of one of the junction tunnels causing serious damage. Problems were identified with the point design and the Northern Line had to be worked as two sections for a couple of months.

A more serious problem for Metronet was the difficulty it had in achieving its ambitious targets which had the effect of hugely increasing its costs. The problems reached the point during 2007 where the overspend was estimated at about £2bn. Appeal to the statutory PPP Arbiter for more LUL funding generated a response that suggested much of the blame was down to Metronet and only a proportion of additional funding was likely. In the light of this the company went into administration on 18th July 2007 and in the short term the Company will transfer to TfL on an interim basis until the long term future of this PPP contract can be determined. While disagreements with LUL over specifications are blamed, a major contributory factor was that Metronet's shareholders were also required to be Metronet's main contractors, putting the company in an impossible position when work wasn't done as required. Nevertheless it has cast doubt about the benefits of this 'flagship' government funding scheme, so hated by the London mayor, and has discredited any remaining belief that any business risks really transferred to the private sector as vast public funds are pumped into the remains to keep train services going. In any event these events are likely to diminish the scale of refurbishment and renewal that will be delivered over the coming years.

Occasionally Underground trains have run in service with overall exterior advertising. A Piccadilly Line train was first, in 1995, advertising United Airlines, and this was followed by a Circle Line train advertising Yellow Pages. In 2005 a Circle Line train and a Jubilee Line train were covered in colourful liveries promoting London's 2012 Olympic bid.

New trains for the Circle, Hammersmith & City and Metropolitan Lines are due to enter service from 2009 onwards. When these lines are completed, further trains of the same design wil take over on the District Line also. They will be the first trains on the Underground in which passengers will be able to walk from one carriage to any other without doors.

The Underground Since 2000

Following the opening of the Jubilee Line extension at the end of 1999, the number of new projects undertaken by London Underground diminished in the face of the impending PPP contracts. In the meantime attention focused on the completion of existing projects. These included some delayed elements of the Jubilee Line extension itself, such as four lifts at London Bridge which finally came into use in January 2001, with two more at Waterloo the following May. The troubled Central Line project also remained incomplete. The last traditional signal box (at Hainault) closed on 21st April 2001 but elements of the project were still in hand on 16th June 2004 when the final section of line (between West Acton and Ealing Broadway) was finally converted to automatic train operation.

Meanwhile the PFI contracts were making some headway. In one of perhaps the most significant, the elderly power station at Lots Road finally came off load on 8th October 2002. The station then operated in stand-by mode for two weeks until the Minister of Transport finally declared the station closed at a ceremony on 21st. As part of this work new bulk supply points brought energy in from the grid and transformed it down to 22kV before injecting it into what in essence was the Underground's existing internal distribution system. After closure all power was drawn from the National Grid and with all below-ground stations fitted with limited emergency lighting from battery backup. Greenwich Generating Station remains available for service in case of catastrophic grid failure with sufficient capacity to supply critical services at all below-ground stations to facilitate evacuation of passengers; it does not have the capacity to power train movements as well. Another huge success came as part of the Prestige ticketing project when 'Oyster' smartcards were launched to the public on 30th June 2003, after many months testing among active and retired staff. Most existing period tickets remained available to be loaded onto 'Touch and Pass' Oyster cards, but the main new facility was the ability to use pre-pay. This method of charging involved pre-loading an Oyster Card with a stored cash value at a ticket office following which the correct fare for each journey would be deducted from this value as a passengers used the system. An especially smart feature was the subsequent introduction of daily 'capping' so that during any one day a passenger never paid more than the cheapest ticket available, such as a one day travelcard. By the end of 2007 over 10 million Oyster cards were in use and passengers could top up cards and renew travelcard facilities from the comfort of their own homes using the internet, the cards automatically being updated when next presented to a ticket gate.

In addition to legacy works, a few substantial new works were started by London

Underground in response to third party requirements, and external funding. The largest of these was the Piccadilly Line extension to Heathrow Airport's new Terminal 5, which itself had just been authorised following an exceedingly long public inquiry. Authority for construction of the Terminal 5 extension was granted in November 2001 and was largely the responsibility of BAA who co-ordinated it with the rest of their terminal project, and picked up the bill. It was handed over to London Underground on 18th July 2007 to allow training and familiarisation to begin prior to opening. To facilitate creation of the new tunnel junctions west of Heathrow Terminals 1,2,3 it was necessary to close the Terminal 4 loop section between 7th January 2005 and 17th September 2006. During this closure all trains ran direct to Terminals 1,2,3 from Hatton Cross, while Terminal 4 was served by a bus link from Hatton Cross.

Another huge job was the complete reconstruction of the upper stations at King's Cross, including a new Metropolitan Line ticket hall beneath the forecourt of St Pancras station and the refurbishment of the Metropolitan Line platforms and the tube ticket hall. Preparatory work on this £300m+ project began on 25th June 2001 and was an essential part of the wider scheme to refurbish St Pancras main line station to handle European and Kent high speed traffic along the new Channel Tunnel High Speed Link. A new 'northern' ticket hall was also planned but construction was somewhat delayed, although contracts were finally let in May 2006; the £115m northern ticket hall and associated connections to the tube platforms are expected to be in service during 2010. Meanwhile the new Metropolitan ticket hall opened on 28th May 2006 with station refurbishment work completed during 2007, including (for the first time) 'within the barrier' interchange between Metropolitan and the tube lines.

The District Line's D stock was the last on the Underground to remain in its original (and now rather tired) unpainted alloy finish with unrefurbished 1970s car interiors which included some non fire-compliant materials – its turn finally came for refurbishment. On 17th July 2002 a single car with a refurbished interior was introduced to test public opinion; externally this car and the flanking motor cars were painted in London Underground's corporate colours. As a result of experience it was decided to proceed on refurbishing the entire fleet, an activity picked up by PPP contractor Metronet. The first two entirely refurbished trains entered service on 2nd June 2005 on the Olympia service and by the end of 2007 most of the fleet had been treated, the work being undertaken by Metronet's rolling stock partner Bombardier.

By the end of 2007 Tube Lines completed upgrades at 47 stations, including refurbishment of finishes, lighting and CCTV systems. Two large projects included reconstruction of Wembley Park in time for the additional traffic generated by the new Wembley Stadium which reopened in 2007. Tube Lines was also responsible for the fitting out of the Terminal 5 extension. One of the larger projects was the construction of additional Jubilee Line cars to lengthen all trains from six to seven cars and provide two complete new 7-car trains to improve line capacity; train lengthening took place over an extended Christmas shut down at the end of 2005. In addition the Northern Line trains PFI contract with Alstom was novated to Tube Lines in order to keep all critical maintenance activities under single control where feasible. Work has also started on the signalling upgrades on the Jubilee and Northern Lines.

The biggest projects on Metronet's agenda are the line upgrades, the Victoria Line upgrade being among the first to be delivered, by 2011. This project includes rolling stock replacement, to which end a prototype train has been built by Bombardier. Work is already in hand for resignalling the line. This is a tricky operation as the new technology has to be overlaid over the existing systems to allow the new trains to be phased in alongside the existing ones. Designs also exist for new rolling stock for the surface lines, the S stock, which will operate in 7- and 8-car formations and whose introduction should begin in 2009. As part of this scheme it is intended to extend the platform lengths between Baker Street and both Hammersmith and High Street Kensington so that trains can be extended from six cars to seven.

Just as the IRA terrorism era drew to a close another menace started to emerge in the form of suicide bombers motivated by extreme religious beliefs; in many ways this threat is more sinister as it is more difficult to prevent. On 7th July 2005 the whole of London was badly hit by a number of co-ordinated terrorist outrages aimed at the London Underground. Shortly before 09:00 London Underground controllers became aware of some major power supply losses and within a few minutes reports of smoke began to arrive. It took several minutes before news of injured people presenting themselves at station exits could be correlated with other facts to suggest that there had perhaps been some kind of awful accident. As soon as it was realised that there were a number of geographically dispersed incidents it became clear that the

In 1997 the Paris Metro began a licensing scheme for buskers following many years of illegal busking. London Underground followed suit in 2002, auditioning busking hopefuls before allocating two-hour slots at suitable positons at central London tube stations.

Underground was the scene of a major terrorist attack and various emergency plans swung into action. About an hour after the first wave of incidents another attack, this time virtually destroying a bus in Woburn Place, complicated matters further as it implied that more attacks were possible, making police very cautious. London was almost immediately paralysed and people were told to stay away from town, or, if already in town, to stay put and await further information. Police and Underground managers established from the confusion of reports that bomb explosions had occurred at Aldgate and Edgware Road, and between King's Cross and Russell Square. The latter was an especially awkward scene to confirm as it was in deep tube between stations, making access and evacuation very difficult. In the end it was found that 52 innocent people had been killed and a further 500 injured, 100 seriously enough to be detained overnight or for longer. In addition to the deaths and injuries the bombs damaged beyond repair each of the carriages in which they exploded, and a second carriage on the Piccadilly Line where the consequences were more severe because of the tube environment.

The problems of recovering the bodies, accommodating the lengthy police forensic investigation, recovering the vehicles and repairing the damaged infrastructure were formidable; included in the damage was the ruptured high tension cable that had originally given rise to the suspicion of a power failure. Train services were hugely disrupted. The Metropolitan ran through only to Moorgate until 25th July, coinciding with the resumption of full Hammersmith & City services; the Circle Line was suspended until 8th August. The dreadful conditions at the Piccadilly Line scene saw services suspended between Hyde Park Corner and Arnos Grove until 3rd August. The attack on the bus was thought to be a result of the bomber having difficulty in getting access to the Underground because of the other attacks.

Overall, the consequences of these co-ordinated bombings were worse than the total death toll of all the Irish terror attacks on public transport in London in the 19th and 20th centuries; the carnage was also on a scale not seen since the Second World War. There were some further attempts to cause explosions exactly two weeks later (at Oval, Shepherd's Bush and Warren Street stations, and on another bus) but the bombs failed to detonate and the perpetrators fled, though some were later caught. Following these attacks the Metropolitan Police were understandably very nervous and under great pressure to catch those associated with the violence and prevent further attacks. On the day after the failed bombings the Police chased a suspect into Stockwell Underground station and shot him in front of passengers as he boarded a Northern Line train, believing the suspect to be about to detonate another explosion. Unfortunately he was found to be an entirely innocent victim of mistaken identity.

One of the largest issues affecting London Underground is that of managing the excessive temperatures of (particularly) the deep level tube network, especially in summer. This has given rise to a substantial project called 'Cooling the Tube'. The problem is that over the years the tremendous heat energy created by train movements has leached into the clay surrounding the tunnels, gradually warming it up. Historically enough heat has been removed by powerful ventilation fans to limit the rate of temperature growth, but in the last twenty years or so the huge increases in train service and installation of electrical equipment on stations have generated far more heat than the installed ventilation plant can remove (and some of that had been neglected and wasn't working). The result is that in winter the stored heat in the clay keeps the system warm, while in the summer even more heat energy is added as the heat cannot be removed fast enough. The system is warming up with temperatures typically ten degrees or more above those at street level and often well over 30 degrees Celsius.

Somewhat to London Underground's surprise the new Mayor for London announced a £100,000 prize for anyone coming up with a workable idea for cooling the tube; according to the Evening Standard the invitation generated 3500 ideas from some 60 countries. After some months evaluating the contributions LUL's assessors concluded that there was little new that was not already being examined and the prize wasn't awarded. The challenge is in fact an exceedingly difficult one. Various measures are being adopted including numerous additional fans (though building new shafts is a problem in central London) and ingenious technological solutions such as using natural groundwater to cool the air and remove heat – some of this is expected to come from the 30 million litres of cool water already pumped out of the system each day. The question of air conditioning is frequently raised but there are difficult issues to address on a deep level system not designed to accommodate it. On trains any air conditioning plant takes up precious space and itself converts electrical energy into heat. More particularly it shifts heat from car interiors to the outside of the train where it is virtually impossible to get rid of, so it merely warms up the tunnels more and re-enters the carriages at every station. A train stalled in a tunnel will instantly be surrounded by an envelope of very warm air and reduce the conditioning effect. If the power goes off there are some serious challenges if the air conditioning goes off too, since the carriages have to be reasonably well sealed if the conditioning is to have any material effect. The problem is that in the tube environment the heat generated outside the train by attempting to cool the interior must not be allowed to increase safety risk under any foreseeable conditions, and disposing of this excess is intractable. Nevertheless current plans are for the new surface 'S' stock to include air conditioning as the problems in the larger sub surface tunnels are considered manageable and the trains are large enough for the equipment.

Following the Railways Act 2005, the Mayor of London was given additional responsibilities for transport in London. After agreement, this included control of the new train services to be operated over the extended East London Line, certain London main line local services then operated by Silverlink Trains (as Silverlink Metro), and finally for delivery of the much-vaunted Crossrail project, given government go-ahead on 5th October 2007. The main line local services under the Mayor's control, branded 'Overground', are those between Euston and Watford, Richmond and Stratford, Clapham Junction and Willesden Junction and Gospel Oak to Barking. Train service operations were competitively tendered to a consortium of Hong Kong MTR and Laing Rail, trading as London Overground Rail Operations Ltd (LOROL), who took charge at 02:00 on the morning of Sunday 11th November 2007. While the stations all remain owned by Network Rail, those served purely by what were now LOROL trains were gradually re-branded 'Overground' following the changeover, with station management placed in the hands of LOROL staff.

The stations between Queen's Park and Harrow & Wealdstone, together with Gunnersbury and Kew Gardens, were also served by London Underground trains. It was decided that London Underground would lease these stations from Network Rail, with Silverlink staff transferring to London Underground from 11th November; London Underground signs were apparent by that date, together with its own publicity. From the same date the Overground-served platforms at Highbury & Islington, West Brompton and Blackhorse Road were also placed under London Underground control (but were branded as 'Overground'). Willesden Junction and Kensington Olympia (where Underground trains use only part of the station) transferred to Overground while management of Barking and Richmond stations remained in the hands of the existing main line train operators. At all these stations, new Oyster 'Pay As You Go' equipment was immediately commissioned where it had not previously been available.

Every working day, commuters are carried to work by the Underground in conditions that are illegal for the carriage of cattle. They may say they have little choice, but in the end no-one forces them into such close and often uncomfortable contact with complete strangers. Londoners love to hate it, but the Underground is indispensable and its station staff almost invariably magnificent. Those who live and work in London owe the mid-nineteenth century underground railway pioneers and the staff we meet on it today a vote of thanks.

The Underground in the 21st Century retains many reminders of the Victorian main line origins of some of its suburban stations. In November 2007, the management of stations between Queen's Park and Harrow & Wealdstone was transferred from Network Rail to London Underground, some ninety years after the Bakerloo first served them.

Index to text and captions